HAW....

ADVENTURES IN NATURE

George Fuller

JOHN MUIR PUBLICATIONS
SANTA FE, NEW MEXICO

John Muir Publications, P.O. Box 613, Santa Fe, New Mexico 87504

Printed in the United States of America.
First edition. First printing October 1999.

Library of Congress Cataloging-in-Publication Data

Fuller, George, 1954–
     Hawaii: adventures in nature / George Fuller.
             p.   cm.
     Includes index.
     ISBN 1-56261-437-1
     1. Hawaii—Guidebooks.   2. Natural history—Hawaii.   I. Title.
     DU623.25.F86   1999
     919.6904'41—dc21   99-33133
                                                              CIP

Editors: Ellen Cavalli, Nancy Gillan
Graphics Editors: Ann Silvia, Heather Pool
Production: Janine Lehmann
Cover and Interior Design: Janine Lehmann
Typesetting: Kathleen Sparkes—White Hart Design, Albuquerque, NM
Maps: Kathleen Sparkes—White Hart Design, Albuquerque, NM
Printer: Publishers Press
Cover photos:
          Front cover: Leo de Wys Inc./Sunstar—Men in outrigger canoe
          Back cover: Phillip Rosenberg/Big Island Visitors Bureau—Kohala Ditch
                   Trail in the Alakahi Valley on the Big Island
Title page: ©John Elk—Kalalau Trail, Na Pali Coast, Kauai

Distributed to the book trade by
Publishers Group West
Berkeley, California

CONTENTS

CONTENTS

ABOUT THIS BOOK

Hawaii: Adventures in Nature is a guide to Hawaii's most exciting destinations for active travelers who are interested in exploring the islands' natural wonders. Along with the best places for hiking and birding and the prime spots for swimming and snorkeling, author George Fuller recommends outfitters and local guides that can provide gear and lead you to the more remote parts of the islands. He also points out places to eat and stay that will help you enjoy local cultures and cuisine.

Like all Adventures in Nature guides, this book emphasizes responsible, low-impact travel. Restaurants, accommodations, and outfitters that are particularly eco-friendly—those that strive to operate in ways that protect the natural environment or support local ecotourism efforts—are highlighted in most chapters.

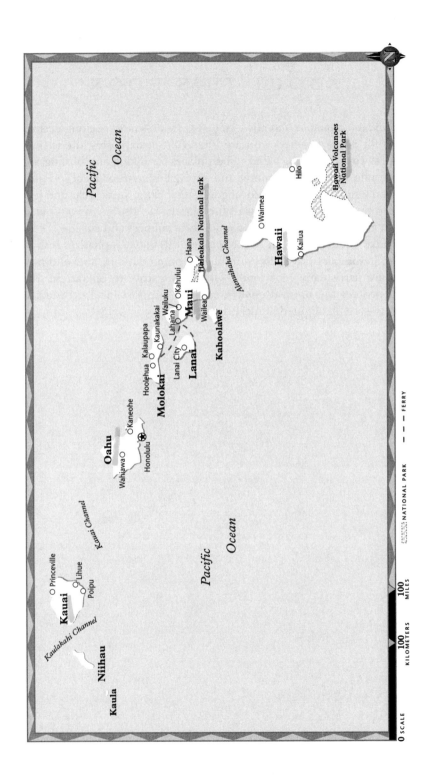

WHY VISIT HAWAII?

This book is the result of the past 15 years of my life, during which time I have had the pleasure and privilege of living in and exploring all sides of Hawaii. Over the years I have spelunked caves in Hana, Maui; paddled kayaks to deserted islands off the coast of Oahu; ridden with a horse communicator on the slopes of Mauna Kea on the Big Island; hiked to secluded beaches on the North Shore of Kauai; mountain-biked down miles of cow trails to empty beaches on Molokai; and swum with spinner dolphins in Hulopoe Bay on Lanai. These are the kinds of adventures you will discover in this book. As such, it will give you a picture of Hawaii like none you have ever seen before.

I have also met some of the best people one could hope to meet on this earth, including coffee farmers, chefs, kahuna and spiritual leaders, writers, photographers, golf professionals, cowboys, and fishermen. We all share one thing: a zest for adventure and an appreciation of the beauty of our home.

Whenever I meet visitors to the Aloha State, I always make a point of asking how they are enjoying their vacations. Interestingly, the response has changed over the past several years. Where once they were happy doing so, today most people no longer wish to spend their entire vacation tanning on the beach during the day and sipping oversweet rum drinks with mini-umbrella decorations at night. Today's travelers, more often than not, say they wish they could find the "real Hawaii"—those unique experiences that put them in touch with the land, culture, and people of these extraordinary islands.

In reality, the opportunities are plentiful. Visitors to the Aloha State can do what the locals do: We snorkel, swim, hike, bike, surf, kayak, get lost, and get found again in one of the most beautiful and remote archipelagoes on the planet. Like everyone else, we marvel at the return of the humpback whales each year on their winter migration. We are in awe at the raw display of nature in Hawaii Volcanoes National Park, where Kilauea Volcano has been erupting for almost 20 years, spewing molten lava into the sea.

We respect and protect the culture of the Hawaiian people. Like our visitors, we go to Hilo each year to see the state's best hula dancers—women and men—compete in the Merrie Monarch Festival. We listen in wonder to the falsetto tones of our finest Hawaiian singers. We visit the Bishop Museum and study the traditions of the Polynesians; marvel at the long red-and-yellow feather cloak of Hawaii's greatest king, Kamehameha I; and learn about the monumental sea voyages that brought the first people to these islands in great double-hulled canoes centuries ago.

All of this and more is available to visitors. Adventure travelers hike to secluded waterfalls, visit the Cultural Learning Center in Waianae at Kaala Farm to hear real Hawaiians teach about traditional fishing and farming techniques, and maybe take a surf lesson just to say they have. They ride the jet stream in hang gliders, swim with green sea turtles, dive with moray eels, and poke their noses into the cave homes of white-tip reef sharks.

When people ask me where to find the "real Hawaii," I steer them in these directions. They are also the kinds of adventures you will find in this volume.

Lay of the Land

The lovely islands of Hawaii are alive—geologically, culturally, and environmentally. Whether you are a hiker, biker, kayaker, angler,

HAWAII AT A GLANCE

Population—1.2 million
State Capital—Honolulu
Statehood—1959
Area—6,425 square miles, with 750 miles of coastline
Main Ethnic Groups—Hawaiian, Caucasian, Japanese, Chinese,
    Filipino, Samoan, and other Pacific Islanders
Currency—U.S. dollars
Average Daily Temperatures
    May through October—85 degrees
    November through April—78 degrees
Average Water Temperature—74 degrees
Annual Visitors—6.9 million
Main Visitor Islands—Oahu, Maui, Kauai, Hawaii (the Big Island),
    Molokai, Lanai
State Bird—Nene goose
State Flower—Yellow hibiscus
State Fish—Humuhumunukunukuapua'a
Humpback Whale–Watching Season—November
    through March
Most-Visited Natural Sites—Diamond Head Crater (Oahu),
    Hanauma Bay (Oahu), Hawaii Volcanoes National Park (Big
    Island), Haleakala National Park (Maui), Waimea Canyon
    (Kauai), Na Pali Coast (Kauai)

snorkeler, sun-worshipper, archaeologist, equestrian, or all of the above, Hawaii will enchant and excite you.

The Aloha State is composed of 132 islands and shoals—only eight of which are inhabited. It stretches from Midway Island, roughly parallel with San Diego, California, down to South Point on the Big Island of Hawaii—the southernmost point of the United States—parallel with

Mexico City. The archipelago covers an area of 6,425 square miles, but has only 750 miles of coastline. It is in the midst of the broadest expanse of ocean in the world, and is closer to Tokyo, Japan, than to Washington, D.C. It is the newest land on earth, and even today a new island, Loihi, is being formed under the surface of the Pacific near the Big Island. (Look for it to be included in guidebooks in roughly 100,000 years.)

Geologically, the islands are drifting approximately three to four inches per year toward Japan. Scientists say that Midway, the second island formed in the chain, was once as large as the Big Island of Hawaii. Over the past 30 to 35 million years, the land mass of Midway has drifted almost 2,000 miles northwest and sunk in the ocean to the point that it is now only a coral atoll.

Visitors will find just about every one of the planet's climatic zones in Hawaii, often very close together. Scientists have thus far identified nearly 150 climatic zones around the world, and most occur somewhere in Hawaii. On the Big Island, for example, you can see the (seasonally) snowcapped peak of Mauna Kea—some 13,000 feet in the sky—from your chair on the beach. With proper planning, you can watch the sunrise from the summit and be tanning on the white sands of Hapuna Beach by midday.

On the same island, Kilauea Volcano has been erupting for close to two decades now, issuing molten lava in fiery rivers to the ocean. Anything in its path is destroyed, given back to Madame Pele, the fire goddess. Just ask the former residents of Kalapana, whose town was burned to the ground by the onslaught of red-hot lava in 1990.

On the other hand, Hawaii is the most beautiful place on earth to live or visit. The trade winds keep the temperatures in check most of the year, and residents and visitors alike enjoy the recreational opportunities this close-to-perfect weather affords. This, combined with a rich Polynesian cultural tradition and a lush tropical environment, make the Hawaiian Islands unlike anywhere else.

The Aloha State has changed much over the years—particularly since 1960, when the first commercial jets began bringing throngs of visitors to these remote islands more quickly and conveniently than ever before. The bulk of these new arrivals stayed in charming and low-key

Waikiki. The liner notes from a Don Ho album of the time proclaimed that Honolulu was, "where it's happening, hun," and only a few adventurous souls ventured afield from Waikiki.

Today most of the state's nearly 7 million annual visitors still begin their sojourns on Oahu. But beginning around 1975, a new trend began to develop: Along with a day or two on Oahu, travelers started hopping interisland carriers and looking for new adventures and excitement on the neighboring islands.

Maui was the first to benefit from this trend, carving an identity for itself in travelers' imaginations. Destinations such as Kaanapali, Kapalua, and Wailea had enormous appeal, as they were quiet and secluded, and boasted great beaches and access to far-flung adventure. Anyone who made it as far as Hana, way out on Maui's eastern hip, took home tales of an undiscovered paradise in Hawaii.

Kauai and the Big Island didn't really start hopping until the mid-1980s, and even at that, with the exception of Mauna Kea and Kona Village Resort—two luxury properties that didn't even need an advertising budget until the early 1990s because their clienteles were so reliable and faithful—"hopping" on the Big Island meant occupancy rates in the 50 to 60 percent range.

Today, things are different. In 1998, the Big Island outpaced Waikiki in more than one month for occupancy rate. Kauai has had a breath of new life after Hurricane Iniki (1992) blew a monkey wrench into its works. And Maui continues to hum along like the Little Island That Could. Even diminutive Lanai has a tourism base, centered around two luxury hotels. Only Molokai—the Friendly Isle—continues to resist luxury development (or any development, for that matter), a strategy that has Molokai Ranch, the island's largest landholder, relying on the budding ecotourism market.

Each of the major islands has a distinct personality. For the traveler interested in natural sites and adventure travel, there are compelling reasons to visit each one: the Big Island, with Hawaii Volcanoes National Park, its lava-strewn Kohala Coast, Mauna Kea, and its observatories; Maui, with Haleakala National Park, the still-remote and beautiful Hana Coast, and the West Maui Mountains; Oahu, with its surf-famous North Shore, dramatic Koolau and Waianae mountain ranges, and its international flavor; Kauai, with the sharp ridges of the Na Pali Coast plunging into the ocean, Waimea Canyon, and Kokee State Park.

Flora and Fauna

Hawaii is a very special place when it comes to flora and fauna. The lush green mountains are vibrantly alive with living things, particularly plants, flowers, insects, and birds. But it has not always been this way. Once, these fertile islands were no more than points of barren lava washed over by the sea.

Since the first lava mounts poked their domes above the ocean's surface millions of years ago, every species of plant and animal found today had to make a long and difficult journey to settle here. Seabirds were likely the first immigrants to arrive, blown on the winds to these remote spots 2,500 miles from any other land mass on the planet. Seedlings were washed upon the shores in the ocean's currents, and over the course of time, ecosystems evolved.

During the course of a day hike on any of the islands you're likely to see a wide variety of native birds, such as the bright red *i'iwi* (honey-creeper), the chubby little brown-and-white *elepaio* (monarch fly-catcher), or the quick red *'apapane* (crimson honeycreeper), as you make your way through the abundance of ferns and ohia trees.

And while it may seem that all of this activity means all is well in the rain forest, it must also be pointed out that Hawaii has more species on the endangered lists than any other place in the world.

For reasons quite similar to those that accounted for the population decline of the native Hawaiian peoples (introduced diseases and cultures), many of Hawaii's native flora and fauna populations have been greatly reduced or forced to extinction over the past 200 years.

Environmentalists point to the following statistics: Hawaii amounts to just .02 percent of the land mass of the United States, yet almost 75 percent of the documented plant and bird extinctions in the United States have occurred in Hawaii. And of all the bird species currently on the endangered list, 40 percent are in Hawaii.

Researchers estimate that in the 1800s, Hawaii was home to almost

Spinner dolphin off the bow of the Navatek II

150 different species of native birds. This estimate is based on bone re-coveries, feather samples, and drawings made by artists aboard visiting ships. Today, of those 150 species, one-half are extinct, 34 additional species are endangered, and roughly one-third of those 34 species are at such perilously low populations that they may very well be beyond recov-ery. Even the state bird, the Hawaiian nene goose, is endangered.

Much the same story is true of Hawaii's flora. In the early 1990s, some 85 Hawaiian plant species were listed on the federal endangered list. This represents roughly 31 percent of the entire nation's endan-gered species. As of 1999, the list had grown to include 263 species of Hawaiian plants. Over the course of the next several years, we can be certain more will be added, provided that the Endangered Species Act is renewed by Congress.

Again similar to the avian species, close to 100 of Hawaii's trees, shrubs, vines, and ferns have fewer than 100 individual specimens

HAWAII'S ENDANGERED ANIMALS AND BIRDS

Hawaii—Animals—34 species as of October 31, 1998
Note: No longer includes non-nesting species of sea turtles that enter state coastal waters.

- *'Akepa, Hawaii (honeycreeper) (Loxops coccineus coccineus)*
- *'Akepa, Maui (honeycreeper) (Loxops coccineus ochraceus)*
- *'Akialoa, Kauai (honeycreeper) (Hemignathus procerus)*
- *'Akiapola'au (honeycreeper) (Hemignathus munroi)*
- *Bat, Hawaiian hoary (Lasiurus cinereus semotus)*
- *Coot, Hawaiian ('alae-ke'oke'o) (Fulica americana alai)*
- *Creeper, Hawaii (Oreomystis mana)*
- *Creeper, Molokai (kakawahie) (Paroreomyza flammea)*
- *Creeper, Oahu (alauwahio) (Paroreomyza maculata)*
- *Crow, Hawaiian ('alala) (Corvus hawaiiensis)*
- *Duck, Hawaiian (koloa) (Anas wyvilliana)*
- *Duck, Laysan (Anas laysanensis)*
- *Finch, Laysan (honeycreeper) (Telespyza cantans)*
- *Finch, Nihoa (honeycreeper) (Telespyza ultima)*
- *Goose, Hawaiian (nene) (Nesochen sandvicensis)*
- *Hawk, Hawaiian (i'o) (Buteo solitarius)*
- *Honeycreeper, crested ('akohekohe) (Palmeria dolei)*

remaining. Sadly, several have but a single specimen that can be found. Add to that the fact that almost two-thirds of the islands' original forest cover has been lost, including roughly 50 percent of its rain forests, and the underlying reasons for the plight of Hawaii's native flora and fauna become clearer.

- *Millerbird, Nihoa (Old World warbler) (Acrocephalus familiaris kingi)*
- *Moorhen (gallinule), Hawaiian common (Gallinula chloropus sandvicensis)*
- *Nukupu'u (honeycreeper) (Hemignathus lucidus)*
- *'O'o, Kauai ('o'o 'a'a) (honeyeater) (Moho braccatus)*
- *'O'u (honeycreeper) (Psittirostra psittacea)*
- *Palila (honeycreeper) (Loxioides bailleui)*
- *Parrotbill, Maui (honeycreeper) (Pseudonestor xanthophrys)*
- *Petrel, Hawaiian dark-rumped (Pterodroma phaeopygia sandwichensis)*
- *Po'ouli (honeycreeper) (Melamprosops phaeosoma)*
- *Shearwater, Newell's Townsend's (formerly Manx) ('a'o) (Puffinus auricularis newelli)*
- *Snails, Oahu tree (Achatinella spp.)*
- *Stilt, Hawaiian (ae'o) (Himantopus mexicanus knudseni)*
- *Thrush, large Kauai (Myadestes myadestinus)*
- *Thrush, Molokai (oloma'o) (Myadestes lanaiensis rutha)*
- *Thrush, small Kauai (puaiohi) (Myadestes palmeri)*
- *Turtle, green sea (Chelonia mydas)*
- *Turtle, hawksbill sea (Eretmochelys imbricata)*

Source: U.S. Fish And Wildlife Service, Division of Endangered Species

Luckily, there is also good news. In addition to the relatively healthy populations of *i'iwi, elepaio,* and *'apapane* birds, several finch species are common. The magnificent silversword plant thrives on the volcanic slopes of Haleakala and Mauna Kea. And 1,800 miles northwest, on Midway Island, the Laysan albatross, the black-footed albatross, and some 13 other species of seabirds outnumber the human contingent by a long shot: 2 million birds to 130 humans. The mighty Pacific humpback whales return to Hawaiian waters every year to calve and frolic. Spinner dolphins are common and plentiful. Green sea turtles have made a comeback after being placed on the endangered list. And the Hawaiian monk seal, also endangered, is slowly repopulating in its protected status.

One thing you will not find in Hawaii is snakes. Although there are some 2,800 species of snakes in the world, not a single one of them calls Hawaii home. Not that the climate isn't right—indeed, what jungle in the world has no thriving snakes? But the combination of ardent management to keep them out and the islands' remoteness from other land masses has given Hawaii a great blessing—jungle without snakes. (But you'd better like geckoes.)

History

It is generally agreed among scholars that the first inhabitants of the Hawaiian Islands sailed north from the Marquesas Islands, 2,400 miles to the south, in great, double-hulled voyaging canoes. This was followed by migrations from Tahiti. The exact dates of this initial migration are uncertain, but most archaeologists estimate that it occurred between A.D. 500 and 1200. Due to the ocean currents, the first land they reached is thought to be Kauai. This speculation is further fueled by the fact that Kauai was the first island "discovered" by the British explorer Captain James Cook in 1778.

Archaeologists cite a good deal of evidence to support the Marquesan connection, including similarities in original language, methods of farming and fishing, and the use of certain distinctive tools. One of these telltale implements is the stirrup-shaped poi pounder, found only on Kauai and in the Marquesas.

The sea voyages from the Marquesas were long, and navigation was not easy. The only maps were the stars, and the original Hawaiians were expert celestial navigators. Although today very few practice the art, it has received great respect since the first voyage of the *Hokule'a*, led by Nainoa Thompson, modern-day Hawaii's premier celestial navigator.

© George Fuller

Hawaii's past is reflected in the Pa'u Parade in Waimea.

Thompson and his crew constructed a 62-foot voyaging canoe as close to the type used by the original Hawaiians as possible, and set sail from the Marquesas to see where the currents would lead. This 1976 voyage was followed by several others.

Cook's arrival in 1778 signaled the first of many tumultuous changes the Hawaiians would endure over the ensuing 200 years, including the loss of their sovereignty and the near-death of their culture itself.

Cook's impact was enormous, as we can only imagine. He had great sailing ships, weapons never before seen, worked metals, and a culture of which the Hawaiians knew nothing. Cook and his ships may as well have come from outer space, and in fact Cook was mistaken for the god Lono when he made landfall on Kauai.

Within a year of his arrival, though, Cook himself was dead, bludgeoned to death by natives at Kealakekua Bay on the Big Island. The natives stole a rudder from one of Cook's ship's small launches, and

GLOSSARY OF COMMON HAWAIIAN TERMS

As a state of the Union, obviously English is spoken here. But Hawaii still clings to its Polynesian roots—and language. Here are some terms you may come across in your travels on the islands.

ali'i—royalty
halau—troupe
hale—house
haole—Caucasian
heiau—sacred ground
kamaaina—one who is "of the land," a local
kane—man
kapu—forbidden
keiki—children
kumu hula—master dancers of the hula
mahalo—thank you
makai—toward the ocean
mauka—mountains
puka—hole
stink-eye—a harsh look
wahine—woman

Cook decided it was "a good opportunity to show these people the use of firearms." They were "rather more surprised than frightened," he wrote in his journal. It was his final entry.

One young Big Island warrior named Kamehameha, however, was savvy enough to see the opportunity European firearms and tools presented. Throughout his life Kamehameha surrounded himself with European advisors, and their influence cannot be minimized in his mostly successful efforts to unite the islands. He is remembered as a wise leader of his people as well as a skilled warrior, as the various statues of Kamehameha around the islands attest.

The economic history of Hawaii has had a great deal to do with its present-day cultural makeup. After Cook made contact with the Hawaiians, other Europeans followed. France, Spain, Russia, and other European nations sent expeditions and then emissaries. An attempt by the Russians to annex what was then known as the Sandwich Islands in 1815 came close to succeeding, and the Russian flag flew over Kauai for more than a year. (Today, the ruins of the Russian fort can be visited near Hanapepe.)

America sent missionaries, the first arriving in 1820. This period of Hawaiian history is well documented, although perhaps it is James Michener's *Hawaii* that still tells the story best. Whaling and trading ships came to port in Lahaina and Honolulu, and with them came diseases previously unknown in the islands, such as tuberculosis, smallpox, and venereal disease.

Tragically, by 1830 the native Hawaiian population was in serious decline because of these introduced diseases. Estimates put the number of Hawaiians at the time of Cook's arrival in 1778 at close to 800,000. Less than 50 years later, that number had dwindled to fewer than 150,000. By 1890, there were only 40,000 Hawaiians and part-Hawaiians left.

At the same time, the American missionaries imposed a set of values upon the Hawaiian people in an attempt to "civilize" them. Women were made to cover their breasts; hula was considered lascivious and thus discouraged; traditional methods of farming, fishing, land distribution, and even warfare—which was an integral part of Polynesian culture—were disrupted and replaced with Puritanical values.

Hawaiians who survived the diseases were put to work on the new sugar plantations that had sprung up around 1850. Because there were not enough Hawaiians left, Chinese and then Japanese and Filipino laborers were brought in. The Portuguese and Spanish also came, bringing with them an equestrian tradition.

Plantation managers were often of European descent, many of them Scots. New plants, animals, recreational pursuits, and cultural habits came to Hawaii. Honolulu was, by 1880, the international hub of the Pacific. Novelists such as Mark Twain had written in glowing terms about the islands, and others such as Robert Louis Stevenson and Jack London would also soon arrive to tell fascinating and delightful tales of Hawaii. Their accounts, published around the globe in newspapers and magazines, drew even more international interest.

Of the three main cash crops grown in Hawaii over the years—coffee, sugarcane, and pineapple—coffee was the first to arrive. The coffee tree was brought to Hawaii in 1813 by King Kamehameha the Great's Spanish interpreter and physician, Don Francisco de Paula y Marin. The Big Island's Kona district proved to be a perfect climate for growing coffee commercially, and Kona coffee is now respected throughout the world for its rich flavor. Other islands in the Hawaiian chain are also growing coffee commercially now, particularly Kauai, where coffee trees are replacing sugarcane in many fields.

Pineapple, the third mainstay in Hawaii's economy for nearly 50 years, has been in decline for nearly two decades, much of the production of the sweet fruit having gone to the Philippines. Even on Lanai, for many decades known as the Pineapple Island due to its abundance of production, luxury resorts have replaced pineapples as the primary employer.

There are still no freeways, high-rises, or traffic lights on Lanai. Life is, except at the resorts, pretty much the same as it was in the 1920s when James Dole—a young Harvard graduate and nephew of the Territory of Hawaii's first president, Sanford Dole—acquired the island expressly to grow pineapple in his successful campaign to make "'Hawaiian' mean to pineapple what 'Havana' means to tobacco."

The tourism industry has now taken center stage in Hawaii's economy, but its volume is relatively new. Soldiers who fought in the Pacific theater during World War II came through Hawaii and went home to tell families and friends about the seductive lure of paradise. Movies such as *From Here to Eternity* reinforced with images what the soldiers were saying.

Then, when Elvis made *Blue Hawaii* and his other Hawaii films—mind you, they were now in living color—tourism roared to all-time heights and did not abate until the early 1990s. Michener's *Hawaii* was published in 1959, the same year Hawaii received statehood. Both events brought widespread public recognition. And commercial jets roared into Honolulu International Airport in 1960, ushering in yet another new era for Hawaii.

But that is not the last era Hawaii will see. With the renaissance of Hawaiian culture that began in the 1970s, a new pride has come to the Hawaiian people; and with pride has come a renewed interest in sovereignty, land rights, and cultural independence. These issues will not disappear. In fact, they are likely to grow stronger with the new millennium.

Sue Hackett

Hawaii's indigenous cultures have made a recent resurgence to include more traditional forms of dance.

Cultures

You may not be able to pronounce the name of our state fish (*humuhumunukunukuapua'a*), or the main road leading from Waikiki to Hawaii Kai (Kalanianaole Highway), or the Kingdom of Hawaii's last royal (Queen Liliuokalani), but it's all part of getting to know the Hawaiian culture.

Hawaii is shared by many cultures with diverse backgrounds. The main population groups today are of Asian ancestry: Japanese Americans and Chinese Americans. There are also many Pacific Islanders, such as Samoans, Tongans, Fijians, and Filipinos; and in the middle of the list of ethnic groups you will find Caucasian (or haole).

But it is first and foremost the Hawaiian culture that makes the Aloha State so special. Happily, the Hawaiian culture itself has enjoyed a rebirth over the past two decades, with Hawaiian-language immersion programs now being a standard part of many schools' curriculum; hula *halau* (troupes) producing immensely talented dancers; and many teachers passing down Hawaiian music, chants, and history to the youth.

One of the most rewarding aspects of this renaissance of culture has been a preponderance of authentic cultural programs within the hotels and visitor industry. Of course, for many years you could go into Waikiki and watch the hula dancers and musicians perform at the Halekulani Hotel's House Without a Key lounge, a most delightful way to spend a sunset.

Now, visitors can also go to an excellent interpretive center at the Four Seasons Resort Hualalai (on the Big Island) and learn about the stars, the seas, and the people of Hawaii. This program won the Hawaii Visitors & Convention Bureau's "Keep It Hawaii" award several years ago when it first opened, and is among the best such programs in the state.

Over on Maui, Kapalua Resort has recently opened the Kapalua Learning Center, where island visitors find exhibits, educational displays, and literature on the island's natural and cultural heritage. On Friday evenings at the Kapalua Shops, resort employees stage a wonderful program of traditional and contemporary Hawaiian music.

Then there are people such as Danny Akaka at the Big Island's Mauna Lani Bay Hotel, Clifford Nae'ole at the Ritz-Carlton Kapalua, and a host of others—many employed by the hotels—whose knowledge of Hawaii's land, culture, and people is generously yours for the asking of a question. They are kind, generous people, reflective of the Hawaiian spirit—the Aloha Spirit.

Other cultures, too, have made a great impression on Hawaii. As discussed briefly in the History section, above, the Chinese, Japanese, Filipino, Portuguese, Scots, and Spaniards have also been prevalent in Hawaii's history, each adding their own culture to the mix.

The Chinese people are still very much in evidence, and have created a wonderful Chinatown near downtown Honolulu. The Japanese have had a big effect on Hawaii over the years, and are heavily influential in politics and business. Senator Daniel Inouye, an American of Japanese ancestry, has been a respected member of the United States Senate since 1962. And since 1975, no people have been more significant to Hawaii's economy than Japanese nationals, whose penchants for tourism and investment abroad are well known.

The Portuguese people brought an equestrian tradition to the islands that lasts to this day. The Filipino people, many of whom originally came to Hawaii as laborers, now make up a population segment that is involved in all phases of leadership and society. The Scots may no longer be in any great abundance, but their knowledge of plantation and crop management as well as their recreational pursuits—they brought golf to Hawaii, for example—had a profound impact upon the Hawaii of 150 years ago, and thus upon today.

Horseback riding on Maui

© Ron Dahlquist

In more recent years, the Thai and Vietnamese people have arrived in significant numbers. Their contribution has thus far been the addition of excellent restaurants and shops, but as their numbers increase, so too will their influence upon Hawaii's kaleidoscopic society.

Hawaii has been called a "melting pot" of cultures. It is altogether true. While some friction does occur—and gang fighting is no small menace in some Oahu neighborhoods—it is relatively peaceful between the many diverse cultures that live in Hawaii.

Nature/Adventure Activities

Hawaii affords more outdoor activities than you'll have time to enjoy, unless you are planning to be here a long while. Further, Hawaii offers all skill levels an opportunity to participate and enjoy.

Surfing is a perfect example of this. Every winter, professional surfers are challenged by the best waves on the planet, on Oahu's North Shore. Competitions draw entrants from California, Australia, and other parts of the globe. Yet on Waikiki Beach, beginners of both sexes can take a lesson and ride gentle two-foot waves under the watchful eye of one of Waikiki's famous beachboys.

THE ISLAND OF NIHOA

By Kenneth P. Emory

Excerpted from *Bernice P. Bishop Museum Bulletin #53*, 1933

The island of Nihoa is located 150 miles northwest of Kauai. An additional 150 miles west of Nihoa, 300 miles from Kauai, is the island of Necker (see page 22). Both are volcanic islands, less than one mile in length, rising steeply from the sea.

Nihoa was "discovered" on March 19, 1789, by Captain Douglas of the Iphigenia. Later, in 1822, by order of Queen Kaahumanu, Captain Alexander Adams set forth to find again the island named in ancient Hawaiian tradition. Then again, in 1857, King Kamehameha IV landed on Nihoa with the intention of annexing it to the Hawaiian Government.

Geographically, the island is nearly one mile long and one-quarter of a mile wide. The north end of the island rises in a sheer cliff three-quarters of a mile long, 350 feet high in the middle, and little over 850 feet high at each end. Nihoa is comprised of 156 acres of land, mostly sloped, except where evened by inhabitants. The landscape is covered with grass and shrubs, and unlike Necker Island, has trees. These trees, called loulu *palms, totaled 515 at the time of the Tanager expedition, and were found in two groves.*

Nihoa teems with bird life. Nearly every foot of the island is covered by birds: Five kinds of terns, three kinds of boobies, Bulwer petrel black-footed albatrosses, wedge-tailed shearwaters, tropic birds, and frigate birds were identified. Also seen were two species unique to the island, the Nihoa finch and the Nihoa miller bird. Seals are occasionally found and turtles are fairly common. Adams Bay is abundant with fish. Lobsters, crabs, and shellfish can be collected on wave-cut terraces of the coast.

Archaeologists found that the gentler slopes were stepped with cultivation terraces and that most level spots were dotted with ruins of house sites. *Every suitable grotto gave ample evidence of occupation; among the evidence were ceremonial structures consisting of stone uprights.*

Evidence showed permanent or semipermanent populations did exist at one time on the island. Of the ruins, at least 25 and no more than 35 were house sites. There were 15 bluff shelters and no more than 15 ceremonial structures. Assuming all shelters were used, and allowing five people to each house site and three to each shelter, a population of 170 to 220 seems possible. Taking all else into consideration, though, it seems unlikely that there were more than 100 people living here at one time.

Many of the terraces cut into the gentler slopes, 12 acres (or 7.7 percent of the total land area) were used to grow crops. The main crop was found to be sweet potato. Experiments at the University of Hawaii over a five-year period found that the average sweet-potato crop yielded four tons yearly. That indicates that only 48 tons of sweet potato could have been grown annually on Nihoa, leaving scarcely enough for predicted populations.

Another mystery was the means by which the populace obtained enough water to survive. Three seeps were found but seemed to provide only salt water.

Religious structures were found at 15 ceremonial sites, which greatly resembled those found in Polynesia. Terraces with uprights, called marae, *signified sacred places, though the formation and quantity of* marae *are uncertain in meaning.*

Artifacts found included hammer stones, grindstones, coral rubbing stones, adzes, knives and awls, dishes, gourds, mortars, fishhooks, sinkers, and squid lures. Some of these artifacts were identical to their Hawaiian counterparts, but what stumped archaeologists was that at the same time, some artifacts resembled those found in other regions of Polynesia.

Two burial caves were also found on Nihoa. One contained bones of an adult male and two infants; the other held the bones of four adults, one of them female.

Hiking is excellent on all the islands. Here again, you can challenge yourself to a strenuous week-long hiking/camping excursion, or you can walk a little, see a lot, and be back at the beach by noon. Maui's Haleakala Crater and Kauai's Kokee State Park offer some of the best hiking trails in the state. Not to be overlooked are the hiking opportunities of Lanai's Munro Trail, where you're not likely to see too many other souls and yet the views from the top of the island are superb.

Ocean sports abound on all islands: windsurfing, kayaking, fishing, snorkeling, and diving. Maui's Hookipa Beach Park is considered the best windsurfing spot in the world.

Horseback riding is best on the Big Island, but Maui has great rides, too. And Molokai Ranch, on the offbeat little island of Molokai, is now developing ecotourism attractions, including some fun *paniolo* (cowboy) activities.

This book describes outdoor activities on each island, and also rates each one's difficulty. The chapters that follow do not attempt to describe *all* available activities, but you will read about the most interesting and/or unusual and those that are run by environmentally conscious outfitters and operators.

The Hidden Islands

If you look at most maps of Hawaii, even in the most thorough guidebooks, you're likely to see just six or seven islands. But actually, there are 132!

The "hidden islands" include several that you're likely to see or visit in your Hawaiian travels, such as Molokini (a crescent moon–shaped islet near Maui, popular for snorkeling visits); the Mokuluas (the two islands off the shores of Lanikai on Oahu, where kayakers can beach their craft and relax in relative peace); and Niihau (which can be viewed from the south shore of Kauai but not visited), Rabbit Island, Flat Island, Mokolii (also called Chinaman's Hat), and Moku Manu (all off the shorelines of Oahu; some you can put your feet on, some you can't).

Only eight of the Hawaiian chain's 132 islands and shoals are now inhabited by humans: the Big Island, Maui, Lanai, Molokai, Oahu, Kauai,

Niihau, and Midway. (And the happy fact that only eight of the 132 are inhabited by humans is just dandy with the frigate birds, monk seals, and other nonhuman inhabitants that call the islands home.)

Of the human-inhabited islands, only Niihau is off limits to all but native Hawaiians. Owned by the Robinson family, Niihau is home to several thousand native Hawaiians. There is no television, no phones, no electricity, no fast food, and no convenience stores or malls. Hawaiian is spoken here. Most Americans would feel isolated and out of place, but Niihau Americans seem perfectly content in their isolation. Their world works pretty much as it did back in 1900.

There is also strong evidence that at least two other "hidden islands" were once inhabited, Nihoa and Necker. A study of these two little-known islands by Kenneth P. Emory, titled "Archaeology of Nihoa and Necker Islands" (see sidebars), revealed interesting facts as well as information about the flora and fauna found here.

Other land masses far from the main group include the French Frigate Shoals, Gardner Pinnacles, Lisianski, and Midway Island.

When to Go

I'm often asked which is the best time of year to visit Hawaii. My answer: When is it coldest where you live?

In other words, it's always the best time of year to visit Hawaii. Our climate is unparalleled. Gentle trade winds blow most of the time, and temperatures hover around 85 degrees May through October; and around 78 degrees November through April. Average water temperature is 74 degrees—more comfortable than a bathtub, and a whole lot more interesting.

My personal favorite time of the year? Whale-watching season. The awesome humpbacks return to Hawaiian waters every year beginning in November, though they are most numerous in February and March.

September through November and January through April are most cost-effective. Most years, these "shoulder" seasons will produce good rates on air and hotel accommodations, and campgrounds are more likely to have permits available on the dates you want.

THE ISLAND OF NECKER

By Kenneth P. Emory

Excerpted from *Bernice P. Bishop Museum Bulletin #53, 1933*

Necker, about one mile long and 400 feet wide, has an area of about 41 acres. Its summit ridge stands at 150 to 200 feet, with culminating points of 278 feet above sea level. Necker is much like Nihoa in length, but is notably narrower, lower, and also more barren. The island is shaped like a fishhook, with the shank extending east and west at 4,000 feet and the barb (the northwest coast) at 600 feet long and 200 feet wide.

Necker's slopes are partially covered by grass, pigweed, a plant resembling a salt bush, and ohia bush. Unlike Nihoa, Necker has no trees. Rainfall is estimated at 20 to 25 inches a year, and Necker hosts the same variety of birds, minus the Nihoa finch and the Nihoa miller. Hawaiian seals have been shot on Necker, and turtles, fish, and crustacea abound.

Necker Island was discovered by the sailing ship La Perouse *as it sailed westward on November 4, 1789, and passed close enough to observe surface features. The island has been claimed by the Hawaiian Government many times since 1845, but President Dole, in an 1894 speech, claimed it was officially annexed in 1857.*

Archaeologists found that Necker seems to have been unchanged since the first human visited. Most marae *on platforms, precariously stacked, are still standing. The* marae *found here even more closely resemble those found in Polynesia.*

Only eight bluff shelters were found, and only one of those, called "Bowl Cave" by archaeologists, contained any evidence of lengthy occupation. The bluff shelters' capacities ranged from one person to some with a capacity for six. It was estimated that the island was inhabited by no more than 24 people total.

Artifacts found within Bowl Cave included grindstones, adzes, chisels and awls, sinkers, bird-snaring perches, containers and vessels, dishes, and wood fragments. Also within the cave were the right and left femurs and tibia from an adult male. The bones seemed to represent a burial, and were the only bones found in the investigation of Necker Island.

Unlike to Nihoa, archaeologists on Necker uncovered images (statuettes) of male human figures. These revealed confusing data, because their arms hung straight down just as Hawaiian images do, yet their large heads and smaller bodies resembled uniquely Polynesian Marquesan stone images.

In comparison, the structures on Nihoa and Necker are similar if not identical. Only one site on Kauai, found in opening an irrigation ditch in 1896, revealed a marae similar to those on Nihoa and Necker.

Adzes on both islands are similar, as are containers and jars obviously made on both islands by the same people because not only are two jars identical to each other, but the remains of the contents are the same as well. Each jar is made of materials found on each island, respectively.

In conclusion, it seems that the Necker population would have to have come from Hawaii because of its proximity, but artifacts overall resemble those from the Society Islands. Punaruu Valley in Tahiti bears marae identical to those found on Necker.

At the same time, there is a distinct connection between Necker culture and Hawaiian culture, unique to all of Polynesia. Adzes point to Hawaii, the Marquesas, the Society Islands, and New Zealand, and seem to exclude Samoa, Tonga, and Niue.

One possibility is that the Necker population was forced out of the main Hawaiian group and resettled on Nihoa, then on Necker. Nihoa was then repopulated later by Hawaiians.

Therefore, it seems that the population of Necker Island was a pure sample of culture prevailing in Hawaii before the 13th century, and that prehistoric as well as historic Hawaiian culture should be considered Tahitian in origin.

How Much Will It Cost?

Traveling in Hawaii can cost you a bundle or it can be a relatively good value, depending chiefly on where you stay and eat. Some backpacker/campers can spend almost nothing once they've arrived here. Good bed-and-breakfasts are plentiful, and will average $100 per night. Hotels, of course, range wildly in price and quality, with average rates in the $250 per night range. If you press you can often get a better rate, particularly during slower months of the year.

Some adventurers prefer to hike around the islands and stay in campgrounds. This can be done, but is not always the easiest way to enjoy the islands. For one thing, many campgrounds limit the number of nights you can stay, as well as the number of people allowed in a given area. So you may find yourself moving from one campsite to the next, or even occasionally stranded. Of course, don't be tempted to camp on private land. Landowners will probably not show you the Aloha Spirit if they catch you. It *is* the United States, and that *is* trespassing.

These factors, combined with wet weather in some areas during winter months, can make camping less than ideal. Still, it is a cost savings and may make some sense. If you are going to camp, use the information and addresses in this book, get the facts for the areas you wish to visit, and make reservations in advance. You'll be glad you did.

Transportation

Honolulu International Airport is the hub of the Pacific. On any given day the runways and tarmac are loaded with flights from all reaches of the globe.

From the U.S. Mainland, flights are frequent and available on almost all major carriers, including American, Continental, Delta, and United. Many charter flights are also available—albeit with far less choice of scheduling—offering travelers a less expensive alternative to commercial airlines.

United Airlines flies most people to Hawaii from the Mainland, with roughly 50 percent of the market share. Their fares are higher, but the routing comes from many major U.S. cities, so United is likely to be convenient from a variety of gateways.

But there are less-expensive alternatives. Hawaiian Airlines is always a good phone call, with fares normally from $289 to $389. Hawaiian is limited in its departure cities, however, with flights primarily from the West Coast: San Francisco, Los Angeles, Portland, and Seattle.

Not much is available in the way of sea passage, unless you're considering a cruise. If this is your choice, quite a few luxury liners make Hawaii a port of call.

Getting from one island to another is easy, with the two main interisland carriers—Aloha Airlines and Hawaiian Airlines—offering frequent daily flights. There are no ferries between islands, except for one that runs between Maui and Lanai.

Once in Hawaii, rental cars and vans—with all major rental companies found at the airports—are the preferred method of transportation. Oahu has a good bus system, called The Bus, and it's one of the best deals in the state. For one dollar, you can ride around the island all day. Unfortunately, the other islands don't have such good public transportation, and taxi fares can add up quickly.

Selection Criteria

I used a simple set of criteria in determining which adventures, accommodations, and dining establishments to recommend. First and foremost, I wanted this book to be user-friendly, up-to-date, and logical in its order.

Where appropriate, each island is divided into areas in which you may wish to spend more time. The Big Island chapter, for example, is divided into three sections—Hawaii Volcanoes National Park, Kamuela to Hilo, and Kona-Kohala Coast. You could spend several days in any or all three. Each area has sufficient adventure, accommodation, and dining choices to allow a full experience even if you decided to go nowhere else in Hawaii.

Before any listing could be included in the book, it had to qualify under a number of points:

1) Is this experience in keeping with the philosophy of ecotourism? And does it strive to preserve and protect the

environment while also providing guests an authentic Hawaiian experience?

2) Are the guides/hosts knowledgeable about Hawaii and are they eager and available to share their knowledge? Or is this an experience that self-guided travelers can find and appreciate on their own?

3) Is the experience safe? Is it well maintained? Is it legal?

4) How long has an establishment been in business? Is it likely to be in business next year?

5) Is the experience worth the asking price?

With these standards in mind, not every adventure you could possibly have in Hawaii is included; nor is every decent restaurant or hotel. But what *is* included is certain to meet the search criteria of the responsible traveler/ecotourist.

In some ways, Oahu is the most difficult island to write about in terms of adventure. It has no spewing volcano like the Big Island does, nor a dramatic mountain that dominates the landscape as Haleakala does on Maui, nor sharp green ridges cutting right down into the surf as the Na Pali Coast does on Kauai. Plus, much of what you can do on Oahu is overcrowded. Two examples of this are hiking Diamond Head, where you'll often encounter several hundred people on the trail and at the summit; and snorkeling Hanauma Bay, where you'll find the same people you saw at Diamond Head now spilling off their tour buses in bathing suits.

So, while I've included hiking Diamond Head in the recommendations (with an appropriate word of warning), most of the Oahu experiences I've included will take you farther afield. Still, if you are looking for adventure travel in Hawaii, Oahu—despite its many charms—may pale in comparison to some of the other islands.

A word about accommodations: On all the islands a variety of choices presents itself to Hawaii's visitors. There are many upscale resorts that are not mentioned in the chapter listings, but that fact does not reflect on their quality. Rather, what you will find recommended here is a selection of favorite bed-and-breakfasts, smaller inns and lodges, and the occasional resort.

You should also be aware that bed-and-breakfasts in Hawaii, for the most part, do not take the "breakfast" part of their names in the same way that many of their Mainland counterparts do. In the Aloha State, "breakfast" can mean anything from a welcome basket of fruit and grain, to a full breakfast, to nothing at all.

Some of the properties listed are represented by Hawaii's Best Bed & Breakfasts. This well-respected company is located on the Big Island, but has properties on all islands.

The dining recommendations are all from firsthand experience. In some ways they were the most difficult recommendations, since there are so many good spots to "grind," as we say in Hawaii. Plus, if you ask 10 locals to name their favorite restaurants, you may very well get 100 different answers. So do try some of the suggestions, but don't hesitate to ask around and go find some good grinds on your own.

Hawaii is home to many ethnicities, and often this means good ethnic restaurants. Chinese, Japanese, and Hawaii Regional Cuisine dominate the listings; the thinking was, Why suggest an Italian restaurant in Hawaii? (There are some good ones, however, if you get the Italian hankering.) For each area, you'll find "eco-conscious" choices, or at least restaurants that serve vegetarian dishes.

Biking is an eco-friendly way to see the Hawaiian Islands.

CONSERVATION AND RESPONSIBLE TOURISM IN HAWAII

2

The myth of the idyllic Pacific has persisted for many years. From the time of the first trading ships that sailed her waters, stories and fables have filtered back to "civilization" detailing the uncompromised beauty of the islands and peoples of the Pacific.

Author A. Grove Day, in his book *Mad About Islands: Novelists of a Vanished Pacific*, writes, "The South Seas myth is highly specific. Each of us has his own Bali Ha'i. Solitude becomes more precious as our population explodes. The dream comprises natural beauty and a perfect climate—there are breakers on the reef and shady nooks by the lagoon. All the irritations of urban existence have vanished: no telephones, no crowded freeways, no smog, no strikes.

"So long as we need to believe there is an escape hatch from the rat cage, we shall read South Seas stuff."

Mark Twain, too, was lured by the islands. He first came to Hawaii in 1866, and returned several times throughout his life. He experienced something similar to what many people experience when they decide to move here. Again, according to Day, "He had gone to visit the somnolent island of Maui, intending to stay for a week. He stayed for five, and in later life remembered Maui as the dream refuge from the pressures of life as a celebrity."

If you're heading to Hawaii to get away from it all, be forewarned. Even here, in this paradise of sorts, we are plagued by our share of urban problems. These islands do have telephones and traffic jams, pollution and smog. Even the occasional strike. And in the outlying regions, unthinking industrialists and tourists sometimes tread heavily on our land and resources. But there are still ways to find the Hawaii of your dreams, just as those who came here in previous centuries found theirs.

When you visit Hawaii you have many tour operators and activities from which to choose—too many, perhaps. Making the right choice is often a challenge. But you *can* find operators who are aware of the vulnerabilities of Hawaii's people, land, and water, and who make every effort to preserve and educate. Many of the most conscientious operators are members of the Hawaii Ecotourism Association, which will be happy to send you information on its members.

Come, visit one of the most pristine environments on earth. Enjoy it, but leave it as you found it. Better yet, if you can, leave it improved.

What Is Ecotourism?

"Ecotourism" may be a buzzword, but it's the wrong word. It implies too much and means too little.

The Ecotourism Society defines it as "purposeful travel to natural areas to understand the cultural and natural history of the environment, taking care not to alter the integrity of the ecosystem, while producing economic opportunities that make the conservation of natural resources financially beneficial to local citizens."

Not at all a bad definition. But to some in the travel industry, ecotourism implies tree-hugging environmentalists out to stop all development in all places. To others it implies a category of tourist who prefers backpacking over beachfront resorts, sipping wheat-grass juice over Chardonnay, and eating alfalfa sprouts over osso bucco.

The truth is somewhere in between. Today's good planetary citizens—and I count myself among them—*are* concerned with the environment, and *are* concerned with the issue of their own health in

A Zodiac trip off Kauai—with responsible operators, one can easily "leave no trace."

their dining choices. And when it comes to travel, we take our concerns with us.

But most people like a little pampering now and again. We are willing to spend our hard-earned dollars on quality products and services—we're even willing to splurge once in a while. But we want certain things in return.

For example, we are interested in finding "authentic" experiences, talking to the residents of a place, discovering who they are and how they live their lives. We want some of our dollars to go back into the community we are visiting. We wish to discover "real" arts and crafts, not just those offered in airports or convenience stores. "Ecotourists," for lack of a better word, want to get deeper inside an experience than that which can be summed up on the front of a T-shirt.

We wish to visit destinations and properties that are concerned with these issues, as well. Who in today's world, for example, would care to visit Hawaii if their only choice was Waikiki? My friends in the

5 EASY STEPS TO PROTECT OCEANS

1. Reduce household pollutants. Cut down on, and properly dispose of, herbicides, pesticides, and cleaning products. These pollutants contaminate the watershed and eventually make their way to the ocean.

2. Protect ocean wildlife. Don't dispose of fishing lines, nets, or plastic items in or near the water.

3. Be considerate of sea-life habitats. Don't feed seabirds, mammals, turtles, and fish, or disturb their nesting grounds. Support marine protected areas.

4. Get involved. Take part in a beach cleanup or other ocean-oriented activities.

5. Care! Pass on your knowledge!

visitor industry in Waikiki may take umbrage at such remarks, but these questions reflect valid concerns. Waikiki is a plastic, fantastic microcosm of Hawaii's worst faults. It's overbuilt, overpriced, overrun, and prone to drugs and prostitution. And if truth be told, Waikiki is all too aware of its own shortcomings and is taking steps to align itself with the rest of Oahu, where more authentic Hawaiian experiences can be found.

With the above criteria in mind, is "cultural tourism" a better phrase to describe the travel experiences readers of this book are looking for? It might be, except it excludes one important segment of travel: respectful adventures in nature.

If today's concerned travelers are looking for authenticity in culture, we are also looking for authenticity in adventure. We want to find the people and companies who are offering adventure off the beaten path. We wish to discover authentic cowboys to tell us the stories of their heritage as we ride the mountain slopes; divers and fishermen who know the ocean's moods and currents because they have been brought up diving and fishing them; dancers who come from the land

and feel the passion of the dances, not the showgirls dancing for paychecks you'll find at many of Hawaii's less authentic luaus and shows. Finally, we are looking for cultural and adventure experiences that take an approach of protection and preservation. This may be called "responsible tourism" or "sustainable tourism," two phrases that do not exactly sing. They do, nevertheless, say a little more about the type of travel presented in this book.

In the end, perhaps "ecotourism," with all its flaws, is the word we will have to live with. At least we're working our way toward a clear definition.

Ecotourism in Hawaii

Surprisingly, despite its obvious connection, Hawaii has been slow-to-glacial in recognizing the possibilities of ecotourism.

Although in 1995 and '96 more than 30 nations around the world reported that they were developing or expanding ecotourism projects, the State of Hawaii was not doing so. Although in 1995 the World Congress on Adventure Travel and Ecotourism estimated that 10 to 15 percent of the total global tourism market centered on adventure travel and ecotourism, Hawaii was not cultivating that segment. Although ecotourism has been flourishing for decades in places such as Costa Rica and Ecuador's Galapagos Islands, the State of Hawaii apparently did not see the trend.

With its clean air, diverse terrain, and pristine waters, Hawaii would seem to many people to be the perfect environment for ecotourism. And it is. Only the State of Hawaii *still* doesn't seem to know that.

Despite the fact that visitors spend some $669 million in Hawaii each year on adventure travel and ecotourism-related activities—that's roughly 7.7 percent of total visitor expenditures—the state government acts as if Hawaii is still just a destination for American conventioneers and Japanese honeymooners wishing to spend their days on overcrowded Waikiki Beach and their evenings shopping at a Chanel boutique.

This course of thinking has undergone some changes recently, as Governor Ben Cayetano in 1997 appointed a panel of resort industry leaders to a new board called the Hawaii Tourism Authority (HTA). The HTA's primary mission is to oversee spending the state's $60 million marketing and promotion budget. Until the HTA came along, these monies, collected chiefly from hotel room taxes, had been under the mostly unquestioned purview of the Hawaii Visitors & Convention Bureau (HVCB). Although the ultimate effectiveness of the HTA has yet to be proven, at least the governor has launched the first grenade into the marketing bunkers.

In their defense, though, Hawaii's visitor industry has historically never asked the HVCB to do much more than put "heads in beds." That challenge was relatively easy to meet over the years, because Hawaii drew vacationers from both sides of the Pacific as well as from around the globe. The Japanese came in droves, the Americans came in droves, the Europeans and Canadians came in smaller droves (and spent less). Throughout the 1960s, '70s, and much of the '80s they all came, and no one cared much about the adventure traveler or the still-to-be-defined ecotourist. The numbers looked good.

Then a couple of things happened. First, in the early 1990s, fear of terrorism during the Gulf War caused widespread visitor cancellations and started a decline in arrival numbers. Next, a malaise set into the American economy, followed by a larger malaise in the Japanese and Asian economies. Simultaneously, other destinations such as Mexico, the Bahamas, and Puerto Rico began to mature, many closer to the United States, less expensive to visit, and with much larger marketing budgets than Hawaii's. That drew even more travelers away from the base.

Fortunately, an entire generation of Americans who were brought up in the 1950s and '60s—many with a heightened sense of environmental responsibility—began to mature into a generation of travelers with enough disposable income to travel to Hawaii. This was a saving grace, because if arrivals from the U.S. Mainland had not been on the rise, Hawaii may well have turned off the lights and hung up the "Gone Fishin'" sign for the last three years of the '90s.

It's what this new generation found when they got here that was troubling. Somewhere beneath the veneer of Las Vegas–style glitz and kitsch, something was missing: an authentic Hawaii. This may have been less troubling in the '50s and '60s because the destination was just emerging, and Elvis on the beach in Hawaii fit nicely into an image of America's newest state as a tropical paradise.

REEF ECONOMY

According to Hannah Bernard, naturalist aboard the Maui Nui Explorer, *Hawaii's coral reefs are mainstays of both the local and national economy. She says nationally an estimated $54 billion dollars in goods and services are derived from coastal tourism, supporting nearly 30 million jobs. Hawaii contributes a respectable proportion to that figure, as roughly 7 million people visit in a typical year, spending more than $700 million dollars on ocean-related activities. So not only is caring for Hawaii's reefs an environmental responsibility, it's also a financial imperative.*

But guess what? Hawaiians never wore coconut shell bras and plastic grass skirts while doing the hula—and never will!

And there were more troubling trends. The Hawaiian language was all but dead; hula had been reduced to bad luau shows; the culture was dying. And if rampant and insensitive development went unchecked, the environment would be next on the chopping block. Already so much had been lost. Consider for a moment that of the 100 species of birds extant in Hawaii in 1898, no more than 25 percent still thrive. The balance are now extinct or are close to it, driven to the end of time by introduced species or humans' imposition on the habitat.

Even today, despite increasing environmental awareness, the Hawaiian islands have more birds, insects, and plants on the endangered species list than anywhere else on earth. Some of our most treasured forests, mountains, and trails are threatened by alien species, such as kahili ginger, Japanese honeysuckle, thorny blackberry, and strawberry guava.

It is unlikely that the untrained eye would even notice there is an extinction going on, however, since these alien species are quite beautiful in their own right. Visitors to Hawaii look at the exotic yellow flowers of the

HAWAII

15 WAYS TO SAVE CORAL REEFS

Excerpted courtesy of the National Oceanic and
Atmospheric Administration; prepared for the International
Year of the Coral Reef, 1997

Coral reefs are living, breathing entities, and in Hawaii we are blessed with some of the most beautiful coral reefs anywhere in the world. The responsibility for sustaining our coral reefs and the marine life they support ultimately falls to all of us. No one will do it for us; we must all do our share. Here are 15 things you can do to save coral reefs:

1. Support reef-friendly businesses. Ask what your dive shop, boating store, tour operator, or other coastal businesses are doing to save the coral reefs. Let them know you are an informed consumer who cares about reefs.

2. Don't use chemically enhanced pesticides and fertilizers. Although you may live thousands of miles from a coral-reef ecosystem, these products end up in the watershed and may ultimately affect the waters that support coral.

3. Volunteer for a reef cleanup. You don't live near a coral reef? Then do what many people do with their vacations: visit a coral reef. Spend an afternoon enjoying the beauty of one of the world's treasures while helping to preserve it for future generations.

4. Learn more about coral reefs. How many different species live in reefs? What new medicines have been discovered in reef organisms? Participate in training or educational programs that focus on reef ecology. When you further your own education, you can help others understand the fragility and value of the world's coral reefs.

5. When you visit a coral reef, keep it healthy by respecting all local guidelines, recommendations, regulations, and customs. Ask local authorities or your dive shop how to protect the reef.

6. Support conservation organizations. Many of them have coral-reef programs, and your much-needed monetary support will make a big difference.

7. Be an informed consumer. Consider carefully the coral objects that you buy for your coffee-table. Ask the store owner or manager: Which country is the coral taken from, and does that country have a management plan to insure that the harvest was legal and sustainable over time?

8. Don't pollute. Never put garbage or human waste in the water. Don't leave trash on the beach.

9. Report dumping or other illegal activities. Environmental enforcement cannot be everywhere, and your involvement can make a big difference.

10. Surf the Net! Many different Web sites exist to link you to information about coral reefs and what you can do to become involved. A good starting point is www.noaa.gov/public-affairs/coral-reef.html.

11. Don't start a live-rock aquarium. Although this living rock is still harvested legally in some places, its collection is devastating to the reef organisms' habitat.

12. Hire local guides when visiting coral-reef ecosystems. Not only will you learn about the local resources, but also you will be protecting the future of the reef by supporting a nonconsumptive economy around that reef.

13. Don't anchor on the reef. If you go boating near a coral reef, use mooring buoys when they are available.

14. If you dive, don't touch! Take only pictures and leave only bubbles. Keep your fins, gear, and hands away from the coral, as this contact can hurt you and will damage the delicate coral animals. Stay off the bottom because stirred-up sediment can settle on coral and smother it.

15. Be a wastewater crusader. Make sure that sewage from your boat, from others' boats, and from land is correctly treated. The nutrients from sewage feed growing algae that can smother and kill corals.

ginger plant, for example, and think it a perfectly natural fit in such a tropical environment.

But, as pointed out in a story by Evelyn Cook on the Kokee rain forest of Kauai, published in the October 1998 issue of *Honolulu* magazine, "These (the ginger, honeysuckle, blackberry, and strawberry guava) and a host of other non-native plants are wreaking havoc upon Kokee's native ecosystem, which gradually evolved over millions of years, in highly isolated conditions, at an altitude that averages 3,500 feet. Aliens are rapidly wiping out vast tracts of rare endemic plants, and destroying the habitats of endangered birds and native insects, which can ill afford the added pressure upon their already precarious chances of survival."

Another example lies in the waters close to our heralded beaches. Our coral reefs are imperiled by every snorkeler who steps on them unaware that reefs are living, breathing life forms. The multicolored fish that live so plentifully in our waters become a little more aggressive toward and dependent upon human contact every time they are hand-fed frozen peas or white bread—two substances that are the fish equivalent of junk food—a practice that is common and encouraged by many tour-boat operators.

"Reefs are refuges, providing food and shelter for other plants and animals, and providing for humans in many ways, as well," says Hannah Bernard, a naturalist aboard the *Maui Nui Explorer*, a tour boat run by Royal Hawaiian Cruises. "Reefs and the beaches they form provide protection from storms and high surf for the exploding human population that crowds along the world's seacoasts. Coral reefs are also a bountiful and convenient source of food for people, providing many coastal populations with daily sustenance. Many Hawaiians still catch their supper on the reef each day."

With the exception of some heavily visited hot spots such as Hanauma Bay and Molokini Island, Hawaii still has healthy reefs. Researchers estimate that perhaps as much as 75 percent of Hawaii's reefs are in good health, compared with only 5 percent of the reefs in the Philippines and even less in Jamaica.

"Reefs everywhere are imperiled," Bernard says. "Scientists predict that less than 30 percent of the world's reefs will be healthy by the year 2036 if we don't take aggressive action now. The United Nations was

A pristine beach at Makena State Park on Maui

concerned enough for the future of the reef and marine ecosystems that it designated two back-to-back years, 1997 and 1998, to raise public awareness: the International Year of the Reef, and the International Year of the Ocean."

The Year of the Reef was widely celebrated in Hawaii with public events, reef surveys, conferences, and field trips. The Year of the Ocean provided another opportunity to bring attention to the larger ocean ecosystem of which the reefs are only a small part.

Clearly, it's time for Hawaii to wake up and smell the Kona coffee. The state is a series of fragile and beautiful ecosystems that all of us— residents and visitors alike—must protect. Is there any other choice? Without pristine ecosystems, we are merely a remote archipelago in the middle of a vast ocean, with little to offer.

Business organizations, such as the Big Island's Kona/Kohala Resort Association, have recognized the opportunity adventure travel provides, and have created programs that allow visitors to take advantage of the natural resources these areas have to offer.

A small grant was recently given to the Hawaii Ecotourism Association by the State of Hawaii's Department of Business and Economic Development and Tourism for the development of a manual for ecotourism outfitters and operators. The State of Arkansas has had such a manual for several years.

Arkansas's manual says, "The United States is steadily becoming one of the recognized destinations for global ecotourism. Vacationers are choosing ecotours as meaningful leisure experiences, and the international travel industry is recommending them more frequently to an enlarging base of interested clients."

The Arkansas manual goes on to point out that, "The Australian government recently committed $11.4 million over four years to its National Ecotourism Program. The Land Down Under is increasing opportunities to experience and learn about Australia's natural environment while making a major investment in environmental conservation and management."

The scorecard: Australia—$11.4 million; Hawaii—$10,000.

The State of Hawaii is investing precious little to protect its precious lot.

Parks and Protected Areas

The report is mixed on Hawaii's parks and protected areas. Some, such as Haleakala National Park (Maui) and Hawaii Volcanoes National Park (Big Island), are in excellent shape, with good educational programs, camping facilities, and hiking trails.

Other areas, such as the Kokee rain forest (Kauai)—where native plant populations fight to survive among introduced species—and the once-immaculate Na Pali Coast (Kauai), are having their struggles. Indeed, while the overall visitor count rose in Hawaii for several decades, imagine the strain placed on fragile ecosystems such as these as more and more people—most well intentioned, I'm sure—descended upon them.

Hanauma Bay, one of Oahu's favorite snorkeling bays, is closed one full day per week to allow the fish and the reef a chance to breathe without a throng of vacationers. Also under discussion is the possibility of imposing a fee to visit and climb Diamond Head; these funds would ostensibly be used for trail and facility upkeep.

On every Hawaiian island are issues of this nature to be faced. It is, perhaps, Hawaii's greatest challenge: How do we educate and regulate without being heavy-handed or discouraging to the visitors who come to our shores?

Conservation Groups

While the State of Hawaii may lag, several organizations and some enlightened individuals have seen the opportunity for a brighter future and have picked up the flag of conservation and responsible travel. The Nature Conservancy, the Sierra Club, and the Hawaii Ecotourism Association are three such organizations, working in concert with outfitters and adventure-tour operators to create a game plan for conservation and responsible tourism.

A woman named Kate Reinard has taken it upon herself to do something about conservation, one weed at a time. Reinard's program (808/335-0924), for which she accepts volunteers, involves going into the Kokee forest and identifying key areas to protect. She and her volunteers then begin the simple, time-consuming task of weeding out the alien species to give endemic species the breathing room and sunlight they need to live.

Programs such as Reinard's are perfect for Hawaii, which has so much to protect and so little assistance from government agencies to do so.

Annette Kaohelaulii, president of Hawaii Ecotourism Association and operator of her own adventure-travel business, agrees. "I led hikes for the Sierra Club, and started Annette's Adventures to lead the same kinds of trips," she says. "I realized I couldn't save the world, but I could make a difference one person at a time.

"I thought that if people came and saw the kinds of problems we have here, they could take some of the same solutions back with them wherever they live, because I think an island is a bellwether.

"If people get out and challenge themselves," Kaohelaulii says, "they start to feel better about who they are, so they can try things they've never tried before."

Tips for Responsible Travel

Adventure travelers have a number of excellent opportunities for responsible ecotourism. There are many operators and outfitters who act with integrity toward preserving Hawaii's natural environment. You will find most of them listed in this book.

As you visit our islands, bear in mind that humans pose the greatest threats to the world's reefs through over-fishing, non–point source pollution, boat anchoring, and sedimentation from land runoff. What it comes down to is habitat degradation—ours as well as that of the sea creatures. Here in Hawaii, resource managers are concerned with the decline of fisheries and the negative impacts humans have made in their land-use and marine-tourism practices. With so many visitors to our reefs, Hawaii can be adversely affected by those who neglect to tread lightly.

"Water quality and reefs can be harmed when people step on or grasp coral, and touch or feed sea turtles and other wildlife for their own entertainment," says naturalist Bernard, who teaches as she leads excursions into Hawaii's waters. "These actions can greatly upset the reef creatures we visit. Feeding wild animals is not helpful but harmful, upsetting the natural balance and turning animals into beggars, dependent on humans."

When she sees someone in the water feeding the fish or standing on a coral head, Bernard will talk to that person, resident or tourist, and explain why their actions are inappropriate.

"What a teaching opportunity, as people engage in all the wrong behaviors, to share my reverence for the coral reef," she says, "to explain that coral is a living creature—one of earth's most ancient life forms, having survived the fall of the dinosaurs, existing in the seas for more than 200 million years.

"And there's even more to marvel at. Hawaii's reefs are some of the most isolated in the world, situated on volcanic slopes in the midst of the mightiest ocean in the world. Because of its profound isolation, many of Hawaii's reef creatures are found nowhere else on Earth. Hawaii's reefs are world treasures simply because of their uniqueness and relative health. In addition, the reefs here are simply gorgeous to view. The islands' volcanic black rocks provide a stunning contrast to the blue, green, white, and yellow coral communities that grow on their surfaces."

As visitors listen to and then dive into the warm, blue waters with her, they begin to feel Bernard's love and enthusiasm for the reefs and oceans of Hawaii, and they begin to understand and feel for themselves how special a place underwater Hawaii really is.

"While living in or visiting Hawaii, there are many ways to be a good steward of the ocean and the reefs," Bernard says. "And these actions can be so much more rewarding than the ones that disturb the natural balance. Once we establish a sense of stewardship for the marine environment, it is easy to take actions to protect it. In Hawaii, there is a saying: *Malama i ka moana*. It means: 'Cherish, take care of the ocean.'

"You can help to *malama* Hawaii's marine ecosystem in so many ways," Bernard says. "Living lightly on the land and swimming gently over the reef will help to preserve its beauty and bounty for generations to come. If you feel strongly about an environmental issue, speak out. Your attitude of respect for the environment is infectious and will positively affect everyone's behavior."

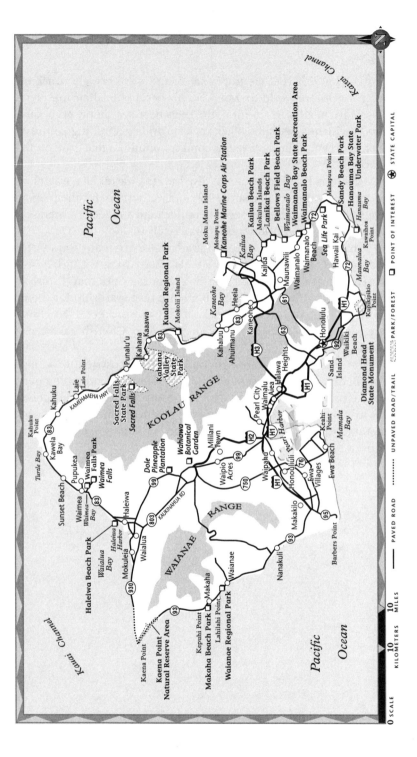

3

OAHU—THE
GATHERING PLACE

Oahu is a difficult island to pin down for adventure tourism, since so much of it seems crowded by freeways, people, and the bustle of an international metropolis at work. Its charms are here, but they are hard to find. If you've been to Hawaii before and spent any time on Oahu, you may wish to skip it altogether on your next visit. But if you've never been to Hawaii, Oahu can be an education that is valuable to take with you on your adventures.

For one thing, here you'll get a sense of the water, the land, and the different cultures in Hawaii. Plus you'll get a valuable lesson in the history of the islands, especially if you spend any time at Bishop Museum.

Orientation/Lay of the Land

The areas you'll want to visit on Oahu are divided into Waikiki/ Honolulu, the North Shore, and Windward Oahu. There are good choices for adventure, dining, and accommodations in each area, and because it takes only 90 minutes or so to get around the entire island, you won't feel isolated wherever you choose to stay.

Here's a good way to pinpoint your choices: If you like nightlife and the bustle of a city, stay in the Waikiki/Honolulu area; if you prefer a more low-key setting in a bed-and-breakfast near the beach, the Windward Oahu area is for you; if you want privacy and the most rugged scenery and adventure, head for the North Shore.

In addition to the myriad nightspots and restaurants, perhaps the most interesting thing to do on the Honolulu side of the island is to study the architecture. Fascinating buildings abound, such as the Honolulu Academy of Arts, which combines indoor/outdoor plantation architecture with pitched Chinese rooflines; the coral block-constructed Kawaiahao Church; and, of course, the Mediterranean-style Royal Hawaiian Hotel—the "pink palace" of Waikiki—which was shunned when it was first built but today is accepted as classic Hawaiian architecture.

When you've had enough city, head for the country, the North Shore. Almost as if it were stuck in time, the North Shore is peaceful and low-key, with quaint villages strung along a beautiful coastline. An easy half-day drive along Highway 83 will take you through the artsy town of Haleiwa; past the surf-famous beaches of Waimea, Banzai Pipeline, and Sunset; around the point at Turtle Bay and Kahuku; and on into Kaneohe past Chinaman's Hat. Along the way are many hikes, beach stops, and knickknack shops.

Windward Oahu boasts the best beaches in the United States, at least according to beach experts Rick Carroll (*Best Beach Vacations: Hawaii;* MacMillan Travel, 1995) and Dr. Stephen Leatherman, of the University of Maryland, who have both published studies on the subject. But Windward Oahu also has some of the best hiking trails and adventure opportunities on the island. There are no hotels, so if you are planning on staying on the Windward side, your best bet is checking in at one of the area's many bed-and-breakfasts.

Nature/Adventure Activities

The hustle and bustle of the Waikiki/Honolulu area may seem to detract from the nature and adventure attractions of Oahu, but this island is teeming with outdoor activities. After all, this is the home of the famous North Shore, a surfer's paradise. And a wide array of diving, snorkeling, and fishing opportunities await you all along the shores. On land, hiking is a major draw, with Windward Oahu standing out not only for its beaches, but also for its trails.

Flora and Fauna

Oahu encompasses an area of 617 square miles. Scientists estimate the island was created by two volcanoes, Waianae and Koolau (both now classified as extinct), some four to five million years ago. Although you may think that an island that compresses 1 million residents into 617 square miles wouldn't have much room left for things natural, that impression is not altogether true. In fact, in the slopes and heights of both the Koolau and Waianae mountain ranges much natural space remains.

One stop you may wish to make before venturing into the wilds is Foster Botanical Garden, on the corner of Vineyard and Nuuanu Avenues just above downtown Honolulu. This lovely area is actually a series of gardens, each set up to provide optimal growing conditions for various groups of tropical plants. An hour's walk through Foster Botanical Garden will help you identify many of the trees, plants, and flowers you'll later encounter in the wild.

The same thing can be said for the Harold Lyon Arboretum in Manoa Valley near the University of Hawaii. Approximately 6,000 species of trees and plants are cultivated and studied here, and the arboretum's scientific contributions have been instrumental in Hawaii's ongoing battle to save species from extinction. A word of friendly advice: Be prepared for rain and take mosquito repellent—both rain and mosquitos are frequent in this lush setting.

As you venture into Oahu's forests, not only will you see many species of palm trees, ferns, and shrubs, but also you'll find that the bird-watching is actually quite good. Aside from the ubiquitous introduced species, such as the northern cardinal, myna, finches, and sparrows, you're likely to see some of Hawaii's endemic and endangered birds. These might include Oahu *amakihi*, *'apapane*, and *elepaio*.

Of course the closer you are to the ocean, the more species of seabirds you'll encounter. Common off Oahu's shores are boobies, sooty terns, wedge-tailed shearwaters, brown noddies, tropic birds, and frigate birds. In the marsh- and pasturelands around the island, particularly on the North Shore, you'll probably see cattle egrets, stilts, coots, and night herons, in addition to a variety of duck species.

History, Culture, and Customs

The island of Oahu is called "the Gathering Place" because it is the first stop for most of the state's 7 million yearly visitors. Additionally, it is home to more than 80 percent of Hawaii's 1.2 million residents and the seat of state government.

But why, you might ask, is Oahu the main island? It is not the largest, prettiest, or most fertile or accessible. The answer is most likely that it is central to the other main islands in the group. The principal seaports at Honolulu Harbor and Pearl Harbor are protected, and the southern shore—Honolulu and Waikiki, all the way out to the Ewa Plain—have always been well suited for growth.

Finally, and perhaps more significantly, when King Kamehameha I was trying to unite all the islands under his rule, Oahu was where he was stopped. He conquered Oahu, but his two attempts to add Kauai and Niihau to his kingdom were ill-fated. And his fallback position was Oahu, which he needed to protect to keep a grip on the kingdom.

Today there is much to see and do on this bustling island. Honolulu and Waikiki are far more crowded than other Oahu destinations, but there are several historical and cultural sights that should not be missed. Foremost among these sights are Iolani Palace, the former home of Hawaii's kings and queens, and Bishop Museum, Polynesia's preeminent educational and cultural steward. There are also good hiking trails in the mountains behind the city.

Honolulu became the seat of government in 1850, when King Kamehameha III moved it from Lahaina, Maui. It was during the ensuing 75-year period that much of modern Hawaii—both good and bad—was shaped. Sugar and pineapple became the primary crops, and with them came an agriculture-based economy. Unfortunately, both crops are now a thing of the past for all intents and purposes, leaving the state particularly vulnerable to the changing tides of tourism.

BISHOP MUSEUM

Bishop Museum, 1525 Bernice St., Honolulu, 808/847-3511, is a must-see for visitors to Hawaii. It is the largest and most respected archive and exhibition space of Polynesian culture and history in the Pacific. Its vast collection of artifacts rotates in and out of exhibition, so what you'll see will vary somewhat from visit to visit. Occasionally King Kamehameha the Great's long red-and-yellow feather cape goes on display—it's one of the museum's treasured possessions. Permanent exhibitions include Polynesian fishing and farming tools, oceangoing outrigger canoes, and much, much more. Bishop also offers a planetarium program. Kids love Bishop, too, because there are a lot of hands-on learning displays. Open daily 9–5 except Christmas.

Also during that critical 75-year span, the native Hawaiian population decreased dramatically, to the point where today there are fewer than 10,000 full-blooded Hawaiians left. Simultaneously, the Chinese, Japanese, and Caucasian populations soared, a fact that is very evident today. In fact, according to a 1992 census study, the largest population bases in Hawaii today are Caucasian, followed by Japanese Americans, Hawaiians/part-Hawaiians, Filipinos, and Chinese Americans. Cultural events, as well as much food and architecture, bear out this multicultural legacy in modern Hawaii.

Hawaii has frequently been called an ethnic melting pot, and nowhere is this more true than on Oahu. In addition to the above-named ethnic groups, many others live side by side in Hawaii as well, including Samoans, Tongans, African Americans, Vietnamese, Thai, Japanese nationals, and others. For the most part, it is a harmonic blending.

Of course, Pearl Harbor has played a significant role in Hawaii's history, as its strategic location in the middle of the Pacific led the United States to annex Hawaii in the first place in 1898. And later, the bombing of Pearl Harbor by the Japanese military led to American involvement in World War II. Today, Pearl Harbor's USS *Arizona* Memorial is among the most-visited attraction in the state. The recent permanent docking of the USS *Missouri*—the "Mighty Mo"—at Pearl Harbor gives Hawaii bookends on WWII: the bombing of the USS *Arizona* is where it began; and the Japanese signing of surrender documents on the Mighty Mo's decks is where it ended.

Visitor Information
The **Hawaii Visitors & Convention Bureau** is always a good source of information. They can provide brochures, maps, and practical tips for travel to all the islands. Contact them before you visit, or drop by when you're in town. They are located at 2270 Kalakaua Ave., Suite 801, Honolulu, HI 96815, right in the heart of Waikiki. Call them at 808/923-1811 or 800/GO-HAWAII. Their Web site is loaded with good information: www.gohawaii.com.

Oahu Visitors Bureau provides a similar service specifically geared to the island of Oahu. They will be happy to send you a packet of information if you call them toll-free at 877/525-OAHU.

Other useful Web sites include the **Hawaii Ecotourism Association**'s locations, www.planet-hawaii.com/hea/, and www.alternative-hawaii.com.

The **Sierra Club** often offers group hikes, 808/538-6616; as does the **Hawaii Trail and Mountain Club** (weekends), 808/488-1161. **The Nature Conservancy of Hawaii** offers occasional outings, 808/537-4508.

Getting There
Honolulu International Airport is Hawaii's transportation hub, and major airlines, including United, Delta, Continental, and American, fly from the U.S. Mainland to here daily. A number of charter flights are available if you're looking for a cheaper alternative to commercial airlines.

Getting around Oahu is pretty easy. Rental cars (and jeeps and motorcycles) are the most convenient option, and The Bus system on Oahu is very good and very economical. If you've got the time, The Bus is a great way to get around and see the island at a leisurely pace.

Camping on Oahu

Oahu has 18 camping areas—some run by the City and County of Honolulu, some by the State of Hawaii Division of Parks. Most of the campsites are located within public beach parks. Although they are free, you must get a permit to camp on Oahu because space is limited.

A word of caution: Several campsites on Oahu are located in urban areas where crime makes them unsafe for outsiders. Those listed below are considered safest and are most popular with tourists, but always take care. Ask other people around the camp if they have experienced any incidents, and inquire of the site's safety at permitting agencies. The likelihood is that nothing will happen, but if you don't feel safe, don't stay. The safety of you and your family comes first.

The City and County of Honolulu oversees 13 beach parks that ring the island, starting at Makapuu Beach Park on the eastern part of Oahu, and extending all the way up the windward coast to the North Shore and around to the leeward coastline. Each beach has a different character, as well as varying surf and weather conditions throughout the year.

All of the county beach parks have bathrooms, showers, drinking water, and garbage disposal sites. Campfires are not allowed, but cooking is allowed on grills (which you provide) or portable stoves. No camping is allowed on Wednesday or Thursday nights.

For City and County of Honolulu sites, permits are free of charge and are issued two weeks prior to the desired date. You may apply in person at the Department of Parks and Recreation, 650 S. King St., Honolulu; information can be obtained by calling 808/523-4525.

The State of Hawaii's campgrounds on Oahu are similar to the City and County's. State sites are at Haleiwa, Malaekahana Beach, Waimanalo Bay, Sand Island, and, inland, Aiea Heights. Limits are 10 persons per campsite and five days. No camping is allowed on Wednesday or Thursday nights.

For state sites on Oahu, reservations are taken 30 days in advance.

These permits are also free of charge and can be obtained one week in advance of your desired date. Write or visit the Division of Parks, 1151 Punchbowl St., Room 131, Honolulu, HI 96813; or call 808/587-0300. See the following sections for information on specific campsites.

WAIKIKI/HONOLULU

Think of Honolulu and Waikiki and you'll think first of a bustling city and a shoreline lined with skyscrapers.

But there's more to this side of Oahu than immediately meets the eye. As you venture away from the beach and toward the green folds of the Koolau Mountains, there's plenty of adventure to be found. The foothills are criss-crossed with hiking trails, and there are some hidden waterfalls and lakes to explore. Plus, several endangered species of endemic birds can be seen in these mountains. Offshore—even off busy Waikiki Beach—the waters are perfect for fishing, snorkeling, and scuba diving.

So if you think Waikiki and Honolulu are just about city life, look a little farther. The city life is there, and it can be exciting, but there's much more to discover.

Orientation/Lay of the Land

The five-mile stretch from Aloha Tower at Honolulu Harbor to Kapiolani Park at the foot of Diamond Head in Waikiki is where most of the commerce and tourist activity on Oahu occurs or originates.

Along bustling Ala Moana Boulevard and Kalakaua Avenue you will find an abundance of luxury hotels, pleasure boats, beaches, restaurants, parks, and shopping centers. It is in this area that many of Hawaii's traditional travelers spend their vacations. If you are interested in water adventures, such as snorkeling, fishing, and scuba diving, these areas are where you'll wish to center your attention.

But if eco-adventures are what you seek, you have to look a little farther, into the leeward foothills of the Koolau Mountains behind Honolulu and Waikiki, for example. Up in the Tantalus/Makiki

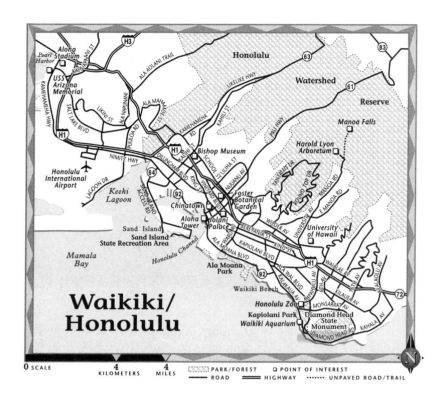

Waikiki/Honolulu

Heights area, in the Manoa Valley, and heading up the Pali Highway you will find hiking trails, bird-watching sites, and scenic overlooks not found on the shoreline below.

It is fairly easy to get around Honolulu and Waikiki without a vehicle. The Bus system is good and inexpensive. It'll even take you to some of the less-traveled areas, such as Makiki Heights and Manoa Valley, where you'll find trailheads for hiking.

The same is true if you are centering your activities on the water. Remember this, too: If you plan on a dive or snorkel tour—in fact a tour of any kind—the tour operators generally have transportation to and from your hotel. If you are not staying in a hotel, they will often meet you at a convenient spot.

CHINATOWN WALKING HISTORY TOUR

Take a fascinating walking history tour of Honolulu's Chinatown, one of the culturally richest areas of town. Conducted by the Chinese Chamber of Commerce, these walks cover the significant historical and cultural spots, go into the shops and markets, and tell the history of Chinatown. While you're there, be sure to sample some of the local foods. Also, on the ocean end of Maunakea Street you'll find interesting antique shops that are worth exploring.

Chinatown Walking History Tours are conducted Tuesdays only, 9:30–noon. Groups meet at the Chinese Chamber of Commerce of Hawaii offices, 42 N. King St., Chinatown, 808/533-3181.

Finally, taxi service is far more cost-effective in Honolulu and Waikiki, due to the shorter distances you'll need to travel, than it is elsewhere on the island or in the state.

History, Culture, and Customs

The Waikiki/Honolulu shore of Oahu has long been treasured for its temperate climate, natural beauty, and bountiful waters. Hawaiian *ali'i* (royalty) used to spend their leisure time in Waikiki. It had the same appeal then as it does today.

Robert Louis Stevenson, Jack London, Mark Twain, James Michener, and other writers came here in earlier days to soak up the magnificent tropical ambiance and write about the lure of the Pacific for readers around the world. And those readers came to the magical shore of Waikiki, first on trading ships, then on steamships and the Pan Am Clipper airliners, and finally on the huge jets that today land 10 to the hour at Honolulu International Airport.

Overlooked by majestic Diamond Head crater, Waikiki is still one

Aloha Tower and Marketplace on Oahu

of the most popular destinations in the islands. A walk down Kalakaua Avenue will reveal many sides of Waikiki. On the historic side, you'll encounter the charming pink Royal Hawaiian Hotel, the recently restored Sheraton Moana Surfrider and its famous banyan tree courtyard, and Waikiki Beach. A little farther down what is called "the Gold Coast" you'll find the Waikiki Natatorium—the saltwater swimming pool at Pacific's edge, once the site of swimming exhibitions by the legendary Hawaiian surfer and Olympian Duke Kahanamoku—as well as the Hau Tree Lanai in the New Otani Kaimana Beach Hotel, where Robert Louis Stevenson sat writing more than 100 years ago.

On the other hand, strolling through Waikiki will make you grip your credit cards tighter as you pass by every high-end boutique known to humankind. Once crowded with Japanese tourists taking advantage of favorable exchange rates, today many of these stores are struggling to survive.

Despite the flaws of overbuilding and the ensuing slam of glitz and traffic, it would be premature to dismiss this side of Oahu as a "been there, done that" thing. Once you emerge from the city, there is plenty of country to be had.

NATURE AND ADVENTURE SIGHTS IN WAIKIKI/HONOLULU

Ala Moana Beach Park

This is a lovely, one-mile stretch of shade trees, grass, and beach between downtown Honolulu and Waikiki. A manmade reef protects a popular saltwater swimming area and makes the beach safe for kids. A trail leading out to the point of Magic Island on the Waikiki end of the park provides a good area for running, walking, or watching the boats enter and leave the adjoining Ala Wai Yacht Harbor. McCoy Pavilion, in the center of the park, often hosts music and cultural festivals. Just to the airport side of the park is Kewalo Basin Harbor, where most of the commercial fishing charters and sunset cruises dock.

Details: *Across from Ala Moana Shopping Center on Ala Moana Boulevard.*

Barbers Point to Diamond Head

Jump aboard a 40-foot sportfishing vessel and go out in search of big game fish. E.L.O. Sport Fishing's Captain Gary Oliver, who was born and raised on Oahu, has more than 20 years' experience finding fish for customers. He'll take you from Barbers Point to Diamond Head lookout, or wherever the fish are biting. You may catch Pacific blue marlin (winter is best for these big boys), striped marlin, yellowfin tuna, skipjack tuna, or mahimahi. Half- and full-day trips are offered.

Details: *E.L.O. Sport Fishing is in Kewalo Basin Harbor, 808/947-5208. Kewalo Basin Harbor is just on the airport side of Ala Moana Park, roughly seven minutes from Waikiki. Trips available seven days a week. Cost is $450 for a half-day with up to six people in the party; full-day trips cost $550 with up to six people; $115/person for full-day share trips.*

Diamond Head State Monument

This may be Hawaii's best-known landmark. It would be difficult to recommend this crowded hike if the views from the top were not so spec-

© George Fuller

Cultural influences in downtown Honolulu

tacular. Busloads of tourists stop here and the trail is often quite busy. Still, it is rewarding—and easy (taking roughly 45 minutes each way)—once you have reached the top, and therefore receives a mildly enthusiastic recommendation. You'll find a series of bunkers near the summit that were built into the mountain face by the U.S. military. These bunkers were originally used as observation posts during World War II, and today serve as a solid platform for your tripod.

Two simple tips will make your visit much more enjoyable: 1) Go early or late in the day to avoid the heat and the bulk of the crowd; and 2) beg, borrow, or buy a flashlight, because once you are inside the tunnels and bunkers it's pitch black until you emerge at the top.

Details: *The entrance to Diamond Head State Monument is found on Diamond Head Road, on the back side of the mountain from the ocean. Gates open at 6 a.m. and close at 6 p.m. There is parking at the foot of the trail. As of this writing, there is no fee for access.*

Kapiolani Park

At the foot of Diamond Head, just past the heart of Waikiki on Kalakaua Avenue, Kapiolani Park is a multi-use park with a tennis center, an archery range, a concert shell, softball and soccer fields, and lots of room for running, biking, working out, and picnicking.

Added bonus: The park is right next door to **Honolulu Zoo** (open daily 9–4). At the zoo, don't miss the African savanna exhibit (hippos, giraffes, cheetahs, lions) and the monthly Zoo by Moonlight (a behind-the-scenes tour with storytelling).

Kapiolani Park is also across the street from the recently improved **Waikiki Aquarium** (open daily 9–5), where you can see many of Hawaii's tropical reef fish in easily viewable exhibits. Affiliated with the University of Hawaii, the aquarium is a research facility as well as a public facility.

Details: Kapiolani Park is located on the Diamond Head side of Waikiki. You can get information about the Honolulu Zoo at 808/971-7171; about the Waikiki Aquarium at 808/923-9741.

Makiki/Tantalus/Manoa Trail Complex

This system includes some 13 trails that lead into the Koolau Mountain Range behind Honolulu. The trails range in length and difficulty, but most are in the one- to two-mile category. Some recommended hikes: the Pu'u Ohia Trail (medium difficulty—two miles) that leads to a beautiful spot overlooking the Nuuanu Reservoir; and the Moleka Trail (easy—.75 mile) that winds around a bamboo grove above scenic Round Top Drive. Many of these looping trails intersect, making it easy to take several different hikes on the same day.

Details: Most of these trails can be accessed at the Hawaii Nature Center, 2131 Makiki Heights Dr., Honolulu, 808/955-0100, which also provides maps and essential information.

Manoa Falls Trail

Take a mild to medium hike up a lovely valley, through a rain forest, to a mountain waterfall. Being at the base of the mountains, this area gets

IOLANI PALACE

The former residence of Hawaii's royal family, today Iolani Palace, near downtown Honolulu, 808/538-1471 or 808/522-0832, is a wonderfully preserved glimpse of what Hawaii was like 100 years ago. Built by King David Kalakaua in 1869, a long-term restoration project has collected and conserved many original palace furnishings. The Throne Room is a high point of the tour, where visitors can see the thrones and coronation crowns of King Kalakaua and Queen Kapiolani. Docents lead the tours and tell the stories, fascinating and tragic, of Hawaii's royal family. Tours conducted Tue–Sat 9–2:15. Reservations recommended.

more rainfall than much of Honolulu, so the trail can get muddy and slippery. But after you've walked the mile it takes to get there, you'll be glad you did—muddy or not—because the waterfall and pool are beautiful and refreshing.

Details: *The trailhead is at the now-defunct Paradise Park, 3737 Manoa Rd., Honolulu. Be sure to wear something you don't mind getting muddy.*

Waianae Shipwreck

The Mahi, sister ship to Jacques Cousteau's *Calypso*, was built in 1942 and used as a minesweeper until the University of Hawaii took her over as a research vessel. In 1982 this 165-foot ship sank in Honolulu's Keehi Lagoon. Later that year she was moved to an area off the Waianae Coast and sunk as an artificial reef, where she lies today at a depth of about 95 feet, with the top of the ship at roughly 60 feet. *The Mahi* is in good condition, and divers can easily explore many of her portals. Spotted eagle rays are common in the area, as are a multitude of fish, eels, and turtles.

*Details: Aaron's Dive Shops, 602 Kailua Rd., Kailua, 808/262-2333, leads these trips. **This dive is for certified divers only, due to the depths.***

Waikiki Beach

Well, this is where tourism in Hawaii started, and no wonder. If you can see past the gazillion tanning tourists, it's a magnificent stretch of white-sand beach in a protected bay with gently curling waves breaking offshore, the whole scene overlooked by majestic Diamond Head. It doesn't get much better for a natural setting, which is why the highrise hotels and condos were built, making this once-tranquil refuge of Hawaii's *ali'i* (royalty) a bustling, hustling destination.

You'll want to visit Waikiki while you're in Hawaii—it would be tough to break the news to Auntie Jo and Uncle Roger back home if you didn't at least look at where they spent their honeymoon. But there are a few things you can do to make your experience a little more authentic. One of the most fun things to do here is ride an outrigger canoe down the face of a five-foot wave, or take a surfing lesson from a Waikiki beachboy.

Details: You'll find Waikiki's famous beachboys hanging out with their surfboards at Kuhio Beach Park, just across the street from the Hyatt Regency Waikiki on Kalakaua Avenue.

Waikiki Reef

This shallow reef dive off the shores of Waikiki is known for its abundance of green sea turtles. The maximum depth is 40 feet, and in this area the bottom is a combination of sand and coral. The turtles are quite accustomed to human contact, and there are also puffer fish, eels, and any number of other sea creatures living in these friendly waters. If you don't want to dive, snorkelers are also welcome.

Details: Aaron's Dive Shops, 602 Kailua Rd., Kailua, 808/262-2333, leads these trips. You don't have to be certified to go on this dive, as a qualified instructor accompanies you and the water on this side of Oahu is gentle year-round. You do, however, need to do an introductory beach dive first that gives you the basics.

GUIDES AND OUTFITTERS

Annette's Adventures, 45-403 Koa Kahiko St., Kaneohe, 808/235-5431, is run by Annette Kaohelaulii, a one-person, full-service travel agent who will customize ecotours and adventure trips on all islands for you. Her specialty is putting together tour packages to Hawaii's off-the-beaten-track destinations of natural and cultural significance. She is also interested in organizing trips specially geared for women.

If you're interested in diving, check out **Aaron's Dive Shops**, 602 Kailua Rd., Kailua, 808/262-2333. With more than 25 years in business and one of the largest stocks of equipment in the islands, Aaron's meets the needs of visiting and local divers. Daily boat dives will take you to all the major dive sites around Oahu, including airplane- and shipwrecks, caverns, caves, and lava tubes. A certified dive guide accompanies every trip. Aaron's also offers four-day PADI certification classes. Snorkelers also welcome.

Another diving outfitter is **Dan's Dive Shop**, 660 Ala Moana Blvd., Honolulu, 808/536-6181. Dan's offers introductory boat dives to shallow Rainbow Reef, off the shore of Ala Moana Beach Park, for those with no experience. There are also daily dives for certified divers.

E.L.O. Sport Fishing, in Kewalo Basin Harbor, 808/947-5208, offers half- and full-day fishing charters available on the south shore of the island. Landlubbers may be interested in **Blue Sky Bicycle Rentals & Sports Center**, 1920 Ala Moana Blvd., 808/947-0101. You can rent mountain bikes here for self-guided riding, or Luis will set up off-road tours for you. Bike rentals run $20 for 24 hours. Off-road tours at additional cost.

CAMPING

For contact and permit information, see the Camping on Oahu section earlier in the chapter.

Keaiwa Heiau State Recreation Area is situated on roughly 385 acres of forested land in the Koolau Mountain Range above Aiea. This camping area is very scenic. It can also be wet and windy, so be prepared for weather. Picnic areas, a five-mile loop trail for hiking, the remains of a Hawaiian *heiau*, and some great city views are the highlights of this recreational area.

Sand Island State Recreation Area is an unlikely location for a campground, Sand Island is known more for being a shipping and industrial area near the airport. Nevertheless, this state-run recreational area is well secured and does boast some pretty Honolulu views. Sunsets are nice, too.

LODGING

As you might expect in a heavily touristed area, the Waikiki/Honolulu region offers a wide variety of accommodation choices. There are many upscale resorts not mentioned in the listings that follow, but that fact does not mean they are lacking in quality or amenities. Rather, what you will find recommended here is a selection of favorite bed-and-breakfasts, smaller inns and lodges, and the occasional resort.

Keep in mind that bed-and-breakfasts in Waikiki/Honolulu, as with the rest of Hawaii, may not take the "breakfast" part too seriously. As with the rest of the Aloha State, "breakfast" can range from a small plate of fruit and muffins, to a full breakfast, to nothing at all.

Some of the properties listed are represented by Hawaii's Best Bed & Breakfasts. You must call this group to make reservations and get directions to the B&Bs.

Colony Surf Hotel, 2885 Kalakaua Ave., Waikiki, 808/924-3111, dwells on Waikiki's Gold Coast. This hotel has several likable traits. First, the beach out front is far less crowded than Waikiki Beach. Next, it has two fabulous restaurants, Michel's and David Paul's Diamond Head Grill. And finally, the 23 rooms in the original hotel building are large, and all have kitchens. It's worth a night or two in one of the oceanfront rooms (900 square feet with kitchen). They are spacious and extremely relaxing, and have a sunset view that is unsurpassed. The 50 rooms in the newer building have been decorated in a Balinese theme. Rates run $224–$385, depending on view and location.

Downtown Honolulu

Also offering a close-up view of the ocean is **New Otani Kaimana Beach Hotel**, 2863 Kalakaua Ave., Waikiki, 808/923-1555. Set on the quiet side of Waikiki, next to the Colony Surf Hotel and the Outrigger Canoe Club, this property is known for its ambiance, for its wonderful beachfront setting, and for offering a good value. The best rooms here look right over the water. They cost more, but the views are superb. The beachfront Hau Tree Lanai is a perfect spot for breakfast (see Food, below). Rates are $115–$220.

Royal Hawaiian Hotel, 2259 Kalakaua Ave., Waikiki, 808/923-7311, is the grand dame on the shore. Built in 1927, Hawaii's historic, 526-room, pink hotel has become a Waikiki landmark. Rooms are pricey, but if you want to stay in Waikiki, this is a good choice. The accommodations are large, and many have good views. In the graceful common areas, you get the feeling that you've stepped back in time. Special treat: Sit at the Mai Tai bar and take in the sunset. Rates run $305–$525.

If you're looking for a homey feel, head over to **Diamond Head Bed and Breakfast** (through Hawaii's Best Bed & Breakfasts), 808/885-4550. A lovely older home in one of Oahu's most desirable

63

residential neighborhoods, Diamond Head Bed and Breakfast is a private residence wonderfully appointed with family heirlooms, koa furniture, and plenty of Old Hawaii charm. It is at the foot of Diamond Head, close to the beach, Kapiolani Park, and Waikiki. There are two spacious rooms available, both with private baths, desks, sofas, and lanais. A full breakfast is included. This place is a gem. Rates start at $100 for a double.

One look at **Manoa Valley Inn**, 2001 Vancouver Dr., Honolulu, 808/947-6019, tells you owner Rick Ralston took great care with this stately Manoa Valley home, constructed in 1919, to restore it to its original grandeur. On the National Register of Historic Places, Manoa Valley Inn has seven guest rooms, each furnished with authentic period pieces: four-poster beds, marble-top dressers, Oriental carpets, carved armoires. The four rooms on the second floor have private baths; the three on the third share a bath. The inn is in the University of Hawaii area, just two miles from Waikiki. Rates run $99–$190.

FOOD

There's so much good "grind" (eats) these days in Waikiki/Honolulu, that it's hard to go wrong. Plus, it comes in every ethnic variety imaginable. Local food comes in plate lunches, and while it's generally not very healthy, it sure can be tasty. In recent years, though, a new style of cooking has emerged called Hawaii Regional Cuisine. Chefs in Hawaii these days have discovered the magic of combining Eastern flavors with Western preparations. You'll find several of the masters of "HRC," as the chefs call it, in Waikiki/Honolulu. Additionally, Thai, Chinese, Japanese, and Vietnamese restaurants have flourished here, giving residents and visitors alike a wonderful menu of choices.

Hau Tree Lanai, New Otani Kaimana Beach Hotel, 2863 Kalakaua Ave., Waikiki, 808/921-7066, is blessed with an oceanfront location, on Waikiki's Gold Coast. Diners sit outdoors under a sweeping *hau* tree—the same tree under which author Robert Louis Stevenson sat more than 100 years ago—watching the swimmers and paddlers on the beach. It's a wonderful spot to enjoy a peaceful breakfast, or catch a sunset later in the day. The food is well prepared, with some good choices such as the crab-cake burger for lunch. But it's the ambiance you're really going for. Breakfast, lunch, and dinner daily.

If you're hankering for Thai food, **Keo's in Waikiki**, Ambassador Hotel, 2028 Kuhio Ave., Waikiki, 808/943-1444, has been recognized as one of Hawaii's best Thai restaurants for many years. Owner Keo Sananikone moved his facility from its original Kapahulu Avenue location to Waikiki several years ago. This has made the prices a little higher, but it's still worth going in for the stuffed Bangkok wings with *sa-te* sauce (a peanut marinade) and the Evil Jungle Prince, a spicy dish simmered with fresh basil, coconut milk, and red chiles, served with shrimp or chicken, or as vegetarian. Keo also offers wonderful curries, from Bangkok-style Panang curry to pineapple and shrimp red curry. Lunch, dinner daily.

To taste the fare of one of the most talented purveyors of Hawaii Regional Cuisine, try **Alan Wong's Restaurant**, 1857 King St., fifth floor, Honolulu, 808/949-2526. Chef Wong's Honolulu establishment is a splurge, to be sure, but very creative and tasty. Daily specials include fresh fish such as steamed *opakapaka* with pork hash, ginger, soy, and truffle. The regular menu features house specialties such as the ginger-crusted *onaga* with miso-sesame vinaigrette, and braised veal shank and smashed taro in poi sauce with *lomi* tomato relish. Recommended appetizer: sliced Chinese-style duck with Asian guacamole and hoisin sauce. Open for dinner nightly.

Specializing in Northern Thai cuisine, **Chiang-Mai**, 2239 S. King St., Honolulu, 808/941-1151, includes lots of vegetarian dishes on its menu, as well as seafood and curry offerings. Recommended appetizers include the calamari with fresh lemongrass and sweet-and-sour sauce; and the Chiang-Mai wings, deboned chicken wings stuffed with mushrooms, long rice, carrots, and spices. The fresh fish curry is very tasty, and can be ordered in red, green, or yellow curry. From the vegetarian menu, try the broccoli with tofu or the mixed vegetables in garlic sauce. Lunch weekdays, dinner nightly.

If you're craving good, basic food, there's **Hawaiian Bagel**, 753 Halekauwila St., Honolulu, 808/596-0638. Since 1979, Hawaiian Bagel has been serving the hard-dough needs of residents and visitors. Lots of varieties of bagels (spinach, sun-dried tomato, jalapeño, plus all the standards), combined with lots of toppings (wild berry cream cheese, Mexican cream cheese, lox spread, etc.) make for a good breakfast. At lunch, you can select just about any sandwich you want, on a bagel, roll, pita, or bread. Sweet-tooth choices galore: cookies, Danish, muffins, and more. Open Mon–Sat 6 a.m.–5 p.m., Sun 7 a.m.–2 p.m.

If you feel like splurging after your morning bagel, **Hoku's at Kahala Mandarin Oriental**, Kahala Mandarin Oriental Hotel, 5000 Kahala Ave., Honolulu, 808/739-8888, can satisfy your desire. This restaurant is simply one of the best in Honolulu. It is a bit pricey for many pocketbooks, but consider it for that special dinner you'll want to have when in Hawaii. Hoku's specializes in various tasty preparations of fresh fish and seafood. The deep-fried fresh whole fish (for two) is highly recommended. Preparations include sweet-and-sour, soy, or black-bean sauce. Also highly recommended from the appetizer selections are the Peking duck spring rolls and the seafood tower. Great bread and dipping sauces, salads, and a selection of fine wines are also offered. Lunch, dinner daily.

Lots of local Chinese people eat at **King Tsin**, 1110 McCully St., Honolulu, 808/946-3273, which gives you a good idea of its quality. King Tsin serves up excellent Northern Chinese/Szechwan cuisine. The eggplant with ground pork in oyster sauce is a treat, as are the cake noodles (which they'll prepare with anything you want). Plenty of vegetarian dishes, and plenty of spicy hot dishes. The pot stickers are not to be missed. Lunch, dinner daily.

To sample real local-style food on this side of the island, there's nowhere better than **Ono Hawaiian Foods**, 726 Kapahulu, Honolulu, 808/737-2275, just outside of Waikiki. It's a hole-in-the-wall kind of place, with only 10 tables, but there is always a line outside the door—and that tells you something. A typical meal here might be the *kalua* pig plate with *lomi* salmon, *haupia* (coconut-cream pudding), rice, and poi (the traditional Polynesian dish of the islands). Other specialties include chicken *lau lau* (wrapped in ti leaves and baked) prepared on Wednesday only, and chicken long rice. Lunch and dinner Mon–Sat.

Several items on the menu at **Sunset Grill at Restaurant Row**, 500 Ala Moana Blvd., Honolulu, 808/521-4409, are highly recommended. One is the deep-fried calamari in black-bean sauce; another is the original-recipe Caesar salad, served whole-leaf. Pasta, fresh fish, and other specials are offered daily. This is a popular lunch spot for local businesspeople, but it's also a nice location to sit at one of the exterior tables and enjoy the sunshine while you dine. Sunset Grill is just across the highway from the waterfront, so a gentle trade wind is often blowing. Good wine list. Lunch, dinner Mon–Fri, dinner only on weekends.

When in Hawaii do as the Japanese do, and if for you that means eating great sushi or sashimi, **Yanagi Sushi**, 762 Kapiolani Blvd., Honolulu, 808/597-1525, is your place. They have every variety of raw fish you'll ever want, and it's all fresh. Start out with a standard such as *maguro* (*ahi* tuna) or king crab California rolls, and move into as exotic a sushi as you like. For example, try the eel or squid with crab eggs if you want something a little different. For non–sushi/sashimi lovers, shrimp and vegetable tempura, chicken teriyaki, and a whole menu of noodles, soups, and other dishes are also available. You can eat at the sushi bar or grab a table. And you can show up late—Yanagi is open for lunch and dinner every day except Sunday until 2 a.m.

Saigon's, 3624 Waialae Ave., Kaimuki, 808/735-4242, is another of those special out-of-the-way finds. Serving Vietnamese foods and French sandwiches, Saigon's is a family-owned and -operated business in a largely untouristed area of town. It's where locals-in-the-know go to satisfy their craving for *pho* soup. This traditional dish of Vietnam is served with oodles of noodles, fresh basil leaves, bean sprouts, and lemon. Add chicken, seafood, tendon, or flank, and you have a meal unto itself. There are lots of other dishes on the menu, including several vegetarian choices. Not much ambiance—but good, authentic, Vietnamese food. Lunch, dinner daily.

NIGHTLIFE

After dark, a different kind of wildlife descends on the Waikiki and Honolulu area. These creatures dance, drink, and make merry. Here are a few entertainment hot spots in Waikiki and Honolulu, where you can observe—and participate in—the local habitat of fun.

David Paul's Diamond Head Grill, 2885 Kalakaua Ave.,

second floor, Waikiki, 808/922-3734, is a chic eatery that features cool jazz along with good food and wine. Music takes center stage after 9 p.m., and patrons can relax at their dinner tables or at the big, curving bar. This is a favorite spot for locals to dine and enjoy. Entertainment Tue–Sat, 9 p.m.–midnight. Another Waikiki institution is **House Without a Key**, Halekulani Hotel, 2199 Kalia Rd., Waikiki, 808/923-2311. This oceanfront lounge at the elegant Halekulani Hotel is a great spot to catch a sunset, listen to Hawaiian music, and watch talented hula dancers. Shows are informal, there is no cover charge, and even locals will venture into Waikiki to meet at House Without a Key. Both lounge and dinner seating available. Entertainment nightly 5–8:30.

In Honolulu, check out **Duc's Bistro**, 1188 Maunakea St., Honolulu, 808/531-6325. This Vietnamese restaurant starts to swing with jazz music on weekends. Duc's is one of the few steady gigs for local jazz talent; here you're likely to hear Tennyson Stevens on piano, joined by vocalist Azure McCall at various points throughout the evening. Both are recommended. Entertainment Fri–Sat, 8 p.m.–2 a.m.

NORTH SHORE

Oahu's surf-famous North Shore has been a mecca for surfers since films such as *Endless Summer* hit our collective consciousness back in the mid-1960s. The 20- and 30-foot high curlers found at Banzai Pipeline and Sunset and Waimea beaches are legendary, and surfers the world over dream of coming to North Shore to test their skills riding the best (and sometimes dangerous) waves anywhere. It is something to see, even if you are not a surfer. Take your camera and hang out.

The North Shore also has some excellent hiking trails, lush scenery, and rugged coastline. It is an area far removed from the bustle on Waikiki and the high-energy of Honolulu. There are few accommodations choices, but camping is good. And with the exception of the artsy town of Haleiwa, there are precious few places to dine.

Still, the North Shore gives you a glimpse of island life not found elsewhere on Oahu. It is a slower shore, with a culture more reminiscent of Molokai than Waikiki. Slow down, relax, and enjoy the charms of Oahu's North Shore.

Orientation/Lay of the Land

The North Shore of Oahu is defined as the stretch of coast from Kaena Point, past Haleiwa, and up to Turtle Bay and Kahuku. For the purposes of logical organization, we have included the area running from Kahuku to Kaneohe in this chapter as well, since most people do not loop back at Kahuku and retrace their steps but prefer to continue on the scenic highway and come out the other side, so to speak, in Kaneohe.

It's pretty easy to get to and from the North Shore. From downtown Honolulu, take U.S. H1 west to U.S. H2 north. You'll pass Schofield Barracks on the left eight miles up U.S. H2; roughly .5 mile after the main entrance to Schofield, turn right on Highway 99 toward Haleiwa. This quaint, artsy town is the gateway to the North Shore. From there, you can drive all the way around to Kaneohe, past much of Oahu's most scenic shoreline.

There is one popular attraction that I have not recommended here, the Polynesian Cultural Center. I consider it a largely gratuitous, commercial effort on the part of the Mormons who run the place to appease the cultural longings of the Pacific Island peoples they have converted.

The North Shore is serviced by The Bus, and if you select that method of transportation you'll find it very economical. But the better idea for this trip may be to rent a car and drive, because you'll want to stop in several places along the way.

Flora and Fauna

One of the best places to view the tropical flora and fauna of Hawaii in one location is 1,800-acre Waimea Falls Park. Across the highway from famed Waimea Bay, the park is known for its faithful restoration

North Shore's famed Waimea Bay

of an ancient Polynesian village and for its garden setting where plants, trees, and flowers from around the globe were planted and thrive.

Near the park's entrance is the Waimea Arboretum & Botanical Garden. Here, you can see more than 5,000 taxa of carefully documented tropical plants, some of which you'll also see on a stroll through the park grounds. But the arboretum's focus is chiefly on the rare and endangered plants no longer commonly found in Hawaii. There is also the fascinating Hawaiian Ethnobotanical Garden that displays a variety of heirloom crops and useful plants that sustained the lives of native Hawaiians for centuries. Researchers and scientists, as well as the general public, are invited to use the library and collection of data on tropical plants.

On the beaches and in the valleys of the North Shore, visitors will discover a wide variety of tropical plants, flowers, and trees. There are serene beach parks shaded by coconut palms, perfect for a leisurely stroll and picnic. And on hikes into the mountain valleys you'll encounter ferns; wild torch ginger; koa trees; banana, guava, and *kukui* nut trees; and much more.

On the western end of the North Shore coastline is Kaena Point Natural Reserve Area. This three-mile hike is worthwhile for the windswept beauty of the dunes, as well as for the bird-watching opportunities it affords. What you'll see here are mainly seabirds, but their numbers are great. Among the species you'll see are wedge-tailed shearwaters, boobies, and Laysan albatross, which are common. If you are lucky you may see a rare Hawaiian monk seal on the beach, or a green sea turtle swimming past.

The Kahuku area contains wetlands that provide critical habitat for many birds, some endangered. Of these, the *koloa* duck and Hawaiian coot are endemic to the islands. Other endangered birds you can see, even from a casual drive-by, are black-necked stilts and moorhens.

History, Culture, and Customs

The North Shore of Oahu is best known for surfing. The three world-class surf spots are Sunset Beach, Banzai Pipeline, and Waimea Bay. All three really start to swell during the winter months, and it's not unusual to see 20-footers curling at the break.

The North Shore has a culture all its own. If you're staying on this shore of Oahu, you sometimes feel as though you are on a neighbor island. The North Shore is more relaxed, surfer-hip, and local. The downside is that there is a lot less to do in the evenings, and fewer restaurant and accommodation choices.

But if you want to get away from it all, spend a few days hiking, beaching, and hanging ten, the North Shore is the place for you.

The North Shore surfing culture traces its roots back as early as 1943, when two young men named Dickie Cross and Woody Brown first surfed Waimea Bay. They had been surfing nearby Sunset Beach when the waves got too big to handle. They thought their best shot was to paddle to Waimea, five miles up the coast. Cross was exhausted by the time they got there, and died trying to surf in. Brown lived to warn others of the dangers of monstrous Waimea Bay.

OAHU'S BEST BEACHES

by Rick Carroll

Author Rick Carroll has studied Hawaii's beaches extensively.
Here are his choices for the best beaches on Oahu.

Best Swimming—Lanikai Beach

This Windward Oahu beach has spectacular sun- and moonrises. Named America's Best Beach in 1996, mile-long Lanikai (it's fractured Hawaiian for "heavenly sea") is excellent for swimming, suntanning, or just hanging out. It's where anyone afraid of water can learn to swim, snorkel, surf, or paddle kayaks and canoes.

A safe, protected beach, Lanikai is great for swimming year-round. The current is mild, the salt water is buoyant and warm, and trade winds are onshore. Olympian swimmers don goggles and fins and churn out to two offshore islets. Others swim laps along the shore or splash in the languid lagoon, home of the championship Lanikai Canoe Club. Everyone gets wet here.

Best Surfing Beach—Sunset Beach

Big-wave surfers drop down the faces of 35-foot waves under blue Hawaiian skies. It's what every surfer worth his Sex Wax dreams of—riding the tube at Banzai Pipeline on Oahu's North Shore.

You can always find surfers at Sunset, especially in so-called winter in Hawaii, when the Pipe rises up with monster sets. That's when this two-mile-long beach becomes an international gallery of spectators.

Sunset isn't only world famous for its waves; it's also a great beach to meet wahines and kanes (women and men), check out the latest swimsuits and surf gear, or watch the sunset.

Best Snorkeling Beach—Hanauma Bay

Sure, it's too crowded, but for smooth, clear, warm water; abundance of fish (more than 150 tropical varieties); scenic beauty; open-ocean protection; and easy access to a gold-sand beach, there's no place like Oahu's Hanauma Bay. It's the best snorkeling spot in Hawaii.

Eons ago this coastal crater lost its seawall, and after the water rushed in so did fish, followed by snorkelers in tour buses. So far, the fish still out-number people, but go early in the day to avoid crowds. Best thing about Hanauma Bay is that everyone, even kids, can join the fun. Just wade in and look down. (Closed Wednesday.)

Best People-watching Beach—Waikiki Beach

An incredibly thin beach covered by nearly naked sun-worshippers bask-ing cheek-to-cheek, world-famous Waikiki Beach often seems to expose more skin than sand. It's Hawaii's best people-watching beach.

On any given day, 30,000 people hit this 1.5-square-mile beach re-sort on the island of Oahu, which attracts the lion's share of Hawaii's 7 million annual visitors. That's a lot of people to watch.

To find your place in the sun, rub on coconut oil and slip into the huddled masses yearning to be tan.

Best Local Beach—Makaha Beach

Expect "stink-eye"—a harsh look—if you're a haole (Caucasian) on Makaha, the most local beach on Oahu, where "da bruddahs" can make you feel like an uninvited guest at their ongoing beach party.

Overcome the mild intimidation (sometimes all it takes is a smile) and you'll discover one of Hawaii's best local beaches, known for surf-ing, diving, and fishing.

Best Beach Overall—Kailua Beach

Oahu's Kailua Beach is two miles of golden sand backed by dunes, shaded by coco palms, and cooled by gentle trade winds.

Home to champion windsurfers, Kailua has an outstanding 35-acre park with a freshwater stream (always teeming with small kids); a boat-launch ramp; affordable beachfront bed-and-breakfasts; a roadside café named Buzz's (even Bill Clinton ate there); and handy, snack-filled Kalapawai Market.

At the beach, the 360-degree view of Kailua Bay and the majestic Koolau Mountains is awesome. This is the quintessential tropical beach.

NORTH SHORE—SURFERS' HEAVEN

Sunset, Banzai Pipeline, and Waimea are the three North Shore surf breaks that brought worldwide fame and recognition to the Hawaiian surf back in the 1960s. Before then, most surfers did not even attempt to ride the three-story curlers that rolled in during the winter months. Even today, only the most skilled athletes should attempt to ride the biggest surf.

Films such as Endless Summer *brought attention to the waves and the men who were riding them. And surfers from around the globe came to try conquering the world's most daunting break.*

And what a break it is. Images of surfers emerging from the perfect curl lodged in the dreams of water enthusiasts everywhere. Surf meets drew international audiences and television coverage, and this once-quiet shore of Oahu began to draw its share of visitors.

You can experience it for yourself at Sunset Beach, Banzai Pipeline, and Waimea Bay. During summer months, these are wonderful beaches for a tan. During winter, try getting in the water only if you're an experienced surfer. If not, join the crowd sitting on the beach watching the best in the world trying to rip curl.

In 1957 some California surfers decided to try their luck: Greg Noll, Rick Grigg, and Peter Cole. Together, they rode Waimea's waves and inspired a whole generation of surfers. Boards were modified specifically to handle Oahu's North Shore.

Films such as Bruce Brown's *Endless Summer* inspired even more young men and women to come to Oahu's North Shore, and a culture was born that lives to this day. Only now the sport has become professional, and surfers the from around the globe come to Hawaii to participate in Eddie Aikau Big Wave Invitational and other surf meets that take place every winter.

NATURE AND ADVENTURE SIGHTS
ON THE NORTH SHORE

Haleiwa Harbor

Shove off from Haleiwa Harbor aboard the *Ho'o Nanea,* a sleek 40-foot catamaran, for a snorkel sail or whale-watch cruise. The best months here for whale-watching are January through May, when the humpbacks frequent the Hawaiian waters to calve. The vessel skirts the scenic North Shore in search of the mammals, which you are almost guaranteed to see.

During non-whale months, the *Ho'o Nanea* takes you to snorkel spots near Waimea Bay, where you'll see hoards of colorful reef fish, turtles, and coral formations. Captain Ray, of North Shore Catamaran Charters, is considered the best of the commercial North Shore sailors.

Details: *North Shore Catamaran Charters, in Haleiwa Harbor behind Aloha Joe's restaurant; call 808/638-8279 for reservations and schedules.*

Kaena Point Natural Reserve Area

On the exposed, western tip of Oahu is Kaena Point. Its landscape is unusual for the islands, in that it is chiefly composed of sand dunes leading to the water. In the 1980s the area was heavily used by off-road vehicles, which did considerable damage to the ecosystem. Today, though, access is restricted to hikers and the ecosystem is starting to rebound.

This three-mile hike from the end of Highway 930 is worth it alone for the windswept beauty of the duneland, but it's also a bird-watching paradise. You'll see mainly seabirds here: Wedge-tailed shearwaters, boobies, and Laysan albatross are common. On occasion, you may see a rare Hawaiian monk seal or a green sea turtle.

Details: *Take U.S. H2 north to Highway 99. Follow Highway 99 north to Highway 930 west. Where Highway 930 ends, a few miles past Dillingham Airfield, you'll find the trail that leads to Kaena Point Natural Reserve Area.*

Kahuku Golf Club

Cheap, fun, and low-key is the way they play golf at this seaside North Shore muni. What's fun here is that only pull-carts are available, and you can play a game the whole family will enjoy. The course was built back in 1937 by sugar-plantation workers. It costs less than $20 to play, and you get four holes (it's a nine-hole course) that run right along the shoreline. Locals love this style of play, and you will, too.

Details: *Kahuku Golf Course, 808/293-5842. In the middle of the town of Kahuku is the Kahuku Superette. When you see it, turn toward the beach, down an unmarked lane. Follow this road a short distance until it dead-ends into the golf course.*

North Shore by Air

If you thought the North Shore of Oahu was exhilarating from ground level, you should see it from a bird's-eye view. People who skydive come back to earth changed, converts to a new religion. **The Pacific International Skydiving Center** will lead you on this thrill-of-a-lifetime adventure from Dillingham Airfield, near Mokuleia Beach. They give you enough instruction to make it safe, then take you up for a tandem dive. Free-fall video and still photos are available.

On the other hand, **Original Glider Rides** offers an experience less vein-popping, but every bit as "air-gasmic." For the past 30 years OGR has been taking passengers up to cruise the thermals in a glider plane. You are towed to altitude by a prop plane, then cut loose (with a pilot) to soar above the North Shore for 20 to 30 minutes. A video camera is bolted onboard, filming both you and the panorama outside. A microphone captures your comments.

Both experiences are highly recommended.

Details: *Pacific International Skydiving Center, Dillingham Airfield, 808/637-7472. Original Glider Rides, Dillingham Airfield, 808/677-3404.*

Sacred Falls

An easy, one-hour hike on a well-worn trail through a lovely valley will lead you to Kaliuwa'a, or Sacred Falls. Once there, you'll find an inviting pool has formed where the waterfall plunges 1,500 feet out of the side of a cliff. Wear something to swim in and don't miss out on the opportunity to cool off. Swimmers play under the waterfall; splash in the fresh, cool water; and picnic on the rocks. The whole hike and swim can be done in less than a half-day.

Details: *Sacred Falls State Park is 21.5 miles past the Haleiwa Bridge on Highway 83 in Punalu'u. A spacious parking area and outhouses are found at the trailhead. Posted signs warn hikers to be careful in rainy weather due to the possibility of flash flooding.*

Note: A landslide in 1999 caused the closure of this popular falls. Check with the state parks department about its current status.

3 Tables

Named for the large, table-like reef formations that lie about 40 yards offshore, 3 Tables is known for its large green-sea-turtle population. The turtles congregate here because it is a "cleaning station," where algae and parasites that grow on them are removed by different types of fish. On this dive, it is fairly common to see several turtles waiting their turn to be cleaned by schools of small fish. Both fish and turtles are mostly undisturbed by the presence of divers. It's quite a sight to see! This is an easy-access dive across a white-sand beach.

Details: *3 Tables is located near Banzai Pipeline. Several outfitters will take you there. One of the very best (and closest) is Surf-N-Sea, 62-595 Kamehameha Hwy., Haleiwa, 808/637-9887.*

GUIDES AND OUTFITTERS

Some travelers may enjoy a bird's-eye view of the island. If you're one of them, check out **Original Glider Rides**, Dillingham Airfield, 808/677-3404, which offers glider and biplane rides over the North Shore. Also giving tourists a lift is **Pacific International Skydiving Center**, Dillingham Airfield, 808/637-7472, which offers skydiving instruction and tandem jumps.

Water lovers can get a hand from **North Shore Catamaran Charters**, in Haleiwa Harbor behind Aloha Joe's restaurant; call 808/638-8279 for reservations and schedules. Captain Ray leads snorkel and whale-watch excursions along the scenic North Shore.

Another seafaring operator is **Surf-N-Sea**, 62-595 Kamehameha Hwy., Haleiwa, 808/637-9887. Here you can take surfing and windsurfing lessons, snorkel tours, dive tours, dive certification courses, and fishing charters.

Back on land, **Raging Isle Surf & Cycle**, 66-250 Kamehameha Hwy., Haleiwa, 808/637-7707, rents top-of-the-line, full-suspension Marin bikes. Their prices are a little higher than other rental locations, but the equipment is better. Cost is $35 for 24 hours, all sizes available. They'll also send you to of Waimea Park's mountain-bike trail.

CAMPING

For contact and permit information see the Camping on Oahu section earlier in the chapter.

The City and County of Honolulu operates the Kaiaka Recreation Area and Kualoa Regional Park. There are spaces for seven tents within the 52-acre **Kaiaka Recreation Area**. A nice coastal location to the south of the town of Haleiwa, Kaiaka is one of the most popular camping areas along this coast. You're near the beach, so it's perfect for all types of water activities as well as exploration into the park itself. Another regional spot is **Kualoa Regional Park**. The island just offshore from this pleasant park and campground near Kaneohe is called Mokolii—Chinaman's Hat. At low tide you can just about walk out to it. There is lots of recreational space at this site, and on weekends the park is quite popular for picnics, barbecues, and playing in the water. Nearby is Kualoa Ranch, where you can horseback-ride and participate in other outdoor activities (for a fee).

LODGING

BackPackers Vacation Inn/Plantation Village, 59-788 Kamehameha Hwy., Haleiwa, 808/638-7838, has been offering affordable accommodations and friendly service since 1979. It is located next to

Waimea Bay on 3 Tables beach, and is convenient to a supermarket and the bus stop. Although the hostel-style accommodations may not be what everyone is looking for, the private rooms and the cottage on the beach are nice, if more costly, alternatives. Volleyball, basketball, boogie boards, and snorkel gear are available, and sailing and diving are also offered at an additional charge.

Rates: Hostel-style beds are $14–$17; private rooms, $35–$40; and apartment/cottages on the beach, $80–$200. BackPackers offers airport pickup at Honolulu International and a great place to snorkel.

Out on the surf-famous North Shore, just north of Waimea Bay, is **Santa's by the Sea** (through Hawaii's Best Bed & Breakfasts), 808/885-4550, a well-maintained cedar home on a stretch of white sandy beach. Attached is a private, one-bedroom apartment, with some very nice amenities: beachfront gazebo, outside shower, barbecue, beach chairs, etc. This is a wonderful location to relax year-round, but if you're there between November and May you're likely to see whales offshore, as well as professional surfing. Rates: $99; two-night minimum stay.

FOOD

Ahi's, 53-146 Kamehameha Hwy., Punalu'u, 808/293-5650, is a find. In this building with its green bamboo facade you feel like you're dining in the jungle—but don't be fooled. This is where the local fishermen bring their fresh catch, and the cook knows what to do with it. It's a good spot to stop by for lunch; try the mahimahi burger or shrimp burger. Also suggested is dinner Friday or Saturday evening, because live Hawaiian music is also on hand. No credit cards are accepted, so bring cash. Lunch, dinner Mon–Sat.

Popular for sunset drinks on the lanai, **Jameson's by the Sea**, 62-540 Kamehameha Hwy., Haleiwa, 808/637-4336, is right across the street from the Pacific. The preparations are nothing fancy, but the fish is fresh and often right off the boat, since the harbor is next door. You'll enjoy the ambiance of the North Shore tradition. Lunch, dinner daily.

For an Italian twist, try **Portofino**, North Shore Marketplace, 66-

250 Kamehameha Hwy., Haleiwa, 808/637-7678. This restaurant serves tasty calzone, pizza, and other dishes from its wood-burning oven. All the breads are baked on premises, too. Recommended for a vegetarian appetite is the Healthy Italian calzone, stuffed with artichokes, black olives, mushrooms, and mozzarella, topped with marinara sauce. Also on the recommended list is the penne *capricciosa*, pasta served with roasted eggplant, tomato, shrimp, mozzarella, garlic, and basil. Lunch Mon–Sat, dinner daily.

WINDWARD OAHU

Windward may be the best area of Oahu for those seeking outdoor adventure. It combines the most popular aspects of the island—good dining, good bed-and-breakfast accommodations, excellent beaches—with an outdoor emphasis that gives visitors just about everything they may want.

Horseback riding, hiking, sailing, fishing, kayaking, biking—all are activities found on the Windward Coast. Here, too, are several of the finest beaches in the United States, Lanikai Beach and Kailua Beach, as rated by Dr. Stephen Leatherman, "the Beach Doctor" from the University of Maryland.

The Windward Coast is charming and fun. It's like being on Maui, but only a short drive over the hill from the nightlife of Waikiki!

Orientation/Lay of the Land

Thirty minutes over Pali Highway from downtown Honolulu, visitors will find the Windward Oahu communities of Kaneohe and Kailua. Kailua is preferred by visitors for its beaches, water activities, and lifestyle. Here, you can hike, bike, kayak to deserted islands, or lounge on the best beach in the United States, Kailua Beach.

The other area of Windward Oahu with great beauty and beaches is along the Waimanalo Coast. Instead of driving over the Pali Highway, head east on U.S. H1 toward Hawaii Kai. Pass Koko Marina Shopping Center on your left, and keep going straight. In this

© George Fuller

Kailua Bay

direction are Hanauma Bay, Sandy Beach, Makapuu Point, Sea Life Park, Waimanalo, and eventually Kailua.

The Bus services Windward Oahu more frequently than it does the North Shore, so you can use public transportation if you only have one or two destinations in mind. On the other hand, if you're planning several stops a rental vehicle may be the better choice.

Flora and Fauna

In this region visitors will find Hanauma Bay State Underwater Park, one of the most popular beaches in the state. In years past, you could come here in relative peace, snorkel, and lie on the beach. But busloads of tourists have overrun the place, causing harm to the coral reef and imbalance in the ecosystem, and causing the state to close Hanauma Bay one full day per week. Despite all this you can still snorkel here and see myriad colorful fish swimming in the protected waters.

If you can stand its commercialism, Sea Life Park actually has some interesting exhibits. Chief among them is the 300,000-gallon saltwater tank that is home to thousands of sea creatures native to Hawaii's waters. Among them are sharks, eels, manta rays, and tropical fish of many species.

This region of Oahu is somewhat arid, but the closer you get to the Koolau Mountains, the greener the landscape becomes.

As for birds, several unlikely spots are actually the best. One is Kaneohe Marine Corps Base Hawaii, where seabirds flourish. Right between the rifle range and the Pacific, for example, is a large nesting colony of red-footed boobies. And less than a mile offshore is Moku Manu Island, where 20,000 pairs of breeding sooty terns reside, alongside wedge-tailed shearwaters, black noddies, some Bulwer's petrels, and masked boobies. The vantage point from the marine corps base is excellent year-round.

On the mountain trails, such as Mount Olomana, northern and red-crested cardinals, finches, and sparrows are common. Less common, but possible to spot, is the bright red *'apapane.*

NATURE AND ADVENTURE SIGHTS IN WINDWARD OAHU

Koolau Golf Club

Here's your chance to play "the most challenging course in the world," according to United States Golf Association ratings. If golf is your game, this course will be the adventure of a golf lifetime. Set in a beautiful, lush landscape at the foot of the Koolau Mountains, it plays over and around ravines and jungle-lined fairways, and past some of the best views on Oahu's windward side. Even for non-golfers the views are worth the price of riding, and besides, you'll enjoy your mate's tribulations as he or she tries to master this tough cookie.

Details: *45-550 Kionaole Rd., Kaneohe, 808/247-7088. Located off Kamehameha Highway between Pali Highway and U.S. H3.*

Koolau Mountain

Climb atop a trusty steed and ride in the majestic Koolau Mountain foothills. A short briefing is followed by a familiarization arena ride, and then off you go. Locals return here because even they have never seen views of Oahu like this. You'll see panoramic vistas of the Mokulua Islands, Rabbit Island, and the Waimanalo Coast. On clear days Maui and Molokai are visible across the water. Trail guides are knowledgeable and share the history of this area, as well as some *paniolo* (Hawaiian cowboy) lore. Kids age eight and older are welcome.

Details: *Correa Trails Hawaii, 41-050 Kalanianaole Hwy., Waimanalo, 808/259-9005. Cost is $49.95 for the one-hour ride.*

© George Fuller

Hanauma Bay

Makapuu Point

The old military bunkers at the top of Makapuu Point were built by renowned author James Jones's *(The Thin Red Line, From Here to Eternity)* battalion when he served in the military in Hawaii. Magnificent views of the Waianae Coast and the coves and inlets near Hawaii Kai await you at the top of this hike. It takes roughly 45 minutes to hike each way, but you'll want to plan an extra half-hour at the top to admire. This is also a wonderful spot for whale-watching during winter months.

Details: *No posted signs mark this hike, but a gate is on the ocean side of the highway 4.4 miles from the intersection of Lunalilo Home Road and Kalananiole in Hawaii Kai; 3.5 miles east of Hanauma Bay entrance.*

Moku Manu Island

Off Oahu's windward coast stands a barren island, with sheer, 225-foot

WINDWARD OAHU BEACHES

Lanikai Beach, Kailua Beach, Sandy Beach, and Makapuu are among the best beaches in the United States, according to Dr. Stephen Leatherman, "the Beach Doctor" from the University of Maryland, and also according to Rick Carroll, an expert on Hawaii's beaches.

Lanikai Beach and Kailua Beach are almost deserted on weekdays, since both are near residential neighborhoods. This makes them perfect for vacationers looking for solitude, a tan, and warm, clear waters in which to swim, kayak, and play. On weekends, both of these beaches come alive.

Sandy Beach and Makapuu are more exposed to open ocean, so both are better body-surfing beaches. Sandy Beach, just past Hawaii Kai, has a grassy recreational area where you can witness the latest in kite technology while enjoying a picnic. And the cliffs above Makapuu are popular with hang gliders, so people on the beach may get a free show. Again, both of these beaches bustle with water enthusiasts on weekends.

cliffs, known to local fishermen and seabirds as Moku Manu. Only 15 minutes by small craft from Kailua Beach, this deserted island is a world removed from civilization. The waters can get a little rough in this channel, but the fishing can be very good in the area around the island. *Ahi* (yellowfin tuna), *aku* (skipjack tuna), mahimahi (dorado), and *ono* are among the fish landed here. Moku Manu is also a birder's delight, as no fewer than 10 species make the island their home. They include an estimated 10,000 to 20,000 pairs of nesting sooty terns, brown and black noddies, red-footed and masked boobies, and the lovely wedge-tailed shearwater. In fact, local fishermen follow the concentrations of terns to find the schools of fish.

Details: *You can charter a fishing boat out of Kewalo Basin Harbor near*

Mokulua Islands

Waikiki. Specify where you wish to fish before booking, as some captains specialize in certain areas and don't wish to venture further afield.

Mokulua Islands

Kayaking to these often-deserted islands off the Lanikai shore is the highlight of many visitors' stay. It takes about half-hour to paddle out, but the surrounding waters are so warm, clear, and calm that you'll want to take all day to do the round-trip. Take a waterproof bag (you can rent them where you rent the kayak) to hold your lunch and other valuables, and take reef walkers and drinking water with you.

You can hike a little around the islands, but be careful of the changing tides and the slippery rocks. Early in the morning is generally calmest, and at certain times of year the sun rises right between the islands. This trip is highly recommended.

Details: Twogood Kayaks Hawaii, 345 Hahani St., Kailua, 808/262-5656, will rent kayaks for a half-day, full day, weekend, or week. Prices run from $25 for a single kayak/half-day rental to $195 for a tandem kayak/full-week rental.

Olomana Peak

Hiking Olomana, the 1,643-foot-high mountain that rises from the base of Maunawili Valley, is one of the better hikes on Oahu. There are three peaks you can climb, and they get progressively harder. Many hikers opt for the first peak only, and even to this summit there are two tricky spots. The most difficult of these spots—a rock face just before the summit—has been eased by fixed cables that provide handholds. At the summit, hikers are greeted by wide, beautiful views of windward Oahu that make the effort well worth it.

The second and third peaks are for advanced hikers only. If you feel like you want to give it a go, be aware that the third peak has a very narrow ridge that leads to the top, and some difficult footing.

Details: The trailhead is located on the entrance road to Luana Hills Country Club, just off Auloa Road. You must park by the side of the road and walk roughly .5 mile to the trailhead, which is marked by a small sign on the left.

GUIDES AND OUTFITTERS

With more than 25 years in business and one of the largest supplies of equipment in the islands, **Aaron's Dive Shops**, 602 Kailua Rd., Kailua, 808/262-2333, meets the needs of visiting and local divers. Daily boat dives will take you to all the major dive sites around Oahu, including airplane- and shipwrecks, caverns, caves, and lava tubes. A certified dive guide accompanies every trip. Aaron's also offers four-day PADI certification classes. Snorkelers also welcome.

Paddlers may want to check out **Twogood Kayaks Hawaii**, 345 Hahani St., Kailua, 808/262-5656. Owner Robert Twogood specializes in single or tandem kayak rentals and instruction. Half-day to full-week rentals are available, and kayaks are delivered to Kailua Beach Park free of charge.

Land adventures are to be had through **Correa Trails Hawaii**, 41-050 Kalanianaole Hwy., Waimanalo, 808/259-9005, which offers horseback rides into the foothills of the majestic Koolau Mountains.

CAMPING

For contact and permit information, see the Camping on Oahu section earlier in the chapter.

The following two sites are run by the City and County of Honolulu. Just north of Waimanalo, **Bellows Field Beach Park** is quite safe. Campsites are located within groves of ironwood trees. Get hold of a kayak and take advantage of these calm waters.

Makapuu Beach Park is one of the most popular camping areas on Oahu, and also one of the best body-surfing and swimming areas. Makapuu can get crowded, but it is safe, and the views of Rabbit Island are wonderful. Makapuu is across the highway from Sea Life Park.

Locals know that the beaches at **Waimanalo Bay State Recreation Area** are among the most beautiful in the state. Warm, aqua-blue water laps gently against long stretches of white-sand beach; a coral reef protects the bay, making the area perfect for swimming. And generally speaking, there's far more space than people out here. The campground itself is another matter. It is used by locals as a permanent residence, and therefore is often crowded; some visitors might feel uncomfortable. Contact the State of Hawaii for more information.

LODGING

The accommodations listed below are only available through Hawaii's Best Bed & Breakfasts. Contact the group for reservations and directions.

Hawaii's Best Bed & Breakfasts picks **Ingrid's**, 808/885-4550, as their top

MIDWAY ISLAND—BIRDLAND

By Marcie Carroll, travel writer

It's midday at Midway. A thin winter sun warms the parade green next to the stone monuments that honor the past war heroes of this tiny, far-flung islet. But my thoughts are on the future of an egg, a grand-daddy of a goony egg, about five inches long, perfectly shaped, khaki-colored. It has rolled away from the place it belongs, which is inside a bowl-shaped indentation on a small hummock where it can be properly sat on by a nine-pound white-breasted Laysan albatross, aka goony bird, moli (in Hawaiian), and Diomedea immutabilis.

I want desperately to pick it up and put it back, but this intervention would not be divine. You don't want to mess with Nature here—this is the Midway Islands National Wildlife Refuge, former Navy base turned ecotourism destination. Still, I touch the egg gingerly. There's only one egg per mother bird per year, and if there's a chance... but it's cold. One of about 30,000 eggs here that won't make it.

So many other eggs are life-bound, tucked safely underneath some 400,000 plump white breasts snugged into their nests, 800,000 if you count the albatross mates who are out in search of food. Those nesting pairs are the most prominent among an estimated 2 million birds here. The Midway goonies include nearly 80 percent of the world's population of Laysan albatross, as well as 44,000 dusky black-footed albatross and one short-tailed albatross or "golden goony." They are drawn by pelagic magic back to the nests in which they were born on the three sandy pinpricks of this small atoll, some 1,300 miles northwest of Honolulu and roughly halfway between San Francisco and Tokyo.

Landing at Midway at night to minimize conflict with birds, our flight is greeted by a friendly human contingent. The goonies are relatively quiet, maybe awed by our noisy metal Big Bird.

We pass goonies in the dark, see the hummocky nests, and watch and hear 50 or so dancing their courtship reel under my window. But it isn't until the next day that I begin to grasp the magnitude of the bird presence.

Birds overwhelm the landscape. They are everywhere on the ground, nesting three or four feet apart on the lawns; by the doors, lanes, bike racks, and walkways; in the lee of buildings; under ironwood trees and hibiscus bushes; in the sand dunes; any place they can scrape up a nest. We heed a warning on the cable TV channel:

"Remember to preflight your vehicle for albatross prior to moving, by checking under tires."

The goonies share the refuge with 13 other species of breeding seabirds, vacationing shorebirds, a sizable pod of spinner dolphins, a couple hundred green sea turtles, an ocean of fish (fishing is banned within a 200-mile radius of Midway), roughly 50 endangered Hawaiian monk seals, and about 130 people who operate the former military base as a cooperative federal/private ecotourism venture. Up to 100 tour guests at any one time can come to see the goony birds nesting in winter and to dive and fish in summer, when the goonies are gone but unusual bird encounters are likely to include a face-to-face with a white tern.

You can't take anything at all, beachcombers and bird-watchers, not even a feather; fisherfolk, it's mostly tag-and-release, except for food fish for island consumption.

The pact between the U.S. Fish and Wildlife Service and Midway Phoenix Corp. is a first in the federal refuge system. Midway Phoenix, which manages the island and runs the air service to Midway, in turn works with Oceanic Society Expeditions (a research and ecotourism organization based in San Francisco) and Midway Sport Fishing (a fishing/diving tour operation) to bring people to Midway. For more information, call 888/643-9291.

accommodations choice on Oahu. Just a mile from Kailua Beach, this one-bedroom apartment is in a quiet neighborhood. It is elegantly appointed, with a partial kitchen, luxurious bath, swimming pool, and private entrance. Rates: $110; three-night minimum stay.

Step back into the golden age of steamships at a restored 1924 bungalow on Lanikai Beach. **John Walker's Lanikai Beach House**; 808/261-7895, is a comfortable and spacious property that features a picnic area and lounge chairs at ocean's edge, and spectacular views of Lanikai Beach and the Mokulua Islands. Rates start at $395.

Another fine B&B is **Lanikai Bed & Breakfast**, 808/261-7895. There are two choices here, the Hale Mahina and Garden Studio. Hale Mahina is spacious, with one bedroom and one bath plus den, tastefully decorated in Old Hawaiian bungalow style with heirloom koa furniture and treetop-level views. The Garden Studio is on the ground floor and has its own patio and entrance. Rates: $95 for Hale Mahina; $80 for the Garden Studio.

Lanikai Perch, 808/261-7895, is a unique accommodations choice high atop the residential area of Lanikai; it features sweeping ocean and mountain views. Watch the sunrise between the twin Mokulua Islands offshore, and the sunset in the other direction. A hammock on the large deck is most people's favorite place to settle in. Rates: $125.

FOOD

If you get a hankering for Italian food while in Windward Oahu, **Baci Bistro**, 30 Aulike, Kailua, 808/262-7555, is the place. Homemade pastas include *agnolotti* filled with lobster, prosciutto, and ricotta in cream sauce, and spinach tagliatelle with porcini mushrooms in cream sauce, both recommended. Several vegetarian risottos are offered, and the chef will be glad to make any request to order. Also recommended is the Sunday brunch menu. Lunch Mon–Fri, dinner nightly, Sun brunch.

Boots and Kimo's Homestyle Kitchen, 119 Hekili, Kailua, 808/263-7929, is a family-owned and -operated kitchen. Select from an array of omelets, such as seafood, "Pakalolo Onolicious" (fresh Maui herbs combined with veggies, honey-cured ham, and cheese), and egg-

Chao Phya Thai

One of the most pleasurable aspects of this Windward Oahu restaurant is getting to know the owner, "Mama Toy" Coppedge. She'll come over to your table, chat, and make sure everything is to your liking.

plant Parmesan. All kinds of egg dishes and pancakes—the macadamia-nut sauce is tasty—round out the breakfast menu. Lunches are local-style, served with rice and macaroni salad, with teriyaki beef or chicken, saimin, and other sandwich choices. Breakfast, lunch daily.

A local hangout near Lanikai Beach, **Buzz's Original Steak House Lanikai**, 413 Kawailoa Rd., Lanikai, 808/261-4661, has been serving up good food, drink, and company for nearly 20 years. What you'll find here is a hard-to-beat salad bar, teriyaki steaks and chicken, and a crowd of people waiting to get in. It's worth it. Put your name on the list and relax on the lanai out front. This is where President Bill Clinton went for dinner after his round of golf at nearby Mid-Pacific Country Club. Bring cash; no credit cards accepted. Lunch, dinner daily.

"Mama Toy" Coppedge runs one of the best Thai restaurants in Hawaii from a suburban shopping-mall location in Kaneohe. At **Chao Phya Thai Restaurant**, 45-480 Kaneohe Bay Dr., Kaneohe, 808/235-3555, she specializes in curries, offering red-curry, green-curry, and yellow-curry dishes. Other items are the vegetable tofu Chao Phya salad (tossed with sweet-and-sour coconut dressing topped with mint), shrimp soup (with lemongrass, kaffer lime, and mushrooms in a clear, spicy broth), and crispy fried mahimahi (in garlic chili sauce). Lots of vegetarian dishes are available. Lunch Mon–Sat, dinner nightly.

Roy Yamaguchi's restaurant, **Roy's**, 6600 Kalanianaole Hwy., Hawaii Kai, 808/396-7697, is a splurge. But there are items on this menu that are worth robbing your piggy bank. The Maryland blue-crab cakes in spicy sesame butter sauce are out of this world. How about seared blue jack *ulua* fish with shiitake oyster cream sauce? Finally, indulge yourself in a chocolate soufflé for dessert—it's simply the best. Dinner nightly.

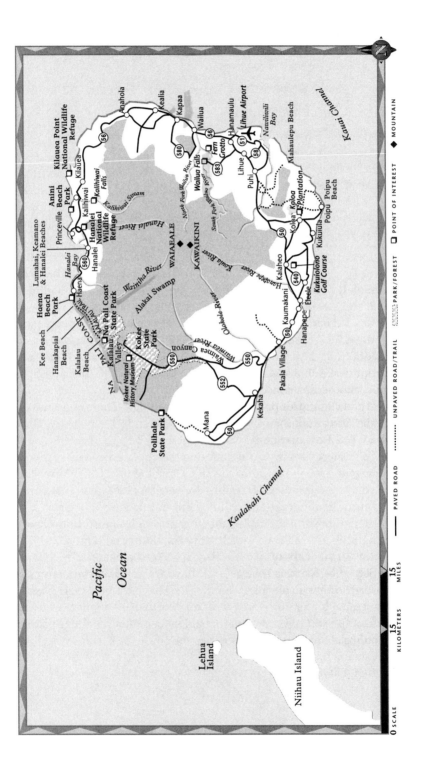

4

KAUAI— THE GARDEN ISLE

While it may not have a star on the Walk of Fame, Kauai is a Hollywood celebrity. Directors looking for the archetypal Pacific island filming location choose Kauai more frequently than any other Hawaiian island. Kauai's idyllic shores have been the settings for dozens of movies, including *South Pacific, Uncommon Valor, Jurassic Park, King Kong* (the remake), *Outbreak,* and *Throw Mama from the Train.*

So how can a Hollywood hot spot be an adventure-travel destination? For the very same reasons the celebs come here: Kauai is beautiful and teeming with nature opportunities for those who thrive on sun, surf, sand, and turf.

Orientation/Lay of the Land

The island of Kauai is basically round, with a large mountain in the center called Waialeale. It is from this wet centerpoint that the island's main geologic features emanate: Waimea Canyon; Alakai Swamp; the dramatic Na Pali Coast; and the State of Hawaii's only navigable rivers, including Wailua River, its longest.

Kauai is by far the greenest of the Hawaiian islands. Indeed, an average of 450 inches of rain falls on the cloud-covered peak of Mount

Waialeale every year, and one look at the myriad waterfalls gushing down its sides makes it clear why Kauai is called The Garden Isle: Everything grows in its lush, marvelously tropical climate. The island even *smells* green.

Kauai is the fourth-largest of the Hawaiian islands, composed of about 555 square miles of land. Yet fewer than 30,000 people live on her shores. It is estimated to be 5.6 million years old, the oldest of the inhabited islands. At one point, it is believed that Kauai and Niihau—"the forbidden island" that lies to Kauai's southwest—were one, and credence is given to that theory by the fact that the channel between the two islands is unusually shallow.

Nature/Adventure Activities

There are adventures of all sorts to be had on every side of Kauai. Na Pali offers a wealth of water-based activities, especially kayaking, sailing, and rafting. Off the island's North Shore there's great windsurfing. Poipu Beach is a haven for divers. And, although the Big Island and Maui may be better known as adventure destinations, in recent years Kauai has quietly made its own mark as a first-rate destination for those seeking fun beyond the beach. Hiking, backpacking, horseback riding, even ultralight flying, are among the popular activities open to ecotravelers today.

Flora and Fauna

Because Kauai is the oldest of the main inhabited islands, its landscape has had a longer opportunity to evolve. Like the others it is a volcanic island, and at one time was as lava-strewn and barren as parts of the Big Island are today.

Over time—and accentuated by the fact that being the northernmost island in the main Hawaiian chain, Kauai takes the brunt of many hurricanes and Pacific storms—the face of the island has changed.

As mentioned above, Kauai's main geologic features emanate from Mount Waialeale, which has been dubbed "the wettest spot on earth" due to that 450-inch annual average rainfall. From Waialeale emerge the close-to-pristine Alakai Swamp, the Na Pali Coast, and Waimea Canyon. And because of the difficult, blustery conditions, much of Waialeale and its surrounding areas remain untouched and largely unexplored. For Kauai's flora and fauna, this is a blessing. Many species of plants and animals that are endangered elsewhere due to habitat destruction, avian diseases borne by introduced insects, and encroachment of human activity, live relatively untouched in these areas, particularly in Alakai Swamp. If you are quite lucky, you may sight one of the extremely rare *puaiohi*, a small thrush native

© George Fuller

Lighthouse at Kilauea Point

to Kauai, whose population is believed to be fewer than 10 birds.

Runoff from Waialeale's eastern flank created the Huleia National Wildlife Refuge, some 238 acres of estuary that are home to almost 30 bird species. Of the birds that call this area home are several endangered species: the Hawaiian coot, Hawaiian *koloa* duck, and Hawaiian stilt.

Kilauea National Wildlife Refuge provides a home to many species of seabirds and animals, perhaps more than any other place in Hawaii. Offshore, you can see humpback whales on their yearly migration, rare monk seals, and large sea turtles. In the seabird department, Laysan albatross make one of their rare stops in the lower part of the state here, along with red- and white-tailed tropic birds, frigate birds, and many other species.

At the top of Waimea Canyon, Kokee State Park encompasses close to 4,400 acres of rain forest. In addition to some excellent hiking trails, the area is a prime breeding ground for Hawaii's only native land mammal, the Hawaiian hoary bat. A walk through the Kokee Natural History Museum at the park's headquarters will show you what the hoary bat looks like, as well as give you a good idea of some of the other flora and fauna found here.

Hurricane Iniki, which devastated much of the island's landscape in 1992 with winds measured at 175 to 200 m.p.h., did damage Kauai's native and endemic flora. But most species have completely recovered, and some are thriving even better than before.

In the Kokee rain forest, this presents as much of a problem as a blessing. Some non-native plants, such as ginger, honeysuckle, blackberry, strawberry guava, and a host of others, have repopulated quickly, wreaking additional havoc upon Kokee's native ecosystem. Aliens are rapidly wiping out vast tracts of rare endemic plants, and destroying the habitats of endangered birds and native insects. Efforts are underway to monitor and control this situation.

History, Culture, and Customs

In 1778 a slight Englishman wearing white breeches and a blue coat with brass buttons sailed his huge ship, the *Resolution*, into Kauai's waters. At the helm was Captain James Cook, whose ship's sails were similar to the banners of tapa cloth that the Hawaiians hung from their own masts in honor of one of their primary gods, Lono. Thus, Cook was accepted by the Hawaiians as the reincarnation of their long-disappeared god Lono.

Kauai was the first island in the Hawaiian chain that Cook "discovered" on his third voyage into the Pacific. He made landfall at Waimea, about 20 miles from today's Lihue Airport, and we can imagine how news of Lono's return must have traveled along the coastline, conveyed from village to village by runners.

Within a year, though, natives on the Big Island rose up against Cook, bludgeoning him to death. They had stolen a rudder from one of Cook's ships; Cook thought he could scare them into submission by demonstrating the power of firearms. Obviously, that didn't work.

By 1796, Kamehameha the Great controlled the entire Hawaiian chain, except for Kauai and Niihau. He claimed the failure of his first assault on Kauai was caused by a storm at sea that stopped his advance and killed many of his men. The warriors of Kauai said that was nonsense,

Koloa Town

that a battle was fought and won—and they produced skulls from the sand to prove their point.

In 1804 Kamehameha planned a second attack, but this time his troops were decimated by an epidemic. So the attack was put aside for another six years when, in 1810, Kauai was finally won by negotiations and a little deceit.

Kaumualii, Kauai's king, agreed to give his lands to Kamehameha as long as he, Kaumualii, remained king. It was an empty title. In 1821, two years after Kamehameha's death, his son and heir Liholiho sailed to Kauai and invited Kaumualii aboard his vessel for dinner, suggesting he leave his warriors ashore. Kaumualii agreed and the ship sailed for Oahu during the meal. From that moment on, the king of Kauai was a prisoner.

Nine days later, Kaumualii was married to Kaahumanu, the favorite of Kamehameha's 21 wives, who had gained extensive power after Kamehameha's death. She also proceeded to marry Kaumualii's eldest son, a Kauaian named Kealiiahonui, who was reported to be almost

THE LEGEND OF THE *MENEHUNE*

Kauai is home to the menehune, *that mysterious race of "small people" who sailed north from Tahiti. Short and squat—and some legends say hairy—and very, very strong, they are said to work on projects only at night, using their great strength and vast numbers to accomplish mighty feats.*

The menehune *are playful and they love games and jokes. They used to carry stones from the mountains to their bathing places, throw them into the sea, and dive after them; the object was to catch the stones before they sank to the bottom.*

Sometimes they built hills solely for the purpose of rolling down them. They are musical, using bamboo nose flutes and Tahitian-style hollow log drums. When they laugh, it is said that they make so much noise they frighten the birds on Oahu.

The menehune *are athletes, excelling at boxing, wrestling, tug-of-war, and foot racing. According to one gatherer of legends, who lived where Kauai Lagoons stands today, two* menehune *were so swift they could run around the island six times in a single day!*

In work, it was with stone that the menehune *excelled. They were said to have built the* heiau *near Wailua, as well as elaborate irrigation systems such as the Menehune Ditch, a job of fitted and dressed stone-*

seven feet tall. Through these manipulations, the Kamehameha dynasty gained title to Kauai. Even today, though, residents of the Garden Isle pride themselves on their independent nature.

At about the same time, missionaries from America began arriving in Kauai. The first puritanical representatives of the Christian god, under the leadership of the Reverend Hiram Bingham, came to Hawaii "to clothe and convert the heathen" in 1820. They set up their mission in Honolulu.

In May of that year two of the missionaries, Samuel Ruggles and work that involved turning the course of the Waimea River and directing the water around a corner of a mountain. That accomplishment still draws respect from vacationing engineers.

Menehune *also built the Alakoko fishpond near Nawiliwili Bay, more commonly referred to as Menehune Fishpond. The way the story goes, a lazy Hawaiian named Pi refused to help build a stone wall around an area that was to be used for the raising of taro and fish. Naturally, his chief refused to give him food in return for work not done.*

That night, Pi wrapped portions of fish and poi and hung them in a kukui, *or candlenut, tree near the unfinished wall, knowing the* menehune *would find his offering when they came after dark to inspect the Hawaiians' work.*

Pi was there to greet the small people, sweet-talking them into helping him finish the job. Soon, Pi was standing by as the menehune *passed stones from hand to hand, completing the wall before dawn. Next day, Pi took credit for completing the work, and his chief sent him quantities of food and elaborate woven mats, proving that sometimes then, as now, there is no justice. Nonetheless, the fishpond remains, a few miles from Kauai Lagoons, giving the Nawiliwili Harbor area one of its most popular visitor attractions.*

Samuel Whitney, visited Kauai and established rapport with the Kauaian people. Both Ruggles and Whitney went on to spend part of their missionary careers in Kauai, as did others who followed them, but it wasn't until 1854 that the first permanent missionary family moved to Kauai—the Reverend and Mrs. William Harrison Rice.

There have been a handful of prominent and influential non-Hawaiian families who have set their imprint upon the island of Kauai over the years. A few were missionary families, and a few others were businessmen's families. Some took their profits (or losses) and left. But

KOLOA PLANTATION DAYS

Koloa Plantation Days began more than 10 years ago to celebrate the 150th anniversary of commercial sugar production on Kauai. The week-long event is still held every July in the cute plantation town of Koloa, just up the road from Poipu on the South Shore. Although sugarcane production has declined in Hawaii over the past decade, this festival is a reminder of an important part of Kauai's history. Cultural events, Hawaiian music, food booths, and a parade are highlights of this fun event. For more information, call 808/332-9201.

others—the Rices, Wilcoxes, Fayes, Doles, Isenbergs, and others—found Kauai a loving home.

When the monarchy ended in 1893 with the house arrest of Queen Liliuokalani, the Rices, Doles, and Wilcoxes became members of what one historian called the "haole inner core"—the small group of missionary descendants, their relatives by marriage, and selected business associates who were determinedly grasping political control of the islands.

At the same time, the group created a social environment that would grip local society in much the same way the Cabots and Lodges and others had dominated the social strata of Massachusetts. Their legacies are still apparent today. The primary hospital on Kauai is Wilcox Memorial; Rice Street is one of Lihue's main thoroughfares; and descendants of these prominent families still live on Kauai.

During the late 1940s and early '50s, Kauai received few visitors. It was an unknown paradise, and even the increasing number of travelers who made their way to Waikiki rarely ventured as far afield as Kauai. But a paradise it was, especially on the northern and eastern shores, where the flora was thick and flowery. Hawaii's longest navigable river, Wailua, was on Kauai, ending in a giant fern grotto. On the other side of the island was Waimea Canyon, a gorge not nearly as big as Arizona's Grand Canyon, but easily as spectacular.

These scenic secrets were known only to a few outsiders. Kauai was off the beaten path, and the people who lived on Kauai liked it that way. In the 1950s, preservation of Kauai's rural lifestyle was not yet a political issue, as one day it would be. From the time of the great tidal wave in 1946 up to statehood in 1959, Kauai was a tropical backwater so remote and determinedly anti-growth that it seemed of all the islands, it was the least ripe for commercial development.

And if it ever *did* develop, many thought the tourist industry would most likely center on the North Shore, near Bali Ha'i beach, where *South Pacific* was filmed. Others picked the region at the mouth of the Wailua River, where the Coco Palms hotel was opened in 1953 and where Elvis Presley filmed *Paradise Hawaiian Style* in 1966. Unfortunately, this landmark "fantasy resort" today stands dark, having never reopened after Hurricane Iniki slashed across the island in 1992.

In fact, although an excellent and world-class resort was developed on the North Shore at Princeville, it has been the Poipu Beach area that has seen much development.

Visitor Information

There are many ways to get the best current information about Kauai. The **Hawaii Visitors & Convention Bureau** is always a good source of information, providing brochures, maps, and practical tips for travel to all the islands. Contact them before you visit, or drop by when you're on Oahu: 2270 Kalakaua Ave., Suite 801, Honolulu, HI 96815, in the heart of Waikiki, 808/923-1811 or 800/GO-HAWAII or check out www.gohawaii.com.

A similar service specifically geared to the island of Kauai is provided by the **Kauai Visitors Bureau**. They will be happy to provide you a packet of information if you call 808/245-3971, fax 808/246-9235, or write to 3016 Umi St., Suite 207, Lihue Plaza Bldg., Lihue, HI 96766.

Useful Web sites include the **Hawaii Ecotourism Association**'s locations: www.planet-hawaii.com/hea/ and www.alternative-hawaii.com. For specific dive information about Kauai, the Web site at www.divekauai.com is very good, as is www.aloha-hawaii.com/seasport.

For current information about hiking on Kauai, write to the

Department of Land and Natural Resources, Division of State Parks, P.O. Box 1671, Lihue, HI 96766. Kathy Morey's book, *Kauai Trails* (Wilderness Press, 1997), is also a very good resource.

Getting There

Getting to Kauai is easy. Most visitors arrive from Honolulu at the Lihue Airport, located on the southeastern shore of the island. United also offers nonstop flights to Lihue from the Mainland's west coast. From Lihue, it'll be far more convenient to rent a car than rely on the public bus system, called Kauai Bus, to get from one adventure to the next. Among the car-rental agencies are Avis, Budget, Hertz, and other major companies.

NATURE AND ADVENTURE SIGHTS ON KAUAI

Alakai Wilderness Reserve

Alakai Wilderness Reserve, at the end of Highway 550 beyond Kokee State Park, encompasses 30 square miles of Hawaii's rarest land. The reserve is a pristine swamp, with a cloud cover that stunts the growth of many plants and trees. Thus, it looks like a dense forest of bonsai size. Since it's so difficult to access most areas of the preserve, rare birds and plants thrive here. Also, the elevation—4,000 feet—is a boon to bird-watching because there are no mosquitos, which transmit avian malaria and have been so damaging to Hawaii's native species elsewhere.

The wet, rugged conditions in many areas are problematic for casual hikers. Therefore, you are *not* advised to explore beyond where the state forestry division has built a boardwalk, or where the going is clearly marked and relatively dry. Be aware that people have become lost in the deepest parts of **Alakai Swamp**.

That said, the areas that are accessible will provide some great hikes through some of Hawaii's precious flora. And if you're lucky you'll see some of the state's most endangered birds, such as the *'apapane* and the curved-beaked *i'iwi*.

The trail most easily traversed through the area is called **Pihea Trail**,

North Shore Beach

roughly 4.25 miles long. It is a forest bog, receiving as much as several hundred inches of rain annually; wet and muddy conditions are the norm. Hiking these days is easier due to the boardwalk that is mostly complete, but you might wish to check first with the Department of Land and Natural Resources in Lihue about the current status of the trail. In any case, take rain gear.

The vegetation you'll encounter here is primarily ohia trees and shrubs, ferns, and maile vines. If you are particularly fortunate and are here on a clear day, the views of Kalalau Valley are superb. But clear days are rare, and often the area is overcast and foggy.

The Pihea Trail intersects the **Alakai Swamp Trail**, and you can follow this a short distance on the boardwalk. But again, it is not an easy hike beyond the point where the boardwalk ends, so we do not recommend it for families or casual hikers.

Details: *Alakai Wilderness Reserve is at the end of Highway 550 beyond*

KAUAI'S BEST BEACHES

by Rick Carroll
Author Rick Carroll has studied Hawaii's beaches extensively.
Here are his choices for the best beaches on Kauai.

Best Beach—Hanalei Beach

Half-moon Hanalei Bay, where sloops anchor and surfers play, opens wide as a Saturday yawn to a beach some call heavenly. Hanalei, in fact, means "heavenly garland." Gentle waves roll up the two-mile beach. Coconut trees line the shore. Sheer volcanic ridges laced by waterfalls rise 4,000 feet to fleecy clouds in the background.

For pure natural beauty there is no finer beach in Kauai, maybe in all of Hawaii. Not just a beach, Hanalei is also a great bay, a wetland refuge for endangered waterbirds, a laid-back ex-plantation town, the locus of North Shore activity—such as it is—and a state of mind. It's my favorite beach town in the islands.

Best Hidden Beach—Keamano

If you see a footprint on Keamano Beach, it's probably yours. You can reach this hidden beach only via helicopter, and then spend only the day.

You'll never forget this mile-long, 100-foot wide crescent of golden sand that rises to dunes on the north shore of the once "forbidden" island of Niihau. Sometimes, folks from Puuwai village come down to say aloha, "talk story," or trade seashells for cash.

On the beach you'll discover Japanese glass-ball fishing floats; tiny, precious Niihau shells; tasty, silver dollar–sized opihi in virgin tide pools; and a view of Lehua Islet, a seabird rookery off Kamakalepo Point.

Best Romantic Beach—Mahaulepu

Grab your sweetie and go on a long, lazy, afternoon picnic at Mahaulepu, the most romantic beach on Kauai. Under jagged ridges of

Ha'upu mountains this two-mile, sun-kissed beach on Kauai's south-eastern shore is made for romantic liaisons—it's secluded, with lots of privacy. There are ocean breezes, sand dunes, and tide pools to explore, a shady forest, and pounding surf. Don't forget the champagne.

Best Kids' Beach—Poipu

A graceful golden sand curve on Kauai's sunny South Shore, Poipu draws a family crowd. It's big, wide, handy, safe, and good looking.

A sand bar divides Poipu into two very different beaches that look like this:)(. On the left, a sandy-bottomed green lagoon embraced by black lava rock is ideal for small children to splash and play. On the right, green/blue waves are big enough to hang ten, yet small enough for gidgets.

Best Hollywood Beach—Lumahai

When Hollywood goes to Hawaii it heads for Kauai, the island with picture-perfect beaches. More than 80 movies have been filmed on Kauai, including Jurassic Park and Raiders of the Lost Ark.

Nominations for best beach in a supporting role are:

- Lumahai Beach, where Mitzi Gaynor sang "Gonna wash that man right outta my hair" while filming the musical South Pacific;

- Kee Beach, at the end of the road beyond Haena, where The Thornbirds was filmed;

- Honopu, the remote Na Pali beach where King Kong (from the remake) fell in love with Jessica Lange; and

- Mahaulepu, where George C. Scott appeared in Hemingway's Islands in the Stream;

And now the envelope please: The winner is Lumahai, of course.

Kokee State Park. No fee is charged, and no permit is required to hike here, but it is smart to let someone know you are going.

Anini Beach

Learn to windsurf at beautiful Anini Beach, on Kauai's North Shore near Princeville. This beach is considered perfect for beginning windsurfers because the lagoon is sandy, shallow, and protected by a reef. Plus, the breeze here is generally steady and gentle, as opposed to an open-ocean area such as Hookipa Beach on Maui, where the ocean is rough and the wind is often howling.

A company called Anini Beach Windsurfing will meet you at the beach park and teach you the basics, and then get in the water with you for open-water instruction.

Details: Anini Beach Park is on Anini Road. You'll want to take a right onto Kalihiwai Road, the first right turn after the bridge on Highway 56 past Kilauea, then a left onto Anini Road. If you reach the Princeville Airport you've gone too far. Lessons and rentals can be obtained through Anini Beach Windsurfing; reservations required by calling 808/826-9463. Cost is $65 for a three-hour lesson; lessons are offered every day. Rentals are $25/hour or $50/all day.

Kalihiwai Falls

There are few more satisfying ways to get up close and personal with the beautiful and lush North Shore of Kauai than on horseback. Several outfitters offer excursions that allow you do exactly that.

The best choice is the waterfall picnic ride, a four-hour round trip where, halfway through the ride, wranglers doff their cowboy boots and blue jeans in favor of swimsuits for a refreshing swim at Kalihiwai Falls. While you're swimming, your tour guide is setting up the picnic for you to enjoy before the ride back to the stables.

Other rides take you to Anini Bluffs and down to Anini Beach, or deep into the Hanalei Mountains. All rides allow you plenty of time to soak up the wonderful scenery of Kauai's North Shore.

Details: Princeville Ranch Stables, 808/826-6777 or 808/826-7473, is where these excursions begin. Stables are just off Highway 56 near the Princeville

Airport. Signs clearly mark the entrance. Cost is $110/person for the Kalihiwai Falls ride; $100/person for the Anini Bluffs and Beach ride; $55/person for the Hanalei Mountains ride. Advance reservations are required. Riders must be over eight years old and in good physical condition.

Kauai by Air

Enthusiasts of thrill-flying can soar over Kauai in an ultralight aircraft. You buckle into a tandem, open-air cockpit with an experienced pilot and take off into the wild blue yonder. But in addition to sightseeing, you're also learning how to operate the craft. Within the first 10 minutes you'll be executing your first banking turn.

The ultralight aircraft are equipped with wing-mounted cameras so you take home photos of yourself gliding above the lovely Garden Isle. Half-hour, one-hour, and two-hour flights are offered. Unless you're an avid thrill-seeker, the one-hour flight should be plenty. Since the airstrip is at Hanapepe, a one-hour flight is enough time to go around the west end of the island and see the Na Pali Coast.

Details: Birds in Paradise offers ultralight flights. They meet you at the airstrip outside Hanapepe, a left turn onto Highway 543 off Highway 50. Reservations are required; call 808/822-5309 (it's a good idea to call a week or two in advance of your visit since flight times fill up during busy months). Cost: $90 for the half-hour flight; $150 for the one-hour flight; and $250 for the two-hour flight. Photos are $25 extra.

Kukuiolono Golf Course

If you like golf, but rail against the high prices charged for rounds at resort courses, you'll enjoy this quaint nine-holer. It's located in wooded Kukuiolono Park above Kalaheo, and is a hidden gem on an island known for great golf. Plus, it's a course everyone feels comfortable playing—no one seems to be in much of a hurry here. You have the option to walk the course (as opposed to renting a motorized cart), and that's the best way to go. Take your time; enjoy the ocean views and the ambiance. The park's benefactor, Kauai sugar baron Walter McBryde, is laid to rest in a peaceful Japanese garden between

holes seven and eight. There is plenty of room to picnic in the park...
after golf, of course.

Details: Turn south off Highway 50 onto Papalina Road in Kalaheo.
You'll see the entrance gates to Kukuiolono Park & Golf Course, 808/332-
9151, on your right in roughly one mile. Follow the signs to the clubhouse. Cost
is $7 to play all day. Clubs are available for rent.

Na Pali Coast State Park

Kauai's Na Pali Coast is one of Hawaii's most spectacular natural attributes. It is located on the northeast shore of the Garden Isle, and
therefore—like the windward shores of all the Hawaiian islands—is
subject to more severe weather than the typically calmer South Shore.

What that means for the traveler is that some activities along the Na
Pali Coast are available—and others are certainly safer—only during the
nonwinter season. Many sea-tour operators and outfitters limit their Na
Pali excursions to the months of May through September.

The other thing to be aware of is that the County of Kauai has been
trying to limit the number of sea-tour operators in Hanalei Bay, once the
preferred launching site for Na Pali Coast excursions. As of this writing,
most outfitters have moved their bases of operations to the South Shore,
and either sail/raft around the west coast, or take people by van to
Haena, a trip of two hours, and launch from there. The best idea is to
call several of the outfitters listed in the Guides and Outfitters section
that follows, get the most current information about the trips, and make
your decision from there.

Those things said, kayaking, sailing or rafting along the Na Pali
Coast is magical. Kayaking (rigorous) or rafting (motorized) allows access into some hidden sea caves and beaches inaccessible by any other
means of transportation, plus a stunning view of the lush valleys, plunging waterfalls, sheer cliffs, and knifelike ridgelines that make this coast
such a visual treat.

Along the way you're likely to encounter dolphins, tropic birds,
and monk seals. Most of the tours and outfitters include snorkeling as
part of their offerings, often at **Kalalau Beach**, and this is also a wonderful experience. The waters here are typically teeming with colorful

Na Pali Lookout

reef fish and green sea turtles, and the occasional reef shark may be spotted in its cave.

Sailing is another popular way to view the Na Pali Coast. This relaxing trip is good for families, or those who wish to see the sights without an exhausting journey. Again, most sails will include snorkeling as well as lunch.

An option that may appeal to the more adventurous is hiking the **Kalalau Trail.** There are several ways to do this, all starting at the Kee Beach end of Highway 560, where you'll find a parking area. (Warning: It is not advisable to leave valuables in your car here, particularly if you are planning to be gone overnight, because thefts have occurred.)

For the most part, day hikes along the trail are more rewarding than camping. This is true for a number of reasons. Although the Na Pali Coast you see from the water is one of Hawaii's most spectacular sights, hiking along the Kalalau Trail can be arduous and sometimes dangerous. The trail is not particularly well maintained, and the campgrounds are overused, mosquito-ridden, and often filthy. It is a shame, but the untrampled beauty and extreme serenity that once were found along the trail and in the camping areas are things of the past.

Still, **Hanakapiai Beach**, four miles from Kee Beach, is a good day hike. A permit is not required for the hike, but one *is* required if you plan to stay overnight. Excellent views of the coast and Kee Beach are to be had from this stretch of trail.

A wonderful way to end the day after this hike is a dip in the ocean at **Kee Beach**. There is often a refreshment table here where you can buy water, soft drinks, and snacks. Kee Beach is calm and protected, but often crowded. Nevertheless, after a four-hour round-trip hike, it's awfully inviting.

The other option for viewing the Na Pali Coast is by helicopter. Many companies offer this tour, most starting from Lihue Airport. Helicoptering over the many valleys and hovering next to plunging waterfalls can be very exciting, plus your flight often takes you over some of Kauai's other visual treasures.

Details: Na Pali Coast State Park and the Kalalau Trail begin where Highway 560 ends, on Kauai's far northwest shore. The best months to visit this area are May through September; in other months the weather can become rainy and the hiking trail and seas more dangerous. Permits are required for hiking beyond Hanakapiai Beach, and also for camping at any of the campsites along the coast. Permits are available from Division of State Parks, 3060 Eiwa St., Rm. 306, Lihue, Kauai, HI 96766; 808/274-3445.

Niihau

Advanced divers can experience the thrill of diving off "the forbidden isle" of Niihau. Local divers say these are some of the most pristine and dramatic dive sites in the Hawaiian islands. You'll find wall dives, lava pillars, and huge caves. Visibility in this region is mostly great. What makes this a spot for advanced divers only is the strong sea currents and the depths.

A typical dive adventure will begin at 6:30 a.m. From Kauai's west shore it's a 20-mile crossing to Niihau that takes about two-and-a-half hours. Breakfast is served. Dive sites include "Keyhole," lava shelves where you'll see lobster, octopus, and monk seals; and "Super Highways," which is known for its caves, swim-through rock formations, and towering lava pillars—home to white-tip reef sharks, tiger cowries, and yellow margin eels. Green turtles and spinner dolphins are normally in this area, as well. Lunch is served, and typically one more dive site is explored before you head back to the Garden Isle. You'll be back on land by around 6 p.m.

Details: Several outfitters offer this dive, and the best of them are listed under Guides and Outfitters, below. This is a summer-season dive. Expect costs to range $220 to $250/person, and to include three dives, breakfast, lunch, and dive gear. All outfitters require advance reservations.

Sheraton Caverns

Located off Poipu Beach, these underwater caverns are considered by many divers to be the best diving on Kauai. In addition to swimming through hollow lava tubes with graceful underwater archways, you are likely to see green sea turtles, moray eels, and the occasional white-tip reef shark in the caverns. This dive is good for less-experienced and occasional divers because the waters here are generally calm and the dive is shallow (35 to 65 feet). Sheraton Caverns is also popular for night dives. Many dive companies offer free introductory classes in a pool to prepare you for the ocean.

Details: Several outfitters offer this dive, and the best of them are listed under Guides and Outfitters, below. This is a year-round dive, but it's always dependent on weather. Expect costs to range $85 to $100/person, and to include snacks, drinks, and dive gear. All outfitters require advance reservations.

South Shore

Kauai features some of the most dramatic shoreline scenery in Hawaii, and there's no better way to see it than from the ocean. Several outfitters offer sailing excursions, but Captain Andy's is the best.

You can jump into the water and snorkel with spinner dolphins off Kauai's South Shore aboard Captain Andy's *Spirit of Kauai* catamaran. Andy also offers a two-hour sunset excursion. Both are wonderful experiences. Perhaps the most exhilarating sail of all, though, is whale-

watching during winter months. If you're lucky enough to spot one of these magnificent mammals close up—and they do come right up to the boat on occasion—it's an experience you'll never forget.
Details: Reservations recommended; call 808/335-6833. Cost: $49/adult, $34/child for sunset sails; $49/adult, $34/child for whale-watch tours.

Wailua River

Kauai is the only island in the Hawaiian chain that has navigable rivers, and Wailua is the largest and busiest of them. On any given day you'll see riverboats, kayaks, and other crafts making their way up and down its waters.

There are two forks of the Wailua River, North and South. The best adventure is to rent a kayak—nearby companies will deliver them for you right to the mouth of the river—and paddle your way up the **North Fork**. An easy, two-hour paddle up the scenic waterway will bring you to a well-marked trailhead, where you beach your kayak and take a half-mile hike through ferns, flowers, and brooks to **Hidden Waterfall**. This is a wonderful spot to break out your sandwiches and have a picnic. Beneath the gently flowing "bridal veil" waterfall you can swim in an idyllic pool.

The **South Fork** is equally lovely, leading to the **Fern Grotto**, an area of natural caves, gardens, and lush jungle scenery popular for wedding ceremonies. A little way past Fern Grotto you'll find a rope swing where you can play Tarzan. Beyond that, if you feel energetic and want to paddle farther, is **Wailua Falls**. South Fork is more commercial with tour boats, but that rope swing sure is fun!

Details: Wailua River access is on Highway 56, the main road leading from the airport to the North Shore, seven miles north of Lihue. There are several kayak rental companies right at the mouth of the river, and several more in Kapaa, five miles north. Some travel outfitters offer guided tours up the Wailua River, but a guide is not really necessary for this trip. There is no fee for using the river.

Waimea Canyon

Called "the Grand Canyon of the Pacific" by author Mark Twain, who visited Hawaii in 1866 and returned to the islands several times

© George Fuller

Waimea Canyon, "the Grand Canyon of the Pacific"

throughout his life, Waimea Canyon is indeed spectacular. It is 10 miles long, a mile wide, and 3,657 feet deep. Like the Grand Canyon, the beauty of Waimea Canyon is in its details. Yes, the whole is immense and inspirational, but it's when you get closer that you begin to appreciate the finer points.

There are several ways to view Waimea Canyon. The drive up to Kokee State Park is the option most people take, because you have to get out of your car only at scenic lookout points. If you don't have a lot of time, or only want the "been there, done that" photo, the scenic drive is the way to go.

But if you're looking for a more insightful encounter with the canyon, hiking is the ticket. There are four or five hikes of varying difficulty and length, beginning in the town of Waimea. One of the more popular hikes is along the Waimea River, starting near the lower end of the canyon. You can go as far as you like—as little as one-quarter mile, or as far as 20 miles. The hiking options begin roughly two miles from the junction of Highways 50 and 550. Parking

113

is on the left side of the road; the trailhead is on the right. Most often, there is no signpost indicating where the trailhead is (they get washed or blown away), so you have to be alert.

From the trailhead, hikers head toward the canyon along the **Iliau Nature Loop**. There are a couple of stopping points where you'll get good views up the canyon ahead. Plus, the plentiful flora here is indicative of what Waimea Canyon has to offer in this regard: *iliau* plants, ohia trees, and koa trees. About 10 minutes into the hike is a hunters' check-in station, and just beyond that is an inviting picnic shelter.

Longer hikes take you along the **Kukui Trail** to Wiliwili Camp, roughly seven miles. The first two-mile section is a fairly easy hike and provides some good views. **Wiliwili Camp** has a pit toilet, a table, and room to pitch a tent (permit required).

The longer hikes up **Waimea Canyon Trail** really begin in the canyon. The area is also used by four-wheel-drive vehicles owned by the sugar companies, as the Kekaha Ditch supplies water for the fields in Waimea Town below. Because of the water here the vegetation tends to be a little heavier, and there are several species of birds that call the area home. The farther you go, the more difficult the hike becomes due to footing and elevation changes.

From the top side of the canyon, beginning at Kokee Lodge, a popular hike is the **Waipoo Falls–Kumuwela Trail Loop**. It's just over six miles but is fairly moderate. The reward is that the hike leads to two waterfalls (one where you can swim in a pool) and provides fantastic views of Waimea Canyon. This hike is highly recommended.

Other hikes into Kokee State Park—and there are quite a few trails available, ranging from .5 to 3.5 miles—reveal some of the fascinating birds that live in the area, including the *'apapane*, the lovely red *i'iwi*, and the white-tailed tropic bird. When hiking in the upper elevations of Waimea Canyon and Kokee State Park, remember that temperatures can drop quickly later in the day, and that rain is frequent. Be prepared... and be careful.

Another popular Waimea Canyon adventure is a downhill bike ride from the 3,500-foot level. Outfitter **Bicycle Downhill** supplies the ride up (complete with Kauai coffee and muffins) and the bikes. It's a 13-mile ride down a winding road, ending up at the ocean. The bikes are made for comfort, with wide, cushy seats; high-rise handlebars; lightweight aluminum frames; and power brakes. Several stops along the way let you enjoy the scenery, rest your rear, and ask questions about the flora and fauna. A van follows the bikes in case you decide to ride by motor instead of muscle.

Details: *Waimea Canyon is off Highway 550, accessed from the town of Waimea via Highway 50. For current information about hiking in Waimea Canyon and Kokee State Park, write to the Department of Land and Natural Resources, Division of State Parks, P.O. Box 1671, Lihue, HI 96766. Kathy Morey's book,* Kauai Trails *(Wilderness Press, 1997), is also a very good resource. Contact Bicycle Downhill at 808/742-7421. Cost is $65/person. You'll meet your group at 6 a.m. at 2827-A Poipu Rd., Poipu.*

GUIDES AND OUTFITTERS

Look up in the sky. It's **Birds in Paradise**, 808/822-5309, a guide company that offers ultralight flying trips. They meet you at the airstrip outside Hanapepe, a left turn onto Highway 543 off Highway 50. Cost is $90/half-hour flight; $150/one-hour flight; and $250/two-hour flight. Photos are $25 extra.

If you're more hydro-inclined, Kauai outfitters offer a host of water-based adventure activities. **Anini Beach Windsurfing**, 808/826-9463, offers windsurfing lessons and equipment rentals on Kauai's North Shore. Cost is $65 for a three-hour lesson, and lessons are offered every day. Rentals are $25/hour or $50/all day.

Divers may want to check out **Dive Kauai Scuba Center**, 976 Kuhio Hwy., Kapaa, 808/822-0452 or 800/828-3483. This outfitter will meet you in Port Allen for all-day trips to Niihau, and also for shorter dives around the South Shore. Dive Kauai specializes in both day and night shore dives to Tunnels, off the beach near Poipu.

Also, look up **Fathom Five Divers**, 3450 Poipu Rd., Koloa Town, 808/742-6991 or 800/972-3078. Half-day, two-tank dive trips with a maximum of six divers per boat are the norm with Fathom Five. They regularly offer dives to some 20 sites around the South Shore of Kauai, and you can also charter a trip to Niihau during the summer season.

Snorkeler at Makua Beach, Haena

David Boynton

They specialize in a night dive to Sheraton Caverns. And **Sea Sport Divers**, 2827 Poipu Rd., Poipu, 808/742-9303 or 800/685-5889, offers Niihau dives (advanced divers only) as well as dives around Kauai's South Shore, such as the popular and less-demanding Sheraton Caverns. Scuba certification courses and introductory diving lessons in a pool are also part of Sea Sport's menu.

Rafting and snorkeling are the domain of **Kauai Z-TourZ**, 808/742-6331. This company specializes in small-group rafting/snorkel tours of the Na Pali Coast (May through September), whale-watch expeditions (December through May), and snorkel trips off the South Shore (year-round). Cost: $120/person for Na Pali Coast trips; $75/person for whale-watch and South Shore snorkel trips.

Another snorkeling option is **Captain Andy's** *Spirit of Kauai*, 808/335-6833. A plush, state-of-the-art catamaran, the *Spirit of Kauai* offers snorkel cruises, Na Pali Coast sailing tours (summer), sunset cruises (year-round), and whale-watch sails (winter months). Cost: $109/person for the Na Pali sail; $49/person for sunset and whale-watch sails.

Holo Holo Charters, 3416 Rice St., Anchor Cove Shopping Center, Lihue, 808/246-4656, has two new catamarans, the 61-foot *Holo Holo* and the 48-foot *Leila*. Both are state-of-the-art vessels. Snorkel cruises to Niihau are a specialty (year-round), and they also offer Na Pali Coast trips (summer). Cost: $119/person for the Na Pali sail; $140/person for the Niihau snorkel sail.

Snorkel tours of the Na Pali Coast aboard the *Na Pali Explorer*, 4469 Waialo Rd., #23, Eleele, 808/335-9909, depart from Port Allen on Kauai's South Shore and motor around the west side of the island. This vessel is small enough to get into the hidden caves, but large enough to be comfortable. Cost: $99/person for the swim and snorkel tour.

A well-respected company that has been in business on Kauai for more than 15 years, **Kayak Kauai Outbound**, Hwy. 560, Hanalei, 808/822-9179 or 800/437-3507, offers guided Na Pali Coast kayak trips (May through September); Kipu Kai guided kayak and whale-watching tours (October through April); Huleia River National Wildlife Refuge paddling tours (year-round); guided kayak tours in the Hanalei River National Wildlife Refuge (year-round); and a six-night, seven-day tour that incorporates most of the above, plus some hiking (year-round). Cost: $130/person for Na Pali tours; $105/person for Kipu Kai whale-watch tours; $55/person for Huleia River tours; $55/person for Hanalei River tours; and $1,350/person for the six-night, seven-day tour (includes all lodging, travel, and dining).

Kayakers, take note of **Outfitters Kauai**, 2827-A Poipu Rd., Poipu, 808/742-9667 or 888/742-9887, which guides kayak trips along the Wailua River (year-round), the Na Pali Coast (summer), and Kipu Kai (winter). Reservations requested. Cost: $78/person for the Wailua River trip; $135/person for the Na Pali Coast trip; $115/person for the Kipu Kai trip.

If you've had enough of water, check out some land-based outfitters. **Bicycle Downhill**, 2827-A Poipu Rd., Poipu, 808/742-7421, guides bicycle rides down from the 3,500-foot level of Waimea Canyon. Cost is $65/person. You'll meet your group at 6 a.m. at Bicycle Downhill. And **Princeville Ranch Stables**, off Hwy. 56 near Princeville Airport, 808/826-6777 or 808/826-7473, offers a variety of horseback-riding excursions on the North Shore.

CAMPING

The County of Kauai operates seven oceanside beach parks that allow camping, although only the two listed below—Anini Beach Park and Haena Beach Park—are recommended. At the others, there have been problems with homeless people; in several cases, such as Lucy Wright Park, the location is right next to a noisy, busy road.

Required permits are $3 per person per night (no charge for children) if you obtain them at the county office, $5 per person per night if you get them at the campsite itself. Maximum stay is four days per campsite, 12 days total if you move from park to park.

For information and a camping permit application, write or visit County of Kauai, Parks and Recreation, 4444 Rice St., Moikeha Bldg., Suite 150, Lihue, Kauai, HI 96766; 808/241-6660; fax 808/241-6807. Permits for Mainland visitors can be obtained through the mail with a certified check or money order. You should allow 30 days for this process prior to your arrival.

A popular day-use area that allows camping is **Anini Beach Park**. It is one of Kauai County's best campsites, located on the North Shore, and offers toilets, showers, cooking grills, and a pavilion. You'll pitch your tent in a grove of ironwood trees just behind the beach. A nearby grassy area is perfect for the kids. The beach, too, is safe for swimming, because it's within a protected lagoon. As you enjoy your time here, you'll have the opportunity to snorkel or learn to windsurf.

Another popular spot is **Haena Beach Park**. This beach park, near the end of Highway 560 on the northern end of Kauai, offers good camping, although it is often crowded with day users as well. The beach is the highlight of your stay here, and there are also some nice day hikes that emanate from this area. You'll find a pavilion, toilets, showers, tables, and grills. You'll enjoy your time at Haena—it's one of Kauai's most beautiful camping sites.

The State of Hawaii operates four parks on Kauai, and all allow camping. All are in wonderful natural settings: Na Pali Coast, Kokee State Park, Waimea Canyon State Park, and Polihale State Park. For information on camping permits in these areas, contact Division of State Parks, 3060 Eiwa St., Rm. 306, Lihue, Kauai, HI 96766; 808/274-3445.

One state campsite is **Kalalau Beach,** along the famed Na Pali Coast. It requires a 22-mile hike along the Kalalau Trail. The trail is often challenging because of the weather and loose footing, and the campground, once you arrive, is often infested with bugs and not well maintained. Still, this is the one experience many adventurers come to Kauai to experience. So if you're determined to go, by all means go; but be forewarned: The camping may not be all you were hoping for. Still, snorkeling in these secluded waters, lying on the wide stretch of white sandy beach, and hiking into Kalalau Valley are all wonderful experiences.

There are several camping areas within **Kokee State Park.** The best of them is **Sugi Grove** campsite, due to its proximity to hiking trails and its wonderful ambiance. Remember to pack warm clothing; at 3,500 feet, this site can get cold at night. Amenities are limited—just a pair of bare pavilions and a pit toilet—but the setting in a grove of cedar trees is peaceful.

Polihale State Park has two camping areas. Amenities are not fancy, but you'll find showers, toilets, barbecue pits, and some tables. The dunes of Polihale, and the *heiau* just north of the beach park area, are considered sacred by the old Hawaiians—it is said this was where the spirits of the dead departed the islands. Polihale Beach itself, on the sparsely inhabited western shore of Kauai, is more than two miles long, by many accounts the longest stretch of beach in the islands. The campgrounds are located in the dunes behind the beach, and one of the best things about camping here is the magnificent sunsets you'll see. If you're lucky and visibility is good, you can sometimes see the uninhabited islands of Necker and Nihoa from Polihale.

LODGING

To make reservations and get directions to many of the B&Bs below, contact Hawaii's Best Bed & Breakfasts.

The Historic B&B, in Hanalei, 808/826-4622, a cute little Victorian-style house right on the main street of Hanalei on Kauai's North Shore, is actually a 94-year-old Buddhist mission that has been transformed into a bed-and-breakfast. Owners Jeff and Belle Shepherd pride themselves on offering some very attractive rates, and on providing a charming and restful stop for the traveler. It's not the fanciest lodging on Kauai, but it is wonderful in its own right. Rates are $68/night double occupancy, $450/week double occupancy.

Another fine B&B is **Kai Mana** (through Hawaii's Best Bed & Breakfasts), in Kilauea, 808/885-4550. A private home on nine acres, nestled on a cliff above a secluded beach, Kai Mana is the home of author Shakti Gawain. The main house has two corner rooms for lease, each with a private entrance. A separate cottage with a full kitchen and ocean view is also available (five-night minimum stay). A hot tub on a deck overlooks the ocean, and it's a short walk to the beach from this home. Rates are $130 double occupancy for the two rooms in the main house; $175 for the cottage.

Also through Hawaii's Best Bed & Breakfasts is **Rosewood**, 872 Kamalu Rd., Kapaa, 808/885-4550. This wonderful property offers several types of accommodations, and is one of the best deals in the state. The premier offering is a Victorian-style cottage with a full kitchen and upstairs loft; a thatched cottage is private and cute, with an outside shower; and several bunkhouse rooms (shared bathroom) are perfect for singles and campers looking for economy. Rates are $115 for the Victorian cottage; $85 for the thatched cottage; and $40–$50 for the bunkhouse rooms.

Marjorie's Kauai Inn (through Hawaii's Best Bed & Breakfasts), Lawai, 808/885-4550, offers three suites on the lower level of a home in Lawai, on Kauai's South Shore. It's a modern-style home with all the amenities: kitchenettes, covered lanais, and an outdoor Jacuzzi gazebo. But the best part about this property may just be the owner. Marjorie is an accomplished adventurer herself, having trekked the Himalayas, backpacked through Greece, and bicycled across the U.S. Mainland. So if you would like a Kauai local's perspective on the Garden Isle's best adventures, just ask Marjorie—she has probably done them. Rates are $75.

Hale Pilialoha (through Hawaii's Best Bed & Breakfasts), in Poipu, 808/885-4550, is a sunny cottage perfect for families or couples traveling together, as it has two bedrooms, two baths, cathedral ceilings, a full kitchen, washer and dryer, and a spacious deck. The master bedroom has a four-poster king-size bed. Nine sets of French doors let lots of sunlight and fresh air in. There is no host on-site and no breakfast provided. It's a short walk to the beach. Rates: $150 double occupancy; $20/night each additional person; plus a $65 cleaning fee. Minimum four-night stay. Weekly rates available.

Those looking for a high-end stay should check out **Hyatt Regency Kauai**, 1571 Poipu Rd., Poipu, 800/233-1234 or 808/742-1234. At this 600-room oceanfront resort, opened in late 1990 and set at the end of the road in Poipu, the architecture and ambiance are exactly what you want from a resort in Hawaii. Strung along 50 acres fronting Poipu's Shipwreck Beach, the Hyatt Regency Kauai is laid out in low-rise buildings with a distinct Hawaiian missionary period flavor—and none of the buildings are taller than a coconut tree, as Kauai's building code mandates. Anara Health & Fitness Spa is a 25,000-square-foot facility at the hotel featuring eight private massage rooms, sauna and steam rooms, and a comprehensive health and fitness program. Rates: $310–$520 single or double occupancy; $785–$2,950 for suites.

FOOD

A Pacific Cafe, 4-831 Kuhio Hwy., Kauai Village, Kapaa, 808/822-0013, is the signature restaurant of Chef Jean-Marie Josselin, and the food preparation fits into the category called Hawaii Regional Cuisine. Basically, that means using local ingredients in preparations combining Eastern and Western influences. Although the menu changes nightly, typical dishes might include wok-charred mahimahi in a garlic sesame crust and a lime ginger sauce; grilled rib-eye steak in a Gorgonzola cabernet sauce; and fire-roasted *hamachi* tuna with a mushroom-eggplant-tomato-shrimp risotto, all in a Thai coconut red-curry sauce. Great food and creative presentations. Dinner daily.

Beach House at Poipu Beach, 5022 Lawai Rd., Koloa, 808/742-1424, serves dinner nightly in a wonderful oceanfront setting. If you get to the Beach House early enough, you'll be treated to a savory sunset. This restaurant serves Hawaii Regional Cuisine, the specialty of its owner Jean-Marie Josselin, who also runs A Pacific Cafe. Dishes might include Pacific

▼▲▼▲▼▲▼▲▼▲▼▲▼

Roadrunner Cafe

Owner Denis Johnston cooks without lard, fats, or oils, and uses all local ingredients at his restaurant. There are also many vegetarian dishes on the menu. You won't find better food on Kauai than here.

▲▼▲▼▲▼▲▼▲▼▲▼▲

coconut clam bisque, followed by a basil-pesto–crusted salmon steak with a slice of grilled wild-mushroom polenta. Presentations are highly creative, and desserts are always tasty. Highly recommended if you're staying on the South Shore.

If you're looking for Italian cuisine on Kauai's North Shore, there's **Cafe Luna**, Hanalei Center, Hanalei, 808/826-1177. Cafe Luna offers a variety of winning dishes, with or without meat. On the vegetarian side are penne pasta with fresh broccoli and spinach in a light olive-oil/red-pepper sauce; and spaghettini in a Gorgonzola cheese, fresh sage, and tomato cream sauce. If you feel like a meat dish, try the osso bucco or the veal piccata. Several pizzas and seafood dishes are also available. Lunch and dinner daily.

An unassuming little deli, **Da'Li Deli**, across from the post office in Koloa Town, 808/742-8824, serves breakfast, lunch, and baked goods. The better items are from the lunch menu, such as the Da'Li Lama sandwich: marinated eggplant, pesto, provolone, tomato, and lettuce on focaccia; and the Hello Da'Li: a fresh roasted turkey sandwich with cranberry relish on French bread. Baked goods include bagels, breads, and pies (try the mango pie!). Coffees and smoothies are also served. Breakfast and lunch daily.

Gaylords at Kilohana, one mile south of Lihue on Kaumualii Hwy. (Hwy. 50), 808/245-9593, is special for both the exquisite food and the historic setting: a restored 16,000-square-foot former plantation home, which also houses several cute shops and a Pottery Barn. Patrons can catch a horse-drawn carriage tour around the lush, 35-acre estate gardens before their meal. But don't linger too long, because the dining is delightful. The dinner menu features baby back ribs that are favorites. Plus, fresh fish of the day, and herb-crusted rack of lamb are specialties. But you're not finished until you've tried the Kilohana Mud Pie: a tall serving of Lappert's mocha and chocolate ice creams layered with fudge and peanut butter on an Oreo cookie crust. Save room! Lunch and dinner daily.

Serving gourmet vegetarian dishes and fresh seafood is **Postcards**, 5-5075A Kuhio Hwy., Hanalei, 808/826-1191. Try the Thai coconut curry with crisp vegetables, tempeh, and a spicy peanut sauce, served over organic rice pilaf. Grilled or blackened fish is offered in several sauces, including honey ginger Dijon, macadamia butter, or peppered pineapple sage. It's also a good spot for breakfast. BYOB here, as they have no liquor license. Open for breakfast and dinner daily.

Another health-conscious eating spot is **Roadrunner Cafe**, 2430 Oka St., Kilauea, 808/828-8226. Denis Johnston owns and cooks at this cute, muraled café near Kilauea Lighthouse. He cooks without lard, fats, or oils, and uses all local ingredients, including his pork and beef. Mostly you'll find Mexican items on the menu, such as an *ahi* tuna "burra" with pickled cabbage, pinto and black beans, and Mexican rice. He also offers vegetarian burras and tacos, and fresh island fish grilled and on salads. Area locals rave about Johnston's food and his approach to cooking.

For a ritzy dinner, head over to **Tidepools at Hyatt Regency Kauai**, 1571 Poipu Rd., Poipu, 808/742-1234. The ambiance in this resort restaurant is special, with dining tables located in thatched huts next to koi ponds and gently flowing waterfalls. The chef specializes in grilled fresh seafood in a choice of sauces. A vegetarian selection is always available. If your sweet tooth is in need of a fix, the chocolate macadamia-nut pie is divine. One other suggestion: After dinner, go up to elegant Stevenson's Library for a game of pool and an after-dinner drink. Stevenson's features either live Hawaiian music or recorded jazz. The price tag on the evening may be close to $100, but if you have a splurge night planned, this is a good place to spend it. Dinner served nightly.

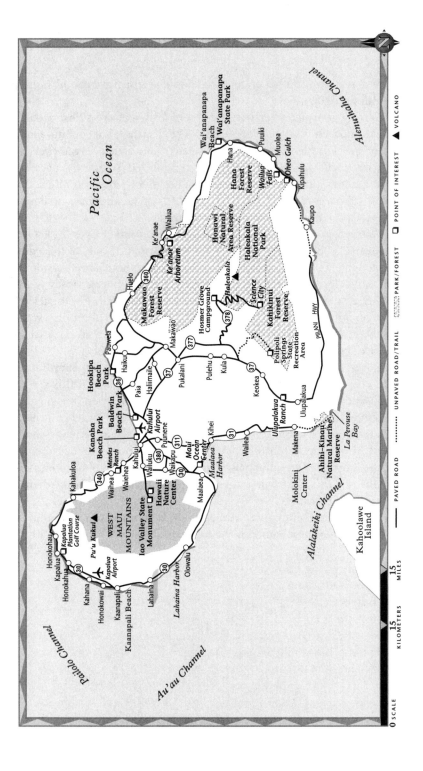

Pacific Ocean

Honokohau
Kapalua
Kahakuloa
Honokahua
Kapalua Plantation Golf Course
Kapalua Airport
Kahana
Honokowai
Kaanapali
Kaanapali Beach
Lahaina
Lahaina Harbor
Olowalu

Pu'u Kukui ▲
WEST MAUI MOUNTAINS
Iao Valley State Monument
Hawaii Nature Center

30
340

Waihee
Mendes Ranch
Waiehu
Wailuku
Kahului
Puunene
Waikapu
Maui Ocean Center
Maalaea
Maalaea Harbor

30
380
311
310

Kahului Airport

Kanaha Beach Park
Baldwin Beach Park
Hookipa Beach Park

Paia
Haiku
Haliimaile
Halimaile

36
360

Huelo
Makawao Forest Reserve

Makawao
Pukalani

37
377
378

Kula
Keokea
Ulupalakua Ranch
Ulupalakua

Pulehu

Kihei
Wailea
Makena

31

Ahihi-Kinau Natural Marine Reserve
La Perouse Bay

Molokini Crater

Ke'anae
Wailua
Ke'anae Arboretum

Wai'anapanapa Beach
Wai'anapanapa State Park

Hana
Hana Forest Reserve
Honawi Natural Area Reserve

Haleakala ▲
Science City
Hosmer Grove Campground
Kahikinui Forest Reserve
Polipoli Springs State Recreation Area

Haleakala National Park

PIILANI HWY

Kaupo

Puuiki
Muolea
Oheo Gulch
Wailua Falls
Kipahulu

Alenuihaha Channel

Alalakeiki Channel

Kahoolawe Island

Au'au Channel

Pailolo Channel

N

0 SCALE
15 KILOMETERS
15 MILES

— PAVED ROAD
.... UNPAVED ROAD/TRAIL
PARK/FOREST
□ POINT OF INTEREST
▲ VOLCANO

5

MAUI—
THE VALLEY ISLE

The people of Maui say, "*Maui no ka oi*—Maui is the best." And it's a pretty quick study to see exactly what they mean.

As soon as you arrive at Kahului Airport, the great mountain Haleakala is before you. A dormant volcano, Haleakala looms over the island, its summit 10,023 feet in the sky. The chill air of dawn draws hundreds of visitors to the summit each day to watch the sunrise from what seems like its source—in fact, in the Hawaiian language "Haleakala" means "House of the Sun."

From this chill and primal force high in the clouds, down the windswept slopes to the sunny shorelines, Maui offers a contrast of climates, and a diversity of pleasures. The visitor centers of Kaanapali, Lahaina, and Kihei complement the more exclusive resort areas of Kapalua, Wailea, and Makena. Combined, these destination resorts offer some of the finest hotels, restaurants, golf courses, beaches, adventures, and scenery in the state.

But to the 100,000 residents of Maui, the island is as much a spiritual force as it is a recreational haven. Maui represents an opportunity to live a lifestyle that is generally free of the congestion and tension of a larger city but is still only a short plane hop from Honolulu. For the inhabitants of Maui, this island truly is the best of both worlds.

The harbor at Lahaina

© Ron Dahlquist

Orientation/Lay of the Land

Maui can logically be divided into West Maui and East Maui, and that's how this chapter is organized. The third section covers Haleakala National Park, which falls geographically into East Maui but is a destination unto itself.

West Maui is where much of the tourism activity on the island began almost 30 years ago. Kaanapali, the first planned resort in Hawaii, started to take shape in the early 1960s, with several hotels, a shopping center, and restaurants to go along with an outstanding stretch of white-sand beach. Kaanapali is still a bustling hub of activity today.

Nearby, the old whaling village of Lahaina—Hawaii's capital from 1802 until 1850—has been transformed into an art and visitor community, but still retains an Old Hawaii charm. Its harbor is where many of the ocean activities meet on this side of the island. From here, whale-watch and snorkel cruises to Lanai are very popular.

Kapalua Resort, on Maui's far northwestern tip, is a multifaceted resort that features excellent nature programs, beaches, golf, and other outdoor activities.

East Maui is several times larger than West Maui, but for visitors the primary areas of interest—excluding Haleakala—can be isolated to Wailea, Makena, and Hana. Like Kaanapali, Wailea and Makena are planned resorts with several luxury hotels, delightful beaches, great golf courses, shopping, and dining. Both areas also make perfect home bases for ocean activities such as snorkel cruises to Molokini.

Hana is a world unto itself. When you get to Hana, out on Maui's far eastern shore, you'll think you've finally found paradise. It's not all that far as the tropic bird flies, but the slow and winding road through rain forests and past gorgeous coastline makes you forget about hurrying. Take your time to get here, stay a few days, and soak up the ambiance of Hana, one of Hawaii's most revered treasures.

Then there is Haleakala. Sunrise on Haleakala summit is a once-in-a-lifetime event. Sure, you get up at 3:00 a.m. to make it on time; sure, it's cold. But there is nothing else like it.

Nature/Adventure Activities

Maui is a big volcanic playground for hikers, climbers, bicyclists, and horseback riders. You can delve into monstrous craters, trek past lava fields, even scale the peak of Haleakala to watch the sun rise. Watersporters will also have a fascinating time snorkeling, diving, and swimming the surrounding ocean and natural pools.

Flora and Fauna

Maui's flora and fauna is as varied as that you'll find on any of the other Hawaiian islands, perhaps more so. From Haleakala National Park—where rare silversword plants thrive in the thin, cold air—down to the warm Pacific waters—alive with humpback whales in the winter months and a kaleidoscope of tropical fish year-round—Maui is a nature-lover's playground.

Haleakala National Park, which stretches from the summit of the mountain down the Kipahulu Valley to the sea just south of Hana, encompasses wide extremes of climate and geology. At the top are gray subalpine lava hills dusted with red volcanic cinder. It is an other-worldly atmosphere. But down at the coast the ecology changes and you are in the midst of a tropical rain forest.

The Nature Conservancy has taken quite an interest in Haleakala, and has established the 5,230-acre Waikamoi Preserve adjacent to park land. In this area are koa trees, raspberry bushes, *ohelo* bushes, a variety of ferns, and the world's only known tree geranium, now endangered.

Several avian species are also seen in Haleakala National Park, including the rare Maui parrotbill, and the *'akohekohe*, a native crested honeycreeper. Oddly, you will also see Hawaii's state bird, the nene goose, which seems to like the atmosphere up here.

Although Haleakala gets most of the attention, the West Maui Mountains are equally fascinating. Iao Valley State Park is a prime example of how interesting this area is. Sharp peaks rise quickly into the clouds, carved over the centuries by wind, rain, and natural erosion. It's only 2,250 feet above sea level, but the clouds that often hang here, and the monolithic look of Iao Needle, make this a very unusual atmosphere.

On the other side of the range, above Kaanapali and Kapalua, the mountains rise to almost 6,000 feet. The top portions of the range are almost all protected by the state and by Nature Conservancy preserves. Up here are several endangered species that are slowly rebounding under their protected status. They include the West Maui silversword, the Maui bog violet, and some rare tree snails.

Birds found here include *i'iwi*, *'apapane*, and *amakihi*. The Nature Conservancy does offer hikes into their preserves in the West Maui Mountains, specifically into the Kapunakea Preserve.

The warm and shallow waters south of Lahaina are favorite birthing and frolicking grounds for humpback whales. And there are several marine conservation districts, such as the Honolua–Mokuleia Bay Marine Life Conservation District, where tropical fish abound.

Certainly, the Hana district is one of Hawaii's most abundant areas for tropical fruits, flowers, plants, and trees. As you travel this region you'll see breadfruit, *kukui*, ferns, hibiscus and pandanus trees, bamboo, and many other species. At the coastline you'll have many opportunities to view seabirds, such as frigate birds, terns, and brown boobies.

EARTH MAUI NATURE SUMMIT

A five-day event focusing on Hawaii's current and future efforts to protect and preserve our land and sea, the Earth Maui Nature Summit began in 1996. It brings together experts, editors, and naturalists to discuss and act upon the issues pertinent to Hawaii's environment.

Not only does everyone talk the talk, but they also walk the walk: Beach cleanups are often scheduled, as are slide shows, seminars, and mountain and ocean tours. This important event showcases the dedication of Kapalua Resort to the environment, and serves as an example to other resorts of what exactly they can do to preserve and protect their respective environments.

For further information or reservations, call Kapalua Nature Society at 800/KAPALUA or 808/669-0244.

History, Culture, and Customs

Maui was formed by two shield volcanoes, officially called the East Maui Volcano and the West Maui Volcano. Most people, however, call them Haleakala and the West Maui Mountains. Haleakala, the newer of the two, covers 570 square miles of land, encompassing most of Maui's eastern coast.

Haleakala is thought to have evolved between 1.5 and 2 million years ago. Its most recent eruption was in 1790, and today it is considered dormant. Geologists think that at one time Maui, Molokai, Lanai, and Kahoolawe—separate islands today—were one large land mass, approximating half the size of the Big Island. This may partly explain why Molokai and Lanai are part of Maui County.

In 1787, French Captain Jean-Francois de Galoup de La Pérouse sailed into Hawaiian waters and became the first European to set foot on Maui. His landfall occurred just south of Makena, at what today is called La Perouse Bay.

Maui Visitors Bureau

Windsurfing on a perfect Maui day

Kamehameha the Great sailed from the Big Island and defeated Maui's King Kahekili and his forces in 1790, bringing Maui into his Hawaiian kingdom. Twelve years later, in 1802, Kamehameha named Lahaina the capital of Hawaii. It remained capital until 1850, when King Kamehameha III moved the capital to Honolulu.

The years from 1819, when the first whaling ship arrived in Lahaina, to 1850, when whaling began to decline, were important for Maui as well as for the Hawaiian nation: Not only did the whaling ships come, but so did the New England missionaries.

At Lahaina's peak in the 1840s, hundreds of whaling ships came into the port every year for supplies and shore leave. It was the shore-leave part that frightened the missionaries into action. They had established a presence at Lahaina and began converting the "heathen." Hawaiian women were made to cover their breasts, and many cultural traditions were forbidden, such as the hula dance, which the missionaries thought to be far too provocative.

The first sugar mill began operation on Maui in 1828, and sugar was

Maui's important cash crop for more than 150 years. The lands in the valley between East Maui and West Maui still grow an abundance of sugarcane. In recent times, though, it is tourism that is the foundation for the island's economy. Today, 2.3 million visitors per year come to Maui.

The evolution of tourism on Maui is interesting. The Hotel Hana Maui was the first resort on the island, built in 1946. In the early 1960s, Amfac, owner of the land on which Kaanapali Resort is now found, decided to diversify their holdings. The land on Maui seemed a perfect location for a resort destination, so plans were developed for one of the first planned resort/residential communities in the United States.

As it developed, and as more and more people started venturing afield from Waikiki, Kaanapali became the destination of choice. It gave Maui an identity apart from Hawaii as a whole, something Kauai and the Big Island have been trying to do ever since.

Nowadays there are four such resort/residential communities on Maui: Kaanapali, Kapalua, Wailea, and Makena. Two are neighbors in the shadow of the West Maui Mountains, Kaanapali and Kapalua; Wailea and Makena are neighbors an hour south.

Visitor Information

There are many ways to get the best current information about Maui. The **Hawaii Visitors & Convention Bureau** provides brochures, maps, and practical tips for travel to all the islands. Contact them before you visit, or drop by when you're on Oahu: 2270 Kalakaua Ave., Suite 801, Honolulu, HI 96815, in the heart of Waikiki; 808/923-1811 or 800/GO-HAWAII; www.gohawaii.com.

A similar service specifically geared to the islands of Maui, Lanai, and Molokai is provided by the **Maui Visitors Bureau**. They will be happy to provide you a packet of information if you call 808/244-3530, fax 808/244-1337, or write 1727 Wili Pa Loop, Wailuku, HI 96793.

The Nature Conservancy of Hawaii can provide information regarding their preserves and hikes on Maui and elsewhere. Contact them at 1116 Smith St., #201, Honolulu, HI 96817; 808/537-4508.

Useful Web sites include the **Hawaii Ecotourism Association**'s locations: www.planet-hawaii.com/hea/ and www.alternative-hawaii.com.

The **Hawaii Wildlife Fund**, a nonprofit educational organization, can provide information on whale behaviors and migrations, sea turtles, dolphins, and monk seals. This type of information helps visitors to Maui know more about what they are viewing. Contact the Fund at P.O. Box 12082, Lahaina, Maui, HI 96761; 808/667-0437.

Information about camping on Maui is available from the **State Parks Office**, 54 South High St., Wailuku, HI 96793; 808/984-8109.

Getting There

You can fly into Maui's main airport, Kahului, on frequent flights from Honolulu on either Aloha Airlines or Hawaiian Airlines. You can also catch direct flights into Kahului on United Airlines from several cities on the Mainland's west coast. Two other options are to fly directly into Hana from Honolulu on Aloha Island Air, or into the West Maui/Kapalua Airport on Aloha Island Air.

Once on Maui, if you are planning exploration, hiking, a Haleakala trip, or a Hana trip, the best bet is to rent a car. All major car-rental companies are found at either the Kahului Airport or near the West Maui/Kapalua Airport. Maui has no public transportation.

WEST MAUI

West Maui is a study in contrasts, where high-style golf resorts nudge up against rugged shorelines, and tourists gape at whales frolicking just miles from uncharted territory. These contrasts can add up to delight for the adventure traveler.

You can obtain general travelers' information on West Maui by contacting the Maui Visitors Bureau, 1727 Wili Pa Loop, Wailuku, HI 96793; 808/244-3530. The Kaanapali Beach Resort Association (2530 Kekaa Dr., Suite 1B, Kaanapali, HI 96761; 800/245-9229) will send you information on Kaanapali and its activities there. Information on Kapalua Resort and Kapalua Nature Society can be obtained by contacting Kapalua Marketing, 500 Bay Dr., Kapalua, HI 96761; 808/669-0244.

© Ron Dahlquist

Snorkeling and sailing at Kaanapali

Orientation/Lay of the Land

West Maui encompasses a land mass roughly half the size of East Maui. Its primary geologic element is the West Maui Mountains, older by far than Haleakala.

The western shoreline boasts some of the best beaches in the state, along with several resort areas of distinction. On the northern tip of the island is Kapalua Resort, known for its golf tournaments, beaches, and exclusive hotels. But Kapalua is also known for its commitment to the environment and as host of the Earth Maui Nature Summit, where topics pertinent to the island's ecology are discussed.

The next main destination down the western coast is Kaanapali, a master-planned resort of hotels, condominiums, golf courses, shops, and restaurants. Kaanapali also boasts a lovely stretch of white-sand beach and a sunny climate.

Further south is Lahaina, an old whaling town turned art capital of Hawaii. Today visitors find galleries galore, restaurants, souvenir shops, and nightlife. Lahaina's marina serves as launching point for many of the water activities on this side of Maui.

On the windward side of the West Maui Mountains is a much different landscape. The higher elevations are rugged and inaccessible, and even though a road circumnavigates the entire mountain range, relatively few tourists venture up the windward coast. If they did, they would find a perfectly scalloped shoreline with wide ocean views. Here are few of the gentle white-sand beaches found on the leeward side, but there are waterfalls, bays, and old Hawaiian villages that feel like they have been frozen in time for a half-century.

By contrast, Maui's county seat is in nearby Wailuku. And just a short drive from Wailuku are Iao Valley and the Iao Needle, a monolithic lava pillar carved to a peak over the centuries and now covered in vegetation. This popular destination is made even more mysterious by the fog that hangs over the valley.

Because there is no public transportation on Maui, and because the sights and adventures of West Maui are considerable distances from one another, it's a good idea to have a rental vehicle at your disposal. Rental cars are available at either the Kahului Airport or the Kapalua/West Maui airport.

Flora and Fauna

It's interesting that parts of the West Maui Mountains are so rugged that they have never been explored, yet they are within 10 miles of bustling resort centers.

The mountains rise to only 2,250 feet above sea level at Iao Valley State Park, but this geologic phenomenon is a prime example of how interesting this area is. Sharp peaks have been carved over the centuries by wind, rain, and natural erosion. Low clouds often hang here, making this unusual atmosphere look a lot like somewhere you'd find Bilbo Baggins and his hobbit friends.

Iao Valley State Park is habitat for several varieties of introduced birds, such as the myna and the northern cardinal, and also provides a close-up look at what centuries of wind and rain can do to a volcanic mass. The Hawaii Nature Center in Iao Valley conducts educational

WHALE-WATCHING

Hawaii's state mammal is the Pacific humpback whale, which commutes 3,500 miles from Alaska to Hawaii to play in the calm water of Maalaea Bay, usually from December to April. Since these behemoths are 45 feet long and weigh four tons, they make a big splash.

You see the cars lined up by the side of the highway and people looking out to sea. You wonder what's going on. Then you see them—humpback whales just offshore. It's a mother teaching her calf how to swim in the shallow, gentle waters. You pull over too, and join the gathering crowd. It is one of the most beautiful and awe-inspiring things you'll ever see, and you are quiet as you watch. Thing is, it's an almost daily occurrence from November through March on many of the Hawaiian islands.

The eight-mile stretch of shoreline just south of Kaanapali is one of the humpbacks' favorite spots. You can do it one of two ways: 1) pack a picnic, pick a nice place to sit on the beach, and wait; or 2) look for the lineup of cars by the side of the highway and join the gathering crowd.

For information on whales contact Hawaii Wildlife Fund, P.O. Box 12082, Lahaina, HI 96761, 808/667-0437; or Pacific Whale Foundation, 101 N. Kihei Rd., Kihei, HI 96753, 808/879-8860.

hikes and presents exhibits designed to teach visitors more about the area's flora and fauna.

As you traverse the windward coast, you are likely to spot quite a few seabirds on the wing. These include the great frigate bird and the split-tailed shearwater.

Across the range, the mountains above Kaanapali and Kapalua rise to almost 6,000 feet. The top portions of the range around Pu'u Kukui, the tallest peak in the West Maui Mountains, are mostly protected by the State of Hawaii and by Nature Conservancy preserves. There are a number of endangered species up here, which are slowly rebounding under their protected status. They include the West Maui silversword, the Maui bog violet, and some rare tree snails.

A partnership has been established between the Nature Conservancy, the State of Hawaii, Maui Land & Pineapple Company, and Amfac/JMB Hawaii for the purpose of protecting the watersheds in the West Maui Mountains. Along with the watersheds, the flora and fauna are also protected. Among those protected species is a native ohia tree that grows only a few inches tall, but whose lehua blossoms grow as large as those found on 50-foot ohia trees elsewhere in the state.

The Nature Conservancy offers occasional hikes into their preserves in the West Maui Mountains, specifically into the Kapunakea Preserve. Among the birds you are likely to spot here are *i'iwi, 'apapane,* and *amakihi.* Write the Nature Conservancy for information on their hikes, tours, and programs at 81 Makawao Ave., Suite 203A, Makawao, HI 96768; or call 808/572-7849.

Golf courses, for all the negative reputation they have garnered over the years, have actually proven to be quite a boon for birds. At Kapalua and Kaanapali, the golf courses provide habitat for many introduced species, including cardinals, sparrows, several finch varieties, and the black-crowned night heron, which likes to hang around the lakes and ponds.

The waters south of Lahaina are warm and shallow, making them favorite birthing grounds for humpback whales. Several marine conservation districts, such as the Honolua–Mokuleia Bay Marine Life Conservation District (above Kapalua), have also been established along this shore where tropical fish of many varieties abound.

History, Culture, and Customs

West Maui's Lahaina has the distinction of having been the only capital of the Hawaiian nation other than Honolulu. The year was 1802, and Kamehameha the Great had sailed from the Big Island and defeated Maui's King Kahekili and his forces 12 years earlier, bringing Maui into his emerging Hawaiian kingdom. Kamehameha named Lahaina the capital of Hawaii, which it remained until 1850 when King Kame-hameha III moved the capital to Honolulu.

Most of the action on West Maui in those days was centered in and around Lahaina. Whaling began in 1819 when the first whaling ship arrived in Hawaii, and soon dramatically changed the lives of West Maui natives. For not only did the whaling ships come, but so too did the New England missionaries.

At Lahaina's peak in the 1840s, as many as 400 ships at a time were berthed in the harbor, with some 1,500 sailors coming ashore for supplies and shore leave. The missionaries, who had established the first high school west of the Mississippi River and installed Hawaii's first printing press in Lahaina, were afraid the sailors would corrupt their new converts. To keep the former "heathens" under strict control, Hawaiian women were made to cover their breasts, and many cultural traditions were forbidden, such as the hula dance, which the missionaries thought to be far too lascivious. The whaling industry began to decline around 1850, but by then the missionaries' work was indelibly marked on the native peoples.

Evidence of these colorful days is everywhere in Lahaina today. Some 55 acres of the old town have been set aside as a historic district, and several buildings have been protected as National Historic Landmarks. Worthy of exploration are the Baldwin Mission House, the old jail, and Lahaina Prison. A whaling museum is housed in the restored two-masted ship *Carthaginian*, permanently moored in Lahaina Harbor.

West Maui is where much of the tourism activity on the island began almost 30 years ago. Kaanapali, the first planned resort in Hawaii, started to take shape in the early 1960s, with several hotels, a shopping center, and restaurants to go along with an outstanding stretch of white-sand beach. Once a playground for Maui's kings and royal families, who liked to surf and canoe-race in the gentle waters, Kaanapali is still a bustling hub of activity today.

This area was important agricultural land as well, with sugarcane and pineapple being the main crops. Although a little quaint, a re-stored "sugarcane train" pulled by a vintage steam locomotive now hauls tourists instead of cane from Kaanapali to Lahaina.

NATURE AND ADVENTURE SIGHTS
IN WEST MAUI

Kapalua

The waters just offshore from Kapalua Resort are popular for kayaking, snorkeling, diving, and swimming. Because Kapalua is set on a lava promontory, the waters are perfect breeding grounds for sea life of all kinds.

Nearby is a turtle reef where "scooter diving"—done with a diver-propulsion vehicle designed to whisk you around underwater—is all the rage. Imagine zooming around like an aquatic James Bond amidst schools of brightly colored reef fish, and looking sea turtles in the eye.

Night dives and beach dives are also popular. If you're here long enough, full PADI open-water certification (a four-day class) is available.

Details: *Kapalua Resort is on Highway 30 at the northern tip of Maui, beyond Lahaina, Kaanapali, and Napili. Most activities meet on Kapalua Beach.*

Iao Valley State Park

At the 2,250-foot level above Wailuku, visitors will discover the wonders of Iao Valley and the Hawaii Nature Center.

The main draw of Iao Valley is **Iao Needle**, a basalt monolith covered in fern and vegetation standing some 1,200 feet above the valley floor. It takes a short and easy hike along a well-maintained path to get to the overlook where this geologic oddity can best be viewed. You'll also be treated to some nice views of Wailuku and Kahului along the way.

There are pools for swimming and trails for hiking. These, combined with picnic tables, a **Heritage Gardens** (Kepaniwai Park), and the **Hawaii Nature Center**, make this area good for every member of the family.

Some trails do venture farther into the valley, but they are more strenuous and for serious hikers only. Be careful if you do decide to go deep into the valley, and check with park officials first: Some trails wash out easily in the rains and can become dangerous to travel.

Details: Follow Highway 32 toward Wailuku from Kahului. Continue on until it becomes Iao Valley Road. This will dead-end into a parking lot, and from there you must hike to the overlook. Ample parking, rest rooms, and picnic tables are located at nearby Heritage Gardens as well.

Lahaina to Lanai

Eco-educator Hannah Bernard of the Hawaii Wildlife Fund and the crew of the *Maui Nui Explorer* lead educational, fun snorkel adventures from Lahaina Harbor to select spots off the coast of Lanai.

Iao Needle at Iao Valley State Park

© Ron Dahlquist

A 48-foot, rigid-hulled inflatable, the *Maui Nui Explorer* takes a smaller group than many of the other snorkel-cruise operators, and trip leaders spend the time to educate passengers about the marine ecosystems they encounter. Turtles, dolphins, and colorful coral are part of the underwater landscape off the renowned Lanai coast. During whale season, it is possible to encounter as many as five or six of these magnificent creatures per voyage.

Bernard has written extensively about Hawaii's whales; her credits include a book and many magazine articles. She is a sincere and dedicated researcher and eco-educator. Her presence, or the presence of the other eco-ecucators from the Hawaii Wildlife Fund, aboard the *Maui Nui Explorer* is part of what makes this snorkel adventure different from, and more valuable than, many others.

Details: Three different trips are offered daily, all leaving from Lahaina Harbor. See Guides and Outfitters for more information.

Whale-watching off the coast of Maui

Mendes Ranch

Like the Big Island, Maui has a long and proud *paniolo* tradition. You can visit and see for yourself several of these ranches on horseback.

One of the best rides on the West Maui side of the island is offered by Mendes Ranch, a 300-acre spread on the windward side near Wailuku. You can ride from *mauka* to *makai* (mountain to sea) and take in all the essential elements of an earthly paradise—rainbows, waterfalls, tide pools, a rain forest, and an ancient volcano.

"I want people to have an authentic Hawaiian ranch experience," says Allan Mendes, a third-generation wrangler who guides riders through herds of Brahma bulls, Texas longhorns, and 300 head of beef cattle, past waterfalls and down to the ocean. During whale-watching season, humpbacks can be seen swimming offshore.

The three-hour ride ends with a high-noon barbecue back at the corral under the old mango tree. A two-hour afternoon ride is also offered, but without the lunch.

Details: Mendes Ranch is at the seven-mile mark past Wailuku on Highway 340.

Pu'u Kukui's Cloud Forest

On 5,871-foot Pu'u Kukui, the legendary highest peak of the West Maui Mountains, you may see—if you are one of 12 lucky hikers chosen each year—the cloud forests of Maui, one of the biologically richest areas in Hawaii. Spiky silverswords and unassuming sedges, rare daisies, wild orchids, and giant ferns flourish in a soggy arboreal sanctuary violated only by a narrow boardwalk.

You'll stand in total silence amid a hundred shades of green. Ohia trees, which normally tower 50 feet or more, barely reach the top of your boots. Almost every growing thing appears stunted, as if some mad bonsai gardener had pruned an entire forest.

The Kapalua Nature Society picks 12 applicants each year as part of the Earth Maui Nature Summit to participate in this rare treat. The area is protected and closed to the public the rest of the year.

Details: Call the Kapalua Nature Society at 800/KAPALUA or 808/669-0244 for further information on the Earth Maui Nature Summit, the Kapalua Nature Society, and these hikes.

Waihee Ridge

One of the best hikes onto the windward slopes of the West Maui Mountains is along Waihee Ridge. It is a short (2.5-mile) hike, but the elevation change is from sea level to almost 3,000 feet. Delightful ocean views are to be had along the way, as well as a high view of the town of Wailuku.

The native vegetation along the ridge is abundant. You start off in a pasture, pass through guava and eucalyptus stands, and then begin to climb into the higher elevations where you'll encounter ferns and other native species.

Take care to avoid some sinkholes near the top of the trail, if you veer from the beaten path. They sometimes have standing water or vegetation growing on top of them. But these can just be "plugs" resting over vertical lava tubes, some as deep as 100 feet. The danger, of course, is walking on a plug and having it give way. If you stick to the trail there is little danger.

You are rewarded at the top of this seldom-traveled trail with a picnic table for having lunch and admiring the wide views.

Details: *Drive north from Wailuku on Highway 340 through the town of Waihee. The trailhead is about two miles north of the town. Just before the Maluhia Boy Scout Camp there is a turnoff on the mountain side of the road. Proceed through a gate (often you have to open and close this gate yourself) and up a dirt road .25 mile to the top of a hill. You must park here and look for the trailhead marker.*

GUIDES AND OUTFITTERS

Maui Nui Explorer, 330 Hukilike, Kahului, 800/852-4183 or 808/661-3776, is an adventure ship that will take you snorkeling with turtles, swimming with fishes, learning about reefs, and whale-watching in season. Each excursion has onboard a trained marine-life naturalist from the Hawaii Wildlife Fund. Three different trips are offered, all pushing off from Lahaina Harbor. Cost ranges from $30/person for the afternoon whale-watch trip (seasonally), to $46/person for the three-hour morning trip (includes continental breakfast), to $69/person for the four-hour midafternoon trip (includes a deli-style lunch).

Another company with seafaring vessels for your adventures is **Trilogy Snorkel Sails**, P.O. Box 1119, Lahaina, HI 96767, 888/225-MAUI. With several identical catamarans sailing simultaneously, Trilogy is able to offer several dives to suit your desires. The Lanai cruise takes you snorkeling off the coast of Lanai, but also pulls up on the sand where you take a short island cruise. A Molokini Crater snorkel cruise takes off from Maalaea Harbor at 6:30 a.m. to beat the crowd. And a Kaanapali picnic sail meets you on the beach at Kaanapali and takes you to several nearby snorkel sites. All gear is provided. Cost is $89/person for the Kaanapali or Molokini sail; $159/person for the Lanai sail.

Take a dip with **Kapalua Dive Company**, P.O. Box 11161, Lahaina,

HI 96761, 808/669-4085, which specializes in dive adventures at Kapalua and nearby waters. Popular are the kayak dives to a turtle reef; and the "scooter dives," where you use the Dacor SV-900 diver-propulsion vehicle to whisk you around underwater. They also do night dives, beach dives, and full PADI open-water certifications (a four-day class). Cost varies depending on choice of adventure, but range from $55 for the two-hour beach dive to $99 for the scooter dive. PADI class is $385.

Land-based explorers, check out **Maui Hiking Safaris**, P.O. Box 11198, Lahaina, HI 96761, 888/455-3963 or 808/573-0168. Randy Warner takes groups of no more than six people on hiking trips all over Maui. Some of his more popular hikes lead you into the lush West Maui Mountains, but Haleakala is also a preferred destination. Offerings range from moderate to strenuous, and from half-day to full-day journeys. Cost varies depending on hike, but ranges from $49/person to $89/person; 10 percent discount for children 13 and under.

Or take a hike over to **Mendes Ranch**, RR1, Box 150, Wailuku, HI 96793, 808/871-5222, to saddle up a horse and enjoy horseback rides from the windward slopes of the West Maui Mountains down toward the glimmering Pacific. A barbecue lunch is served upon your return to the corral. Cost is $130/person for the three-hour ride (lunch included); $85/person for the two-hour afternoon ride (no lunch).

CAMPING

There is no legal camping in West Maui. See Camping listings in East Maui section.

LODGING

There are many fine luxury hotels along the coast in Kaanapali, and many condominium choices in Kaanapali, Napili, and Kapalua—too numerous to mention. What follows are the best resorts that fall into the "ecotourism" category, plus several of the unique smaller inns and bed-and-breakfasts in the area.

143

MAUI'S BEST BEACHES

by Rick Carroll

Author Rick Carroll has studied Hawaii's beaches extensively.
Here are his choices for the best beaches on Maui.

Best Beach—Kapalua

Of all the 80 beaches on Maui, none are finer than Kapalua. A small crescent of gold sand on Maui's northwest shore, the beach sits in the embrace of two black lava fingers at the foot of a royal coconut grove under Pu'u Kukui, the 5,871-foot West Maui peak that ancient Hawaiians called "the junction between heaven and earth."

Soft, warm, and clear, the water is full of tropical fish and some-times sea turtles. Across the channel the island of Molokai appears to be a mirage.

This beach resort hosts the Kapalua Wine Symposium and out-door concerts by the sea. A path leads up to the Kapalua Bay Hotel & Villas and the elegant Ritz-Carlton Kapalua, recently named America's favorite tropical resort hotel in a travel-magazine readers' poll.

Prettiest Beach—Wai'anapanapa

Near Hana, you will find a shiny black-sand, horseshoe-shaped beach with jade-green jungle on three sides and cobalt-blue water lapping at its feet. Welcome to Wai'anapanapa State Park—a place so pretty people

Within **Kapalua Resort**, 800 Kapalua Dr., Kapalua, 800/KAPALUA or 808/669-0244, are two hotels, some villas and condominiums, and some private homes that you can lease. The hotels are the **Kapalua Bay Hotel & Villas** and the **Ritz-Carlton Kapalua**, both exquisite luxury properties with pools, restaurants, and shops. The Kapalua Bay rents condominiums and private homes, which are great for families or longer stays because they are equipped with kitchen and laundry facilities. Anyone staying at stop and stare. *Then they discover it's also the cheapest beach digs in Hawaii—a dozen cabins go for $14 a night. It's not only the prettiest beach, but a pretty good deal.*

Best Tourist Beach—Kaanapali
Everybody's a tourist at Kaanapali, the beach that made Maui famous. Four-mile Kaanapali Beach, designed solely for tourists, is the centerpiece of this 600-acre beach resort full of folks in matching aloha wear.

The gold-sand beach, at the foot of the West Maui Mountains, includes 85-foot-high Keka'a Point, where daring young men take swan dives. Out across Au'au Channel the island of Lanai appears like a lump of brown rock. First-time visitors spin in the sand with videocams, trying to capture the sense of place.

Best Windsurfing Beach—Hookipa
Hookipa Beach is known as the windsurfing capital of the world, and as soon as you get out of your car you'll understand why. Whether you want to watch or get on the water and skim with the big dogs, this is the best it gets for windsurfing. It's probably a good idea to stay on the shore and watch the pros go at it. They'll come flying over the peak of a wave, somersault high in the air, and come down in shape to catch more waves just like the last one.

It's all good fun to watch.

Kapalua has access to the recreational facilities, which include tennis courts, three championship golf courses, three beaches, and water activities of many kinds.

If there is a prime example of a "green" resort on Maui, it is Kapalua. In addition to its world-class amenities, Kapalua Resort has taken the initiative to create a number of preservation programs, including the Kapalua Nature Society and the Earth Maui Nature

Summit. Rates: All of the accommodations at Kapalua fall into the luxury category, but from there the rates vary greatly according to what you are looking for; it's best to call for information.

A lovingly restored, 12-room, Victorian-style inn, **Lahaina Inn**, 127 Lahainaluna Rd., Lahaina, 800/669-3444 or 808/661-0577, is one of the best in historic Lahaina Town. It is wonderfully appointed, with many antiques and period pieces from the 1860s through the early 1900s in Maui. Furnishings include four-poster beds, leaded-glass lamps, and carved armoires. Downstairs is the delectable David Paul's Lahaina Grill. Rates: $99–$159; $10/night more during peak season (December–April).

Another special property is **Old Wailuku Inn**, 2199 Kahookele St., Wailuku, 800/305-4899 or 808/244-5897. A restored 1940s-style inn with six rooms, it is decorated in classic Hawaiian plantation style. Furnishings include colorful and authentic Hawaiian quilts on the beds. Each room has a private bath, and some have whirlpool tubs. A full breakfast is included in the price. Old Wailuku Inn won the "Keep It Hawaii" award from the Hawaii Visitors & Convention Bureau in 1998. Rates: $120–$180 for two persons.

For a more rustic lodging choice, there's **Pioneer Inn**, 658 Wharf St., Lahaina, 808/661-3636. A historic inn in the heart of old Lahaina, the Pioneer is a two-story wooden structure that takes you back in time. Built around a courtyard, all guest rooms are on the second floor. Shops and a restaurant are on the ground level. A lanai off the street-facing rooms gives guests a view of the action down below—and there's plenty of it. This wonderful, historic property is reminiscent of Lahaina's busy days as a whaling port. Rates: $120–$165 for the suite.

FOOD

Avalon, 844 Front St., Lahaina, 808/667-5559, is open for lunch and dinner daily. Owner Mark Ellman is committed to buying the best local organic produce whenever possible. In addition, his talents in the kitchen and the wonderfully tropical ambiance of the restaurant make this one of Maui's best choices. Try it for dinner. Salad specialties include lemongrass chicken or tofu salad, and Chinese chicken or tofu salad. Entrées include luau-style roasted garlic seafood, pesto-crusted mahi, and, for two people, a whole fresh wok-fried *opakapaka* with fresh vegetables in a Thai coconut lemongrass sauce. You'll find a local crowd here, as well as tourists-in-the-know.

For a nouveau cuisine twist on Hawaiian fare, tray **David Paul's Lahaina Grill**, 127 Lahainaluna Rd., Lahaina, 808/667-5117. Start with the Kona lobster crab cakes, or maybe the smoked-salmon hash-brown appetizer. Move to a salad of Hana tomatoes with buffalo mozzarella. And for an entrée try the mahimahi stuffed with Kula spinach and garlic mashed potatoes and topped with a Gorgonzola crispy pancetta; or perhaps the black-truffle risotto with Kona lobster, tiger prawns, and roasted tomatoes. Of course there is no guarantee any of these items will be on the menu, since it changes daily, but you get the idea: This place is great! Open for lunch and dinner daily.

Hula Grill, Whaler's Village, Kaanapali Beach, 808/667-6636, is Peter Merriman's Maui restaurant, featuring Hawaii Regional Cuisine. If you've been to Merriman's in Kamuela on the Big Island, Peter's first restaurant, you'll know what to expect at Hula Grill: quality and creativity. You can get salads, sandwiches, and entrées for lunch, but come here for dinner. The dim sum appetizer menu includes a Puna goat cheese, macadamia nut, and shrimp quesadilla that's not to be missed. Entrée specialties include firecracker mahimahi baked with chili and cumin and served with black-bean, Maui onion, and avocado relish; and many other seafood items. Hula dancers nightly. Lunch and dinner daily.

Wonderful ocean and golf-course views add to the pleasure of dining at the elegant **Plantation House Restaurant**, at Kapalua Plantation Golf Course, 808/669-6299. Breakfast and lunch are the best times to enjoy the vistas, and you can even spot whales swimming offshore during winter months. For breakfast, enjoy granola, fruit, or a plate of eggs Benedict to your liking. Breakfast is served until 3 p.m. For lunch, sample the goat-cheese salad, *ahi* sandwich, or any of the other tasty salads or sandwiches on the menu. Open for breakfast, lunch, and dinner daily.

Although **Rusty Harpoon**, Whaler's Village, Kaanapali Beach, 808/661-3123, is good for lunch and dinner, the serene water views are most relaxing in the morning. Come here for breakfast. You can get fresh fruit, freshly baked muffins, espressos, or a Bloody Mary (if last night lasted too long). Full breakfasts, too. The lunch menu features burgers—the mahimahi burger is popular—gourmet pizzas, sandwiches, and salads. If you're here for dinner, try the sushi and seafood bar, and save room for the island-high macadamia-nut cream pie. Open for breakfast, lunch, and dinner daily.

EAST MAUI

If any one word can encapsulate East Maui, it is "diverse." The geology, flora, and fauna of this region vary as widely as the adventure opportunities. Whether you ride horseback in the scenic upcountry, explore an ancient lava cave, or snorkel on East Maui's sunny side, you'll be sure to experience the variety of wildlife and nature that gives this region its flavor.

Information on all of East Maui can be obtained by contacting the Maui Visitors Bureau, 1727 Wili Pa Loop, Wailuku, HI 96793; 808/244-3530. The **Maui Ocean Center** will also send you information; write to 192 Maalaea Rd., Maalaea, HI 96793, call 808/270-7000, or log onto www.coralworld.com/moc.

Orientation/Lay of the Land

East Maui encompasses a large area, made to feel larger because you cannot drive completely around it, and also because Haleakala is smack in the middle of it.

On the sunny southeastern shore—sunny because it's in the lee of Haleakala—are three resort areas: Kihei, Wailea, and Makena. Many of Maui's favorite beaches are found along this stretch, and many water adventures begin here. Molokini Crater is just offshore from Makena, for example.

Upcountry from the beach resorts, on the slopes of Haleakala, sev-

MAUI OCEAN CENTER

With loads of hands-on learning exhibits, the Maui Ocean Center, 192 Maalaea Rd., Maalaea, adjacent to Maalaea Harbor, is great for kids and family activity—but chances are parents will learn just as much about Hawaii's ocean life. Highlights of the facility are a 750,000-gallon Open Ocean exhibit with a walk-through acrylic tunnel where you can peer tiger sharks right in the eye... in complete safety; a touch pool where you can see what a sea cucumber feels like; a stingray cove that provides an up-close view of the graceful sea creatures; and a whale discovery center with plenty to learn in a fun setting.

This state-of-the-art marine center is a "don't miss" while on Maui. Call 808/270-7000 for more information. Two restaurants and a gift shop are on the property. Admission is $17.50/adults; $12/children 3–12.

eral wonderful towns and ranchlands are found. Ulupalakua Ranch is probably the best known of the ranches, but the entire area is equally lovely. Panoramic views of the Pacific, Kahoolawe Island, and Molokini Crater make this a great spot to pull to the side of the road for a picnic. A visit to Tedeschi Vineyards, specializing in pineapple wines, is also a treat.

Across the mountain, on just about the opposite coast, is Hana— lovely, remote, lush Hana. The drive to Hana is legendary because of its many hairpin turns as well as its tropical beauty.

Once you reach Hana you'll find that getting there was only half the fun. This laid-back community is in a world all its own. Celebrities such as George Harrison, Kris Kristofferson, and Jim Nabors own homes here, and are at ease walking into the general store since no one here really cares about their fame. Charles Lindbergh's grave is in Hana, not well marked or easy to find, and that would have suited the solitude-seeking aviator just fine. Quite refreshing, really.

Highway 360 continues on from Hana, turning into Highway 36 and ending just beyond Puuiki. Access to Seven Sacred Pools and the Kipahulu entrance to Haleakala are found just above the village of Puuiki. Four-wheel-drive vehicles can continue on Highway 31 from here, presuming the weather is not too wet, past the town of Kaupo and Kaupo Gap and along the rugged southern coast of Maui before emerging several hours later in the Kula area.

Since the area is so varied, and since there is no public transportation on Maui, rental car or four-wheel-drive is the only way to go.

Flora and Fauna

East Maui is as diverse as the Big Island of Hawaii, but in a much smaller area. The land mass is dominated by Haleakala, and thus has a distinct dry side and green side. The flora and fauna of East Maui reflect this diversity.

On the hiking trails of Polipoli Springs State Recreation Area, in the upcountry on Haleakala's western slope, redwood, eucalyptus, Monterey pine, and cypress trees abound. The area is also good bird-watching territory, with 'apapane, finch, cardinals, and *pueo* owls commonly seen.

With perhaps as diverse a sea-life population as anywhere in Hawaii, the waters off East Maui include the Molokini Shoal Marine Life Conservation District. A popular dive and snorkel area, here you'll find giant manta rays, pufferfish, butterfly fish, octopi, and the occasional reef shark. The area also boasts some great examples of antler coral.

The Ahihi–Kinau Natural Marine Reserve is far less visited than Molokini, but no less fascinating. In fact, since there are fewer visitors, some of the more reserved fish species are found here in greater numbers than at Molokini. In all, more than 100 species thrive in these coastal waters, as do many species of spiny coral.

As the southern coastline turns east toward Hana, the land becomes more barren and few species call it home. The waters get rougher, too, as you move into the channel between Maui and the Big Island, one of the roughest channels in the world.

The other side of the volcano, however, is a completely different story. Lush and green, the windward side of East Maui will reveal more types of fern, flowers, and trees than you ever thought existed. Many of them can be seen at Keʻanae Arboretum, a stop along the Hana Highway. On display here are species such as the *hau* tree, *kukui* nut tree (Hawaii's state tree), breadfruit, and coconut palms, most of which are used in traditional Hawaiian lifestyle for one thing or another. The fauna of windward East Maui is chiefly avian. Great frigate birds, black noddies, and other seabirds frequent the coastline. In the mountains of the Kipahulu District, added to Haleakala National Park primarily to protect the rare endemic avian populations, you are likely to see common myna, spotted dove, cardinals, and Japanese white eyes at the lower elevations. The upper elevations, mostly closed to the public, are where the endemic birds are found.

Of note is an ambitious project called the East Maui Watershed Partnership, which brings federal, state, and county government together with the Nature Conservancy, Hana Ranch, Haleakala Ranch, and Alexander & Baldwin. The partnership oversees 100,000 wilderness acres from Kaupo (on Maui's eastern tip near Hana) to Makawao; and from the summit of Haleakala to the Keʻanae coast. Through conservation easement, resource management, and the removal of destructive alien species, the East Maui Watershed Partnership protects one of the largest remaining tracts of native forest in Hawaii, as well as the highest concentration of rare and endangered birds in the world.

History, Culture, and Customs

The first resort on Maui—Can you name it? Most people would guess Kaanapali, but the answer is the Hotel Hana-Maui, which opened in 1946. It is still today one of the most serene and exclusive retreats in the Hawaiian islands.

Why build a resort in remote Hana in the 1940s? Hana in those days was different than Hana today. Sugarcane was king back then. The first sugar mill was opened in Hana in 1849, and by 1883 there were six sugar plantations.

The Hana Highway was completed in 1926, making the area far more accessible than it ever had been before. By 1940 there were 3,500 residents in Hana, almost twice the size it is today. And in 1944, Paul Fagan started Hana Ranch with 14,000 acres.

In 1946, however, a tidal wave hit the Hana coast, killing 12 people. That same year the last of the sugar plantations closed, marking the end of the sugar industry in Hana. Many families who were dependent upon the plantations for their livelihood moved to the other side of Maui, where sugar was still going strong. And Fagan, in an effort to attract tourists to Hana and bolster the shaken economy, opened Hotel Hana-Maui.

The other resort areas of East Maui—Kihei, Wailea, and Makena—are more recent, each having started to come into its own in the 1970s. In these areas residents join tourists in a commotion of activity and nightlife, and except for the fact that the weather is better in Maui, you might think you were in California.

But as you veer away from the beach, into the upcountry, for example, you'll discover Maui has many different facets. Traditionally farming and ranching communities, Maui's upcountry now blends cowboys and artists, farmers and craftspeople. Communities such as Makawao, Kula, and Haliimaile feature charming collections of coffee bars, shops, and eateries.

Smaller communities such as Haiku dot the coast, providing refuge for those in search of solitude and beauty. And there's even an old Hawaiian settlement at Ke'anae, where residents prefer a traditional lifestyle of fishing and raising taro, guava, and bananas while the world passes them by.

The ethnic mix is similar to that on most of the Hawaiian islands, and the percentages are roughly the same as well: 36 percent Caucasian; 23 percent Japanese; followed by Filipino, Hawaiian, and Chinese. But one cannot overlook the influence of the Portuguese population, which made up much of the upcountry *paniolo* community, and built the bright white octagonal Holy Ghost Church in 1894. It has recently been restored and keeps watch over the Kula district.

Paia, on the Kahului end of the Hana Highway, is one of those towns unique to Hawaii, where one industry faded and another rose from its ashes. In this case the sugar industry, so long an institution in the lives of Paians—as it was elsewhere on Maui—gradually declined. But today you'll find that Paia is not boarded up and depressed but a lively, artsy village of windsurfers and youngsters seeking to follow the sun in Maui.

NATURE AND ADVENTURE SIGHTS IN EAST MAUI

Haleakala Slopes

One of the best ways to get onto the slopes of Haleakala above the Wailea and Makena resort areas is by horseback. Doing so affords you wide views of the mid-Hawaiian islands and the glimmering Pacific.

The only company offering these rides to the public is **Makena Stables**. Located in an old Ulupalakua Ranch stable at La Perouse Bay—at the end of the highway past the Maui Prince Hotel—Makena Stables leads horseback rides through the 20,000-acre, open-range Ulupalakua Ranch onto the lower slopes of Haleakala.

Owners Pat and Helaine Borge lead the trips into the rugged country on this end of the island, and share with you the history of *paniolos* on Maui, Ulupalakua Ranch, and Maui's beautiful upcountry.

Wildlife-lovers are likely to see axis deer, goats, and Franklin quail. During winter months this is a perfect vantage point to watch humpback whales swimming offshore.

Details: *Makena Stables is at La Perouse Bay at the end of the road past Makena Resort. See Guides and Outfitters for more information.*

Hana Cave

Chuck Thorne regularly goes underground—and he'd like to take you with him. His business is Hana Cave Adventures, and it involves spelunking in some extraordinary lava caves. You'll come across cathedral chambers 50 feet high, and crawl on your belly (only a short distance on an optional tour) through skinny lava tubes. You'll explore several miles of pristine lava caves, Maui's largest cave system. Replete with abundant stalagmites, stalactites, and skylights, and more "wows" than you've had in years, this is one unforgettable Hawaii adventure. Highly recommended.

Details: Two-hour and four-hour cave explorations are offered, and Thorne supplies the hard hats, gloves, flashlights, and water. All you need is courage. See Guides and Outfitters for more information.

Kahului to Hana

Many people simply call it "The Drive." It may sound like a John Elway come-from-behind victory, but it's better than that. From the Kahului Airport it's only 53 miles, but what a 53 miles it is. Driving time is two-and-a-half hours because of the hairpin turns, scenic views, and gawking at the natural splendor of the land—and that's if you don't stop along the way.

You cross 54 bridges—many of them one-lane—wind around 600 hairpin curves, and utter at least 50 "Wow, would you look at that"–type phrases. Yellow ginger blooms along the roadside, set amid rock walls and fern grottos, bamboo forests, and waterfalls.

You really should stop along the way, though, to sample the fruits and smell the flowers at the wayside stands, visit the **Ke'anae Arboretum**, where you'll see species such as the *hau* tree, *kukui* nut tree, breadfruit, and coconut palms growing; and admire the awesome coastline vistas. Don't forget your camera on this road to heavenly Hana.

Details: Pick up Highway 36 out of Kahului, near the airport. It passes Paia and Haiku before you really hit the stretch of hairpin turns. A round trip can be made in one day, but start early and take your time. Remember that there is only one way back—the same way you went in—and it takes just as long on the return trip.

La Perouse Bay to Molokini Wall/Lanai Caverns

Diving off the coast of Maui is a rich and rewarding experience, and Ed Robinson's Diving Adventures will take you to the best sites (see Guides and Oufitters section for details). They include **Molokini Wall**, a dive on the backside of the crater that plummets 200 feet to the ocean floor, with the crater towering 200 feet above the surface; **Lanai Caverns**, which takes you to the waters off the island of Lanai to the renowned Cathedrals dive site; colorful **La Perouse Bay**, where you'll encounter turtles, frog fish, and many other unusual species; and an adventurous, three-tank trip for more experienced divers.

But the one dive that really gets people talking is the sunset/night dive. Offered only on Thursday evening, this is a two-tank excursion that provides a whole new meaning to the word "nightlife." The reef animals act differently this time of day (don't we all?), performing fascinating mating rituals, feeding, and becoming easier to approach as they become sleepy.

After a catered meal and time to digest, you then dive into another world of creatures that only come out at night, such as lobsters, crabs, octopi, and others. It's an experience you will truly value.

Details: *These are popular dives with a popular company. It's a good idea to book the dates and dives you prefer well in advance of your travels. See Guides and Outfitters for more information.*

Makena Shore

The sunny Makena shore of Maui boasts some wonderful, secluded beaches and coves, many of which are not on the beaten tourist path. There's no better way to find them than with a local guide, either.

Dino Ventura is one such guide. Born and raised on Maui, Ventura is owner and operator of Makena Kayak Tours. He takes a maximum of six people per kayak adventure so he can easily interact with everyone and "talk story" with them. By the time you arrive at your destination you'll have gained a new understanding and appreciation of Maui, and made a new friend in Dino.

Trips go to several destinations:

© Ron Dahlquist

Sea kayaking off Makena Shore

155

Makena Landing, La Perouse Bay, and **Ahihi–Kinau Natural Marine Reserve.** All include swimming and snorkeling in the tepid, clear-blue waters. Commonly seen in these areas are giant Hawaiian sea turtles and many varieties of colorful tropical fish; not uncommon is an occasional school of spinner dolphins. Kayaking is done in either one- or two-person kayaks. It is certainly among the most relaxing ways to find hidden Hawaii.

They are all splendid, but the best of these trips is to La Perouse Bay. What you see above the water is a rugged terrain, primarily consisting of black lava flows. What you see beneath the surface is 180 degrees the opposite of that. The waters here are alive with turtles, reef fish, and an unusual 60-foot monolith called La Perouse Pinnacle at the north end of the bay at which divers and snorkelers marvel.

Details: Makena Kayak Tours is listed in the Guides and Outfitters section. Trips of two-and-a-half and four hours are offered. The longer trips include lunch; all include drinks and all necessary gear.

Molokini Crater

What looks on the surface of the water like a lovely little horseshoe-shaped island is actually the rim of a sunken volcanic crater. With some of the most colorful and abundant undersea life in Hawaii, this is a very popular snorkeling and diving destination. Ships sail here with regularity from Maalaea Harbor, Kihei, and elsewhere on Maui, loaded with passengers eager to get in the bathtub-warm water and swim with the fish.

It's just a short trip any way you do it, but the payoff is great. The shore of the island is protected as a seabird sanctuary, so landing is prohibited. But inside the protected bay, where the snorkel boats moor, the **Molokini Shoal Marine Life Conservation District** is alive with a wide variety of sea life, including giant manta rays, pufferfish, butterfly fish, the occasional octopus, and the even-more-occasional shark. There are also some great examples of antler coral.

Divers tend to moor outside of the crater, as a shelf drops off nearly 350 feet there rather quickly. It's good diving, but the currents can be rough.

During whale season you may be treated to up-close-and-personal

© Ray Mains

Molokini Crater

encounters with humpbacks on the trip in and out, as these waters are among their favorite.

Details: Some of the best outfitters get here quite early in the day when the crowds are thin and the water is calmest. They are listed in the Guides and Outfitters section, below.

Wai'anapanapa State Park

Wai'anapanapa, located near Hana in East Maui, is a lovely state park that offers something for everyone. If you enjoy hiking, there are trails; if you prefer the beach, you can sit it out on one of the prettiest black-sand beaches on Maui; if you wish to take a picnic and kick back against a tree, the many trees are friendly.

For many people the hikes are the best part of Wai'anapanapa. They range from easy to intermediate in difficulty, and from one to four miles in length. Some wonderful scenery is afforded the hiker here. You'll find black lava with caves and cool lava tubes to explore in several areas. Some trails traverse rocky areas at the shoreline. This is

157

particularly beautiful in good weather, and particularly dangerous in bad weather, as the rocks can get slippery. Other trails lead onto the cliffs above the ocean, through a forest of *hala* (pandanus) trees. The views from the cliffs are quite nice, stretching as far to sea as the eye can see. ***Details****: Wai'anapanapa State Park is on the Hana Highway between Ke'anae and Hana, roughly one mile from Hana. There are some camper cabins and a campground for use (see Camping section), but they must be reserved well in advance of your visit. There is a parking area, but word has it that this is a favorite place for thieves; leave nothing of value in your vehicle.*

GUIDES AND OUTFITTERS

One of East Maui's most environmentally conscious outfitters is **Pacific Whale Foundation Eco Adventures**, 101 N. Kihei Rd., Kihei, 800/ WHALE-11 or 808/879-8811. Leaving from Maalaea Harbor near Kihei, the foundation offers turtle-, dolphin-, and whale-watching eco-adventures, plus snorkel trips to Molokini and Lanai. Trips emphasize a sensitive, cautious approach to marine-life observation, and marine research naturalists are onboard every excursion to educate passengers. They provide all the gear, and will lead you to all the fun. Cost ranges from $30/person for the two-hour whale-watch cruise; to $54 or $74/person for five-hour snorkeling trips to either Molokini or Lanai.

Ed Robinson's Diving Adventures, P.O. Box 616, Kihei, HI 96753, 800/635-1273 or 808/879-3584, is a well-respected dive company that offers quite a variety of diving options. Three-tank adventure trips, sunset/ night dives, and Molokini Crater dives are just three of their offerings. Each dive is considered a "guided nature tour" of the colorful undersea life in the waters off Maui. Two boats leave from Kihei Boat Launching Ramp. Cost varies depending on trip, ranging from $105 to $145/person.

Born and raised on Maui, owner/operator Dino Ventura guides small groups on kayak and snorkel tours where sailboats do not go. His **Makena Kayak Tours**, P.O. Box 1855, Kihei, HI 96753, 808/879-8426, offers trips to several destinations, including Makena Landing, La Perouse Bay, and Ahihi–Kinau Natural Marine Reserve. Tours last two-and-a-half and four hours. Cost is $55/person for the two-and-a-half–hour tour; $85/person for the four-hour tour.

The Silent Lady, 150 Hauoli St., #405, Wailuku, 800/450-2033 or 808/875-1112, is a lovingly crafted replica whaling ship offering whale-watch, Molokini snorkel, and sunset sails. You sail in complete luxury, with three mainsails full of wind and an experienced captain and crew who tell you the stories of yesteryear on the Hawaiian waters. Shoving off from Maalaea Harbor, this sturdy schooner takes you to Molokini Island and Turtle Reef for snorkeling, then serves a gourmet lunch on the way back to shore. Sunset sails are also offered. Cost is $88/person for the Molokini snorkel sail; $44/person for the sunset sail.

If going underground in Hana sounds like a good way to get far away from it all, it is. Spelunking is Chuck Thorne's specialty, and his caves are remarkable. Through **Hana Cave Tours**, P.O. Box 40, Hana, HI 96713, 808/248-7308, he offers two-hour and four-hour explorations. The two-hour trip is pretty easy walking and good for the whole family. The four-hour trip is for those seeking a bit more of an adventure. Cost is $50/person for the two-hour tour, with children 7–17 half-price with two paid adults; $100/person for the four-hour adventure, no one under 18 permitted.

Makena Stables, 8299 S. Makena Rd., Makena, 808/879-0244, at the end of the road past the Maui Prince Hotel, offers horseback rides onto the lower slopes of Haleakala. Owner Pat Borge leads several types of trips, some geared to experienced riders, some to beginning riders and children as young as 12. The Pacific views are phenomenal. Cost is $99/person for two-hour introductory rides; and $110–$160/person for longer rides.

CAMPING

East Maui offers unique camping opportunities. Although there are not as many options as on some of the other islands, those that are available are quite good.

Maui County has three parks for camping—Baldwin, Rainbow, and Kanaha Beach—all on East Maui. The parks have room for 15 to 20 people each, at a rate of $3 per day. Maximum limit is three days at each park. All have water and restroom facilities. For further information, reservations, or permits, contact or visit the Maui Parks and Recreation Department, War Memorial Center, 1580-C Kaahumanu Ave., Wailuku, HI 96793; 808/243-7230.

Near the ocean in Paia, **Baldwin Park** campsite is popular with windsurfers who like riding the waves at nearby Hookipa Beach. Baldwin has a nice beach of its own. **Rainbow** is upcountry near Haliimaile, on the lower slopes of Haleakala, and is a good base for exploration of Haleakala National Park and Maui's green upcountry with their beautiful trees and flowers. There are some picnic tables and a pavilion here. Close to Kahului Airport, **Kanaha Beach Park** is also just across the jetty from Kahului Harbor. It's busier and more in the middle of town than many of Hawaii's beach parks.

The State of Hawaii operates two campsites on Maui, and both have cabins. Camping is free. The fees for cabin use at either site are $45 for one to four persons; $5 for each additional person. Maximum stay is five nights at both sites, and reservations are taken one year in advance. For more information, reservations, or permits, contact or visit Division of Parks, 54 S. High St., Wailuku, HI 96793; 808/243-5354.

At **Wai'anapanapa State Park** are ocean-view campsites and 12 cabins for use here. The cabins house six people each, and are equipped with linens, cooking facilities, and utensils. This state park is quite popular and features good hiking trails as well as a black-sand beach. It's located roughly one mile from the town of Hana, where all supplies can be purchased.

One lone cabin is located at **Polipoli Springs State Recreation Area**. The cabin sleeps 10, but is somewhat difficult to reach. Getting to it, on the upper western slopes of Haleakala, in the Kula Forest, requires a four-wheel-drive vehicle. The turnoff for Polipoli Springs is from Route 337 (Upper Kula Road), near the southern junction with Highway 37 (Kula Highway). Hiking trails lead through a eucalyptus, Monterey pine, and cypress forest. The Polipoli and Redwood Trails are known as good bird-watching trails, with 'apapane, finch, cardinals, and *pueo* owls commonly seen.

It's best to purchase a hiking guide or hiking map to Maui and study it while walking through Polipoli, as the trails are not all that well marked. Remember when planning a camping excursion here that you'll be at the 6,200-foot elevation, and it gets cold when the sun goes down. Plan ahead.

LODGING

There are many fine luxury hotels along the coast in Wailea, one in Makena. The best include the Four Seasons Resort Wailea, and the Maui Prince Hotel. The many condominium choices in Kihei are too numerous to mention. What follows are several of the area's unique smaller inns and bed-and-breakfasts.

Those interested in specific information on the hotels and activities of Wailea can check with Wailea Resort Company, 3750 Wailea Alanui, Wailea, HI 96753; 808/879-4465. Similarly, if you'd like more information regarding Makena Resort and the activities in this area, contact the Maui Prince Hotel, 5400 Makena Alanui, Kihei, HI 96753; 808/874-1111. Contact Hawaii's Best Bed & Breakfasts for more information on the B&Bs they represent.

Hamoa Bay Bungalow (through Hawaii's Best Bed & Breakfasts), in Hana, 800/262-9912 or 808/885-4550, is a neat Balinese-style romantic cottage. Hamoa Bay Bungalow features a full kitchen, Jacuzzi tub, and lots of wonderful Balinese art and statuary. The setting is tropical and colorful, with the cottage tucked in a banana-and-fern grotto. A 10-minute walk and you're at Hamoa Bay. Rates: $150, three-night minimum stay.

Paia is a peaceful little corner of Maui, an artsy surfer village on the road to Hana, just 10 minutes from the airport. There you'll find **Mama's Beachfront Cottages**, 799 Poho Pl., Paia, 800/860-HULA, or 808/579-9764. Mama's cottages are nicely furnished duplexes set in a coconut grove overlooking the beach. All cottages have full kitchens, but they are just a short walk through the trees to Mama's Fish House, where you are offered a 20 percent discount (you need it—the restaurant is good but overpriced). It's another short walk to Hookipa Beach, the windsurfing capital of the world. Rates begin at $90 for the one-bedroom garden view cottage, and go to $225 for the two-bedroom cottages on the ocean. Three-night minimum stay.

Nearby is **Honopou Lodge** (through Hawaii's Best Bed & Breakfasts), near Paia, 800/262-9912 or 808/885-4550. Set in the green ranchlands near Paia, a pool, Jacuzzi, and uninterrupted ocean views distinguish these three studio offerings just off the Hana Highway. They are part of a series of architecturally modern octagons designed to take advantage of the views. The two pool-level studios have kitchenettes. From this base you can explore the Paia area, take the drive to Hana, or wander to waterfalls and freshwater pools nearby. Rates: $125 for the lower-level studios; $95 for the upper-level studio.

At the end of a bumpy dirt road 20 minutes from Paia is **Huelo Point Flower Farm** (through Hawaii's Best Bed & Breakfasts), in Huelo, 800/262-9912 or 808/885-4550, a unique gazebo set on a cliff overlooking the ocean. The gazebo itself is bright and airy, with three glass walls allowing maximum views of the Pacific. Although the interior bathroom is small, guests have a private outside shower (which also has an ocean view), plus use of a pool and Jacuzzi. Rates: $110, two-night minimum stay.

FOOD

Located in Maui's cool upcountry, Bev Gannon's **Haliimaile General Store**, 900 Haliimaile Rd., Makawao, 808/572-2666, is a delightful find. You'll find the menu reflects the more hearty lifestyle of the area, while at the same time the preparations are divine. For example, the rack of lamb is served Hunan style, in a hoisin, sesame, and black-bean sauce; the one-pound rib-eye steak is pepper- and herb-rubbed and grilled. You will also find meaty barbecue ribs. Lunch is good, too, with sandwiches, burgers, and house specialties on the menu. Open for lunch and dinner Mon–Fri; dinner only Sat; brunch and dinner Sun.

There are not many good restaurants from which to choose in Hana, but luckily there's the **Hotel Hana-Maui**, Hana, 808/248-8211. The setting is pleasant; the food is good. The continental dinner menu includes lamb chops, local fish, and local beef. Breakfast is from the

▼▲▼▲▼▲▼▲▼▲▼▲▼

Raw Experience Paia

If you're into totally healthy food, this is the place for you. Located in Paia in East Maui, Raw Experience serves fresh juices, smoothies, and organic homemade breads. It's good and good for you.

▼▲▼▲▼▲▼▲▼▲▼▲▼

menu or buffet-style fruits, cereals, eggs, and such. Lunch is more limited, but it's worth stopping to have a bite and a tour of this historic property. Open for breakfast, lunch, and dinner daily.

Raw Experience Paia, 42 Baldwin Ave., Paia, 808/579-9729, is an organic restaurant that was started by a 22-year-old woman whose love of Maui and healthy foods merged in the seaside town of Paia. Fresh juices, smoothies, and wheat grass can start you out in the morning; spreads and deli items go nicely on the organic homemade breads; and a variety of super-healthy "rawiches" will take care of you for lunch. Those seriously into organics and healthy foods will love Raw Experience. Open for lunch and dinner daily.

Great ocean views in this elegant golf clubhouse add to the enjoyment of your lunch or dinner at **Sea Watch at Wailea Golf Course**, 100 Wailea Golf Club Dr., Wailea, 808/875-8080. After-golf favorites include the Seawatch club sandwich, the *ahi* sandwich, and the burgers. The dessert specialty is a *lilikoi* cheesecake with a macadamia-nut crust. This is a wonderful vantage point from which to take in the sunset. Try doing so with a mai-tai from the bar. Open for breakfast, lunch, and dinner daily.

When it's time to splurge, **Seasons at Four Seasons Wailea**, 3900 Wailea Alanui Dr., Wailea, 808/874-8000, is one excellent restaurant at which to do so. Located in an ocean-view corner of the Four Seasons Resort Wailea hotel, Seasons serves Hawaii Regional Cuisine. The food is as good as the view here. Entrée specialties include *onaga* (longtail snapper) baked in a Hawaiian salt crust; star anise rotisserie duckling in two courses; and charbroiled Kona lobster with Molokai sweet-potato puree. A selection of soufflés, including mango, bittersweet chocolate, and coconut, should finish you off. Open for dinner only Tue–Sat.

HALEAKALA NATIONAL PARK

It's known to the National Geologic Survey by its formal name, the East Maui Volcano, but most people just refer to it by the name of the crater at the summit, Haleakala. A volcanic wonderland, Haleakala National Park offers numerous adventure-travel opportunities. To get some general information on this area, contact Haleakala National Park, P.O. Box 369, Makawao, HI 96768; 808/572-9306. The National Park Service is in the Prince Kuhio Federal Building, 300 Ala Moana Boulevard, Room 6305, Honolulu, HI 96713; 808/541-2693. They can provide information on Haleakala and all national parks in Hawaii. A good Web site specifically about Haleakala and other Hawaii volcanoes is produced by the U.S. Geological Survey. Check it out at www.hvo.wr.usgs.gov/volcanoes/haleakala/.

Orientation/Lay of the Land

Haleakala's mass covers some 570 square miles of land, including most of the inaccessible (except by four-wheel-drive) eastern coast of Maui.

The park has two access points, one leading to the crater from Kahului, and another from the Hana side, called Kipahulu. Each year more than one million people visit Haleakala Summit area and 500,000 visit Kipahulu. There is no highway linking the two areas of the park.

With visitors from around the world, it is important that everyone help protect their national park by using only designated trails, leaving all natural features in their place, and using proper trash receptacles. This good behavior can be an example to others visiting a national park for the first time.

Haleakala National Park extends from the 10,023-foot summit of Haleakala Crater down the southeast flank of the mountain to the Kipahulu coast near Hana. Much of the area is wilderness, some of which is open to the public, some closed as a preserve.

And what wilderness it is! There is much for visitors to the House of the Sun to do. Many people opt only for the sunrise spectacular,

164

then either get in their cars and drive back to bed at their hotel, or get on a bicycle and go for a thrill-ride downhill to the lowlands.

More thorough exploration is possible, too, with hiking trails, horseback rides, camping facilities, and cabins available for use. However you choose to visit Haleakala, you will not go away disappointed. It is at once mythical and ecologically amazing.

The weather at Haleakala's summit is unpredictable. Temperatures commonly range between 40 and 65 degrees, but can be below freezing at any time of year with the wind-chill factor. Weather changes rapidly at Haleakala's higher elevations. Intense sunlight, thick clouds, heavy rain, and high winds are possible daily. Wear lightweight, layered clothing that will keep you warm even in wet weather, and sturdy, comfortable shoes.

Pregnant women and people with heart or respiratory problems should check with their doctors before coming to the park, given the reduced oxygen at the higher elevations.

On the other hand, the weather in Kipahulu is usually warm, although rain is still common. Flash flooding of the pools and streams can be hazardous to swimmers and hikers. Always check with park rangers before entering the pools, and never swim if flood warnings are posted. Mosquitos can be prevalent in this area, so be prepared with repellent.

Several private companies operate tours within the park. Trips include downhill biking on the park road, horseback tours of the wilderness, and guided hikes. Access to Haleakala National Park is by car or by tour vehicle.

Flora and Fauna

The park preserves the volcanic landscape of the upper slopes of Haleakala and protects the unique and fragile ecosystems of Kipahulu Valley, the scenic pools along Oheo Gulch, and many rare and endangered species. Bird- and wildlife-watching are great at Haleakala. In fact, Haleakala National Park is one of the best places in the state to see rare Hawaiian forest birds. Walk along Halemauu Trail or through Hosmer Grove on your own, or join the guided Waikamoi Hike offered on Monday and Thursday, 9 a.m.–noon at Hosmer Grove.

Some of the more plentiful birds you are likely to spot in these areas include *pueo* (short-eared) owls, *i'iwi*, and *'apapane*. The numbers of these birds at the heights of Haleakala are encouraging, considering they are somewhat scarce elsewhere in Hawaii. This is also one of the few easily accessible areas where you may just get a chance to spot a rare Maui parrotbill, which could be making a comeback up here. They have been seen on more than one occasion in recent years.

Nene geese are plentiful in this area. The state bird seems to pay no mind to the traffic around park headquarters; in fact the nene seem to like it, and frequently interact with visitors.

Hosmer Grove is plentiful with ohia and *mamane* trees. Blooming colorfully all year long, they are favored feeding grounds of several of Hawaii's honeycreepers. After dark, watch the treetops on moonlit nights for one of only two native mammals in Hawaii, the *peapea*, or Hawaiian hoary bat.

On summer nights stop at Leleiwi Overlook and listen for the rare *'ua'u*, or dark-rumped petrel, calling for its mate along the cliffs below. These petrel are seabirds, really, known to breed only in Hawaii and the Galapagos Islands. They were driven to the brink of extinction in their former oceanside habitat by a variety of predators, including humans, pigs, dogs, rats, mongeese, and disease-laden mosquitos. So the birds moved upcountry, and though they're rarely seen, their calls can sometimes be heard. Thus we know they are still with us.

A good idea for anyone with more than a casual interest in birdwatching is to take a guided hike. There are so many different species of birds, plants, and trees, that the well-informed guides can be extremely helpful in pointing out and differentiating them.

Inside Haleakala Crater the distinctive silversword plant is found. Feral goats once roamed freely inside the crater, eating plants and trees, rendering the silversword a rare species. Nowadays the goats have been herded away and protective fencing has been raised around 32 miles of the crater rim, giving the silversword a fighting chance for propagation. Mature silverswords in bloom may stand up to eight feet tall, with misty silver fingers emanating from a center stalk. The plant blooms only once, often after decades, blossoming in hundreds of small purple flowers, then dies.

During winter months humpback whales can be seen from the porch of the Kipahulu Ranger Station.

History, Culture, and Customs

Originally part of Hawaii Volcanoes National Park—which now encompasses only Mauna Loa and Kilauea on the Big Island—Haleakala was redesignated as a separate entity in July 1961. In 1980 Haleakala National Park was named an International Biosphere Reserve. Of its 28,655 acres, 19,270 are wilderness.

The most dominating geologic feature of Maui, Haleakala figures prominently in Hawaiian mythology. Some stories have the demigod Maui, superman of Hawaiian myth, coming to Haleakala Crater to lasso the sun, making it travel more slowly across the sky—thus Mauians had more sunshine to enjoy their days.

Still other stories have Maui climbing the mountain and lassoing the sun after his mother, Hina, complained that she had too little sunshine to dry her tapa (a cloth made from pounded bark). He let the sun continue on its path only after it promised to cross Maui's skies more slowly.

In ancient times, Hawaiian women are said to have descended into Haleakala's sacred crater to give birth. This story is credible due to some historical records that umbilical cords were left at a pit called Kailinau, which is in keeping with the *piko* ceremony of the old Hawaiians. In this ceremony the infant's umbilical cord was left in a sacred place; if it was still there when the mother returned, the child would live a long and prosperous life. If it was gone, however (they assumed a rat had taken it), it was thought the child would grow up to be a thief.

The upper Kipahulu Valley portion of the park, accessed from the Hana coast, contains some of the most pristine rain forest in Hawaii. It is closed to all except park researchers, giving the rare species of birds, trees, and plants that make the area their habitat a chance for survival without human interference. This area is still considered sacred by the old Hawaiians, who value the life-giving waters that once fed their lower valley soils.

NATURE AND ADVENTURE SIGHTS IN HALEAKALA NATIONAL PARK

Haleakala Crater

If you want to see the inside of Haleakala Crater, but don't want to hike in and out, your other option is by horseback. This way, your trusty steed can worry about the footing while you relax and marvel at the "otherworldliness" of the crater.

Pony Express Tours is the only company offering horseback rides onto the crater floor, and they allow just eight people per trip, allowing maximum opportunity for guides to interact with guests. Along the journey you'll learn about the flora and fauna, the mythology, and the geologic diversity of Haleakala.

Details: Riders meet at 9:30 a.m. at the crater rim. Two types of rides are offered, shorter and longer. The shorter rides last until 2:30 p.m., the longer until 5:30 p.m. Both include lunch. No saddlebags are provided, so bring a day pack if you wish to carry a camera, food, or water bottle.

Haleakala Summit

Imagine: You're taking a leisurely drive up to the summit of Haleakala one morning when suddenly, around the corner comes a swoop of bicyclists, dressed boots-to-hairdos in bright yellow haz-mat suits, space helmets strapped to their heads. What, you wonder, could possibly be going on?

Take heart. It's not an evacuation from Science City, just tourists engaging in one of the most popular activities on Maui: the 38-mile downhill bicycle ride after viewing sunrise at the summit of Haleakala.

You can do it, too. The sunrise tour collects you at your hotel between 2 and 2:30 a.m. You are ferried up to the summit; fed coffee, juice, and a continental breakfast while you watch the sunrise; and then suited up for a bike ride down to Makawao for a full breakfast.

You then get back on your bike and continue your downhill trek, past pineapple fields, horse and cattle ranches, and through historic villages. The tour ends in the seaside town of Paia, where you are met by a van and returned to your hotel.

If you just cannot bear the thought of rising so early—and sunrises

SUNRISE AT THE SUMMIT

The visual horizon in many places in Haleakala is up to 115 miles out to sea. Even cloudy skies can offer amazing sights, including rainbows, moonbows, and halos around your shadow. Haleakala offers one of the most easily accessible places to watch planets, stars, and moons when it's dark. Rent a pair of 10x50 or 7x50 binoculars at one of the island dive shops, pick up a star map at Park Headquarters or Haleakala Visitor Center, and see if you can find the moons of Jupiter.

Sunrise and sunset are both amazing events, but sunrise is more crowded. Arrive at least 30 minutes before each to watch the colors change. A flashlight will come in handy, and warm clothes are a must! Good sunset locations include the Halemauu Trail and the Summit. Sunrise can be seen from Leleiwi or Kalahaku Overlook, the summit, and Haleakala Visitor Center.

Special evening star-watching programs are conducted in the summer months. Occasionally, special all-day and half-day hikes, three-day service trips, or full-moon hikes are offered. Check at Park Headquarters or call 808/572-9306 for current schedules.

In the Kipahulu area, cultural demonstrations are occasionally offered. Check at the Ranger Station or call 808/248-7375 for current schedules.

are not in your realm of thinking—there is also an organized tour that will pick you up around 7 a.m. It's essentially the same ride, ending in Paia for lunch.

Biking on your own can also be done on the park road, but not on any trails. Lights are required before dawn and after dusk. Helmets are strongly recommended. Gloves and rain gear will make your ride safer and more comfortable. Bikes can be rented on the island.

Details: Mountain Riders offers these downhill bike tours. They are listed in the Guides and Outfitters section, below.

Haleakala Visitor Center and Park Headquarters

Haleakala Visitor Center and Park Headquarters have cultural and natural history exhibits. Books, maps, and postcards are for sale. Rangers are on duty during business hours to answer questions and help you make the most of your visit. These locations are open daily year-round. Hours: Haleakala Visitor Center, sunrise–3 p.m.; Park Headquarters, 7:30–4.

The centers offer guided walks and programs on the geology and natural and cultural history of the area. At the summit, 15-to-20-minute presentations are given daily in the Summit Building at 9:30, 10:30, and 11:30 a.m.

There is a guided **Cinder Desert Hike** on Tuesday and Friday at 10 a.m. The hike covers two miles and takes about two hours. Meet at the Sliding Sands Trailhead at the end of the Haleakala Visitor Center parking lot. In addition, a guided **Waikamoi Cloud Forest Hike** takes place on Monday and Thursday at 9 a.m. This three-hour, three-mile hike goes through The Nature Conservancy's Waikamoi Preserve. Meet at Hosmer Grove, just inside the park entrance.

Details: The summit area of Haleakala is a three-hour round trip drive from Kahului via roads 37, 377, and 378. Follow the signs posted along the highway. An admission fee of $10 per vehicle is charged at the entrance to the summit area of the park. Bicyclists, motorcyclists, and hikers are charged $5 each. The entrance fee is good for seven days.

Halemauu Trail

From the summit to the coastline, the park is laced with more than 30 miles of incredible hiking trails. Aside from the areas adjacent to the visitor center that are easily accessed, strenuous hiking is one of the few ways to explore inside Haleakala Crater. Unlike Kilauea on the Big Island, there are no highways leading through this park. Hiking trail guides are available at Park Headquarters.

This hike begins at the 8,000-foot parking lot 3.5 miles above

Park Headquarters. The first mile gradually descends through native shrubland to the valley rim. Two miles of switchbacks then descend 1,400 feet to the valley floor. Sliding Sands and Halemauu trails eventually join after about nine miles, and are also connected with short spur trails.

One of the most popular spurs is the **Silversword Loop**, roughly a one-mile side jaunt that leads through an area where you'll see one of the greatest concentrations of the silversword plants in the park. This trail is particularly lovely in spring and early summer.

Remember that the hiking trails inside the crater are strenuous, rugged, and at high altitude. Be prepared for cold weather, and be equally prepared with sunscreen—it's easy to burn at this altitude when the sun is shining.

The **Sliding Sands Trail** starts at the Haleakala Visitor Center parking lot, and you descend 2,500 feet through a cinder desert to the valley floor in four miles (about 6½ hours). The return trip is difficult due to the steep grade, elevation, and reduced oxygen. Allow twice the time to hike out that it takes to hike in.

Many hikers choose to descend to the valley floor via the Sliding Sands Trail and exit via the Halemauu Trail, which is not as severe. If you do this, you will need to arrange to have an extra vehicle or someone to meet you at the Halemauu Trailhead on Route 378.

Details: Hikes into Haleakala Crater should be planned allotting ample time. A full exploration can take up to three days and can cover as much as 20 miles. Ask at Park Headquarters or Haleakala Visitor Center about alternatives for shorter hikes; even short walks offer spectacular views on clear days.

Kaupo Gap Trail

Serious hikers can opt to take the Kaupo Gap Trail from the crater all the way to the coast. The views along this 18.4-mile hike are magnificent, and it's a perfect opportunity to get a close-up look at several different ecological zones on the mountain. This is considered one of the premier hikes in Hawaii.

The trail drops some 10,000 feet in elevation and ends at the remote village of Kaupo, beyond Hana on a four-wheel-drive road. Some

ardent hikers have been known to traverse this trail in one long day, but you'd best be in good shape to do so. If you'd prefer to split the hike in two, hike from the summit to the Paliku campground. This is a 10-mile trek and takes five to six hours. From there, descend the rest of the way to Kaupo Trailhead on Highway 31. This nine-mile portion is extremely beautiful, passing through meadows and woods, with views out to Mauna Kea and Mauna Loa on the Big Island. It should take four to six hours.
Details: *Check with Ranger Station on trail conditions before setting out.*

Kipahulu Ranger Station
Like the Haleakala Visitors Center, the Kipahulu Ranger Station offers a number of guided hikes through the park. Programs include a one-mile hike to the **Bamboo Forest** at 9 a.m. Daily half-mile hikes or orientation talks are offered at 12:30, 1:30, 2:30, and 3:30 p.m.; and a four-mile round-trip hike to **Waimoku Falls** takes place Saturday at 9:30 a.m.

On your own you can take the **Kaloa Point Trail**, an easy .5-mile loop that goes toward the ocean, along pools and waterfalls, and back to the ranger station. Kaloa Point is a windy bluff overlooking Oheo Gulch. Crashing surf and views of the Big Island are a five-minute walk from the ranger station. Enjoy a picnic on the grass next to the remnants of an ancient fishing shrine and house site. Explore a *lau hala* thatched building and envision an earlier time.

If you decide to take the other trails that start from the Ranger Station, be sure to check at the station for current trail and swimming conditions. Be alert to water conditions—flash floods can occur within minutes. Obey posted warning signs.

Kipahulu Ranger Station is open daily 9–5.
Details: *The Kipahulu area of the park is at the east end of Maui between Hana and Kaupo. It can be reached via Highway 36, a curvy, often wet road. Kipahulu is about 90 miles from the resort areas of Wailea or Kaanapali, and 60 miles from central Maui. Driving time is about three to four hours each way. An extension of this road, Highway 31, goes around the dry side of the island, past Kaupo and on to Ulupalakua. This road is only partially paved and can be hazardous or closed during periods of stormy weather.*

Oheo Gulch

Still called Seven Sacred Pools on some maps, this area of Haleakala National Park is accessed from the Kipahulu district. There are actually some 24 pools and there is no evidence to suggest they were ever sacred, but they sure are pretty.

The most popular area is the lower pools, on the left side of Highway 31. A path leads from a parking lot to the pools. Down here the ocean views are magnificent, and on clear days you can see the Big Island across the channel. Take a swim in these lovely pools, but be wary if the weather is bad as it can become dangerous. Otherwise, even though they are not sacred they certainly are refreshing.

Oheo Gulch on the road to Hana

The two pools closest to the ocean are connected by an underwater lava tube. You can swim through the lava tube from one pool to the other if you are a good swimmer.

If you don't mind a bit of a hike—four miles round-trip—to more remote and less crowded pools, a trail from the parking lot leads to Makahiku Falls Overlook and Waimoku Falls. A short side trip leads to a pool in which you can swim up a gorge to another pool.

A visit to the pools at Oheo Gulch is highly recommended.

Details: Ten miles south of Hana on Highway 31 you'll find a parking lot on the left side of the road. Park and take the footpath that leads to the lower pools.

Papwai Trail

Papwai Trail is a moderately difficult four-mile (round-trip) hike through the rain forest up to Waimoku Falls. The trail ends upstream, near the base of 400-foot Waimoku Falls. Take a picnic lunch, snack, insect repellent, and drinking water along on this three-hour hike. It is extremely beautiful in this region, and shows off the wide variety of flora on this side of Maui.

Details: *Check with Ranger Station on trail conditions before setting out.*

GUIDES AND OUTFITTERS

Mountain Riders, P.O. Box 6222, Kahului, HI 96733, 808/242-9739, offers two daily bicycle tours down from the summit of Haleakala, a sunrise journey and a day journey. They pick you up at your lodgings, provide a continental breakfast at the summit, and after sunrise, wave as you leave on your bike. The trip is 38 miles, all downhill. Riders stop for breakfast or lunch along the way. Bikes, helmets, windbreaker suits, and gloves are provided. Plan on seven hours before you can crawl back in bed. Cost is $110 for the sunrise journey; $105 for the day journey; includes admission fees to park and breakfast or lunch.

Specializing in eco-cultural hikes, **Paths in Paradise**, P.O. Box 667, Makawao, HI 96768, 808/573-0094, takes trekkers on half- and full-day hikes. Full-day hikes include excursions to the crater floor of Haleakala (eight miles) or through the entire crater (12 miles). Half-day hikes include a family adventure on Hosmer Grove Nature Trail (one mile). Cost ranges $75–$115/person, depending on hike; $50–$85 for children 12 and under.

If you want something else to hoof it to the crater floor, check out **Pony Express Tours**, P.O. Box 535, Kula, HI 96790, 808/667-2200. This is the only company offering horseback rides into Haleakala Crater. Only eight people are allowed per trip; make a reservation so you don't miss this rare opportunity to ride inside a dormant volcano. Riders meet at 9:30 a.m. at the crater rim. Two types of rides are offered, shorter ('til 2:30 p.m.) and longer ('til 5:30 p.m.). Both include lunch. No saddlebags are provided, so bring a day pack if you wish to carry a camera, food, or water bottle. Cost is $130/person for the shorter ride; $160/person for the longer ride.

CAMPING

Within Haleakala National Park are several camping areas and wilderness cabins. A good camping choice is **Hosmer Grove Campground.** This campground near the summit can be used without a permit. It's located just inside the park entrance and to the left, and has picnic tables, barbecue grills, and outdoor pit toilets.

Kipahulu is a primitive campground near the ocean and is available without a permit on a first-come, first-served basis. No drinking water is available; you must bring your own. The campground has picnic tables, barbecue grills, and an outdoor pit toilet.

There are two wilderness campgrounds inside the park. **Holua** is a four-mile (one-way) hike down the Halemauu Trail, and **Paliku** is 10 miles (one-way) down either the Sliding Sands Trail or the Halemauu Trail. Both campgrounds are primitive, with only pit toilets and nonpotable water. Campers should have provisions and equipment appropriate for possible cold, wet weather. No open fires are allowed in the wilderness, so portable camp stoves and a fuel supply are recommended. Some form of water treatment is required.

These two campgrounds require a permit, available at Park Headquarters between 8 a.m. and 3 p.m. daily. There is no additional fee for these permits. Space at both campgrounds is limited, and no advance reservations are taken for wilderness camping. Stays are limited to three nights per month, with no more than two consecutive nights at any one campground.

Three wilderness cabins are maintained by the National Park Service for visitor use, available by advance-reservation lottery. To reach the cabins, you must hike a minimum of four miles to **Holua**, six miles to **Kapalaoa**, and 10 miles to **Paliku**. Each cabin is allocated to one party as a unit, with a capacity of 12 people per night.

Fees for the cabins are based on the number of people in the party: $40/one to six people; $80/seven to 12 people. At least one member of the party must be 18 years of age or older. Stays are limited to three nights per month, with no more than two consecutive nights at any one cabin.

To enter the reservation lottery, write to Haleakala National Park—

Attn.: Cabins, P.O. Box 369, Makawao, HI 96768, at least 90 days prior to your trip. Include your first and alternate choices of dates and cabin preferred. The more flexible your request, the better your chance of winning a reservation. Keep in mind that weekends are more requested than weekdays. Cabin cancellations are occasionally available. To fill a cancellation, call the park at 808/572-9306 between 1 and 3 p.m. daily to check on availability. You will need a Visa or MasterCard to secure a reservation by phone.

LODGING

The accommodations in Maui's upcountry are smaller inns and bed-and-breakfasts, none of which are within the park. There are no luxury resorts up here. The weather is cooler, particularly at night, so pack a warm sweater and get ready to experience a part of Hawaii many people never see. Contact Hawaii's Best Bed & Breakfasts for B&Bs they represent.

Bloom Cottage (through Hawaii's Best Bed & Breakfasts), in Kula, 800/262-9912 or 808/885-4550, is a good base for exploration of Haleakala National Park and upcountry Maui. At the 3,000-foot level of Haleakala, this private, one-bedroom cottage shares an acre of land with your hosts' home. Wide views of the Pacific Ocean and the West Maui Mountains, a cozy fireplace, handmade quilts, and a brightly decorated interior distinguish Bloom Cottage. Rates: $105, two-night minimum stay.

Also on the slopes of Haleakala at the 3,000-foot level, **Silver Cloud Guest Ranch** (through Hawaii's Best Bed & Breakfasts), Kula, 800/262-9912 or 808/885-4550, commands some of the best views on Maui. There are six bed-and-breakfast rooms in the main house, formerly the home of the ranch manager. Each room has a private bath and some have ocean views. Next door is spacious Lahaina Cottage, which has a full kitchen, wood-burning stove, and ocean-view lanai. Horseback riding is also next door. You can either while away some lazy days in this serene ranch setting, or set out to explore Haleakala. Either way, this place is a treat. Rates: $85–$150 for two persons.

FOOD

There are no dining facilities within the park boundaries. There are, however, several nearby towns where you can find restaurants and stores. See Food listings in East Maui section.

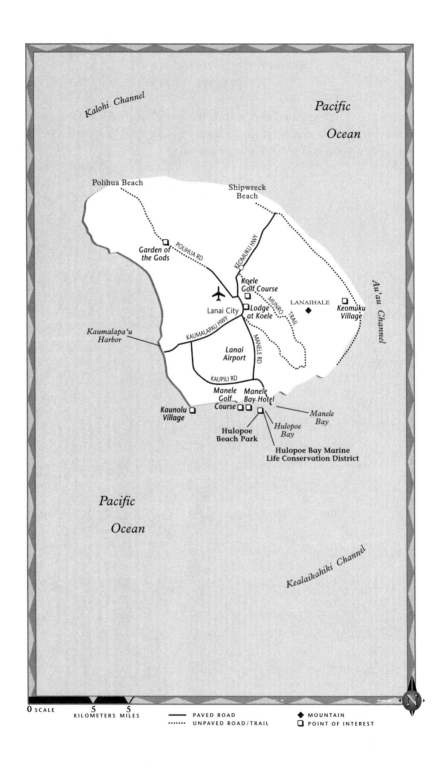

LANAI— THE PINEAPPLE ISLAND

6

Until recently there were few reasons for travelers to visit Lanai. And if they did visit, they managed to keep this beautiful little island retreat a secret. There was a funky 10-room hotel, a nine-hole golf course, the best snorkeling in the islands, a fantastic camping beach called Hulopoe Bay—and lots and lots of pineapple fields.

Funny thing is, all of this—except the pineapple fields—still exists. But so do lots of other options.

Orientation/Lay of the Land

As you approach Lanai from the air, you get a sense of how small this island really is at 141 square miles. But as soon as you touch down you are immediately infused with the next important sense of this remote corner of paradise—serenity.

Long, rolling fields of pineapple; softly blowing winds; tall rows of pine and eucalyptus trees; cliffs that drop off to the sea; red dirt, and lush greenery—these are the elements that define the landscape. Stepping off the plane in Lanai, just slip your watch off your wrist and put it in your pocket for the duration of your stay. You won't need it here.

179

Sheila Donnelly & Associates

Four-wheeling on Munro Trail

There are only a couple thousand residents on Lanai, and the map will tell you that it's one of the Hawaiian chain's smallest efforts. But, like those who live on Molokai, the people who live on Lanai are understandably glad to be here. There are no freeways, no high-rises, and still no stoplights. Instead, you will find people who are genuinely glad to see you, and a whole lot of relaxation.

There are only a few roads on the island. From the airport you have but two choices: up to Lanai City, or down to Manele Bay. Another road leads from Lanai City down to the northeast coast and Shipwreck Beach. And one other road leads down to Kaumalapa'u Harbor, which serves as the island's principal seaport.

Aside from that, there are only four-wheel-drive roads, and that's where the fun begins. With a four-wheel-drive vehicle you can get to the far northern tip of the island, Polihua Beach, known as a prime turtle-nesting area. Or you can get much of the way around the northeastern and eastern shores, which boast beautiful and deserted beaches, traditional Hawaiian fishponds, and the remains of an abandoned sugar town.

The other option afforded by a four-wheel-drive is exploration of the Munro Trail, named after George Munro, who was a ranch manager in the 1930s. Munro began a program of reforestation for the island, planting many of the Norfolk pines that you'll see along the central mountain ridge.

Nature/Adventure Activities

Hiking is popular on Lanai. The distances are not that great and for the most part the going is fairly good. What you need to know about Lanai, though, is that unlike Molokai (see Chapter 7), the native flora and fauna have been overrun by stronger introduced species. Still, hiking on Lanai affords spectacular views and some very interesting geologic formations.

Flora and Fauna

At one time much of Lanai was covered with dryland forest. But so many of the island's native plants and trees were destroyed by imported ranch animals, such as sheep, goats, and cattle, that little of the original ground cover remains.

One area that does remain relatively intact is the Kanepu'u Preserve, a Nature Conservancy tract in the west central portion of the island. This dryland forest area now harbors some 48 native species, including endangered Lanai sandalwood, rare Hawaiian gardenia, and some local species of olive and persimmon.

Much of the original preservation work was done by a New Zealand ranch manager named George C. Munro, who arrived on Lanai in 1911. Seeing what was happening to the native species, Munro constructed fences and removed grazing animals from the areas of greatest danger. For the ensuing 30 years he continued his efforts, and today these are among the only areas of surviving native species on Lanai.

Along the eastern central ridge the Munro Trail is named in George's honor. In this area he planted Norfolk pines to prevent erosion. The pine trees are apparently not on the menu for the estimated 10,000 axis deer that live on Lanai, and so the trees survive with little disturbance. Little else does, though, particularly on the lower mountain slopes. At the higher elevations koa trees, *naupaka* shrubs, climbing pandanus, various ferns, and other species thrive.

Unfortunately, spotting endemic birds on Lanai is not so good at any elevation. The only known endemic left is the *'apapane*, and these swift red honeycreepers are not common.

In the waters of Hulopoe Bay, swimmers, divers, and snorkelers will find exciting underwater life. The Hulopoe Bay Marine Life Conservation District is a unique find. The area is distinguished by unusual volcanic spires and pinnacles, some rising as high as 70 feet from the seafloor.

Imagine examining these towering geologic phenomena, admiring the galaxy of rainbow-colored fish, when out of nowhere comes a school of spinner dolphins to examine and swim circles around you. It sounds like a movie fantasy—but this is the experience many people have at Hulopoe Bay.

History, Culture, and Customs

It's easy to compare Lanai to Molokai, both of them being diminutive islands in the middle of the Hawaiian chain, both with little development. Both are also part of Maui County. Many guidebooks lump them together.

But the reality is, although they are neighbors in the Pacific, they could not be much more different. While the population of Molokai is largely native Hawaiian, the population of Lanai is largely Filipino, families who came to work the pineapple fields in the early 1900s. While Molokai boasts some of Hawaii's most pristine natural area in its eastern mountains, Lanai's ecosystems consist chiefly of introduced species. And while Molokai has steadfastly resisted development over the years, Lanai went from an agriculture-based to a tourism-based economy in a very short time.

Of course the 2,800 residents had little choice in the matter. Lanai is largely privately held (98 percent) by Castle & Cooke, Inc., nee Dole Pineapple, and has been since 1921. That was the year that James Dole, a young Harvard graduate and nephew of the Territory of Hawaii's first

president, Sanford Dole, acquired the island expressly to grow pineapple, in his successful campaign to make "'Hawaiian' mean to pineapple what 'Havana' means to tobacco."
Thus, despite its size, the island of Lanai played a significant role in Hawaii's agricultural economy. At the height of the industry, Lanai was the world's single largest source of pineapple, with some 16,000 acres planted in the sweet fruit.
By 1993, however, pineapple was phased out. Nowadays, with the pineapple industry gone south from Hawaii, the island of Lanai has embarked upon a change of habit—destination resorts and affiliated businesses. With Castle & Cooke still at the helm, two luxury resorts have opened, the Lodge at Koele in 1990 and the Manele Bay Hotel in 1991. Many of the residents have been retrained from pineapple industry jobs to resort industry jobs.
Even with all the change going on about them, the residents of Lanai are still among the nicest people you will meet in Hawaii. They seem to have retained a sense of the true meaning of "aloha," a lesson that could well be learned in some other parts of the state.

Visitor Information

The Lanai Company, part of Castle & Cooke, can provide quite a bit of pertinent information on the resorts of Lanai. Contact them at P.O. Box 310, Lanai City, HI 96763, or phone 800/321-4666; www.lanairesorts.com. **Destination Lanai** (P.O. Box 700, Lanai City, HI 96763, 800/947-4774 or 808/565-7600) will give you a broad perspective of what is available on the Pineapple Island.

The **Maui Visitors Bureau** provides brochures, maps, and practical tips for travel to Lanai. Contact them at 1727 Wili Pa Loop, Wailuku, HI 96793; 808/244-3530. Good Lanai information is provided by the **Hawaii Visitors & Convention Bureau** at www.gohawaii.com.

The Nature Conservancy of Hawaii provides information about their preserves on Lanai. Contact them at 1116 Smith St., #201, Honolulu, HI 96817; 808/537-4508.

Anyone with a desire for knowledge of the culture of Lanai can visit **Kaupe Culture and Heritage Center** in Lanai City, 808/565-3342.

Getting There

Daily flights to and from Lanai are scheduled by Aloha Island Air and Hawaiian Airlines. Shuttles between the airport and the resorts, and from one resort to the other, are frequent and very good. Ferry service runs between Lahaina, Maui, and Manele Bay on a regular basis.

To be able to take advantage of the off-road experiences on Lanai, consider renting a four-wheel-drive. A couple of companies have them available, including Lanai City Service and Red Rover Lanai.

If you are not interested in negotiating the off-highway areas by yourself but still wish to experience them, there are some outfitters who will take you. See Guides and Outfitters section for more information.

NATURE AND ADVENTURE
SIGHTS ON LANAI

Hulopoe Bay Marine Life Conservation District

This is the prime snorkel and dive spot on Lanai. Snorkelers will discover unusual volcanic spires and pinnacles, some as tall as 70 feet over the seafloor.

A galaxy of rainbow-colored fish, a resident school of spinner dolphins, gentle waves, picnic tables, and barbecue grills make Hulopoe Bay a perfect day's outing. The other thing people of all ages thoroughly enjoy is exploring the tide pools on **Hulopoe Beach**. You will find everything from starfish to sea urchins to sea cucumbers in these singular ecologies.

Hulopoe Beach is also the only camping area on the island.

There are several spots on the north coast to snorkel or dive as well, although the best of these areas can be busy with boats from Maui on day cruises. Nevertheless, the coral formations, sea turtles, and other marine life in these areas are considered among the best in the state.

Details*: Several outfitters offer snorkel tours that include Hulopoe Bay. But it is the type of experience you can easily do by yourself, particularly if you wish to stay for a while on the beach to picnic or swim. Hulopoe Bay is next to the Manele Bay Hotel.*

LANAI'S BEST BEACH

by Rick Carroll
Author Rick Carroll has studied Hawaii's beaches extensively.
Here is his choice for the best beach on Lanai.

With gold sand, swaying palms, bold headlands, black-lava tide pools and soft, buttery light, especially at sunset, **Hulopoe Beach** looks too good to be true. Spinner dolphins play in ultra-clear water. Pacific humpback whales spy-hop offshore. The bay is a marine preserve full of tropical fish.

In summer's gentle swell, Hulopoe is great for swimming, snorkeling, or just lolling in the surf. Beware the mouth of the bay, where strong ocean currents (one is called "The Way to Tahiti") can sweep you into the far Pacific.

Koloiki Ridge Trail

Hiking on Lanai is one of the best ways to see the island and drink in some delightful views of practically the entire state. Because the island is only 18 miles long and 13 miles wide, and its highest elevation is the 3,370-foot Lanaihale, hiking the height, length, and breadth of Lanai is mostly possible.

This trail starts behind the Lodge at Koele and heads 2.5 miles north to the high ridges of Lanai. There are plenty of Norfolk pine in this area, as well as axis deer, wild turkey, and other introduced birds. When you reach the top you'll hear the vast silence of the mountains and feel the trade winds blowing as you gaze across the valleys and across the channel to Maui and Molokai. Your only choice is to return the way you came.

A longer hike takes you to the west-central portion of the island, to **Kanepuʻu** and the **Garden of the Gods**. This is roughly a 13-mile trek from Lanai City and back. **Kanepu'u Preserve** is a dryland forest Nature Conservancy tract that now harbors some 48 native species, including endangered Lanai sandalwood, rare Hawaiian gardenia, and some local species of olive and persimmon.

Nearby, the Garden of the Gods is a little like England's Stonehenge, in that unusual rock formations seemingly sprout up from the middle of nowhere. At Garden of the Gods the lava rocks have been coated with layers of red volcanic dust, which at dawn and dusk look particularly eerie.

Details: Koloiki Ridge is a moderate hike. It should take three to four hours to complete the loop. Hiking to Kanepu'u and the Garden of the Gods from Lanai City is an all-day trip. Start early.

Lanai Coast

The 28-foot Omega sportfisher *Spinning Dolphin II* will take you to some of Hawaii's best and least-fished waters. You're likely to catch marlin, *ahi* (tuna), mahimahi, barracuda, and *ono*. Once back in harbor, experienced deckhands will cut the fish for you, so you can present it to the chef at your hotel for tonight's dinner.

Spinning Dolphin II takes a maximum of six people per charter to allow greatest comfort and personalized service. If you like, you can combine your fishing trip with some whale-watching or coastline sightseeing. The tall red cliffs of Lanai are particularly beautiful when viewed from sea.

Details: Contact numbers are in the Guides and Outfitters section, below.

Lanai Ranch Trails

Although the *paniolo* tradition on Lanai is not as well-known as it is on some of the other islands, Hawaiian cowboys worked these ranges, too. In fact, before pineapple took over, Lanai Ranch was the island's main employer.

Many of the old ranch trails survive to this day, and are now used by riders to enjoy the wide plains and stunning vistas from the old ranchlands. The most popular ride will lead you through groves of guava and ironwood trees before emerging at panoramic viewpoints.

▲ Waipoo Falls on Kauai (David Boynton/Kauai Visitors Bureau)

▲ Chinaman's Hat from Kualoa Beach Park on Oahu (© George Fuller)

▼ Sea kayaking off Lanai (Island of Lanai Visitors Bureau)

▲ The endangered nene goose (© Unicorn Stock Photos/Robert Hitchman)

▼ Plumeria on Maui (© Leo de Wys, Inc./Everett C. Johnson)

▲ Makawao Rodeo on Maui
(© Ron Dahlquist)

▲ Haiku Stairs on Oahu
(© George Fuller)

▼ Kohala Ditch Trail in the Alakahi Valley on the Big Island
(Phillip Rosenberg/Big Island Visitors Bureau)

▲ Pineapple blossom on Oahu (© Leo de Wys, Inc./J.P. Nacivet)

▼ Black-crowned night heron (© Unicorn Stock Photos/Dede Gilman)

▲ Windsurfing at Hanalei off Kauai (David Boynton/Kauai Visitors Bureau)

▲ Hiking near Painted Pots in the Haleakala Crater on Maui (© Ron Dahlquist)

▼ Bicycling on Molokai Ranch (© George Fuller)

▲ Waimea Canyon, "the Grand Canyon of the Pacific" on Kauai
(© George Fuller)

▲ Kilauea Lighthouse off Kauai (© George Fuller)

Sheila Donnelly & Associates

Hiking opportunities abound on Lanai.

Along the way you're likely to encounter wild turkey, axis deer, quail, and cattle grazing in the lush green pastureland.

Rides are generally tailored to beginning riders, but for the more-experienced equestrian, faster and more adventurous rides are also available, as are lessons.

Details*: The Stables at Koele, located next to the Lodge at Koele, is the choice for horseback riding. See Guides and Outfitters for more information.*

Lanaihale

This is a lovely hike accessed from the Munro Trail. If it's foggy or raining, think about doing this hike another day, as one of the treats of this trail on the high ridgeline of the island is the wide panoramic views. On clear days you can see five different islands from this vantage point. In total, this hike is roughly 11 miles round-trip from the Munro Trail.

Lanai Eco-Adventure Centre

Kayaking is a popular activity on Lanai.

You can also choose to head down the eastern side of the mountain via the Awehi Trail and end up three miles later at the beach. This trail is steep and can be treacherous after a rain. *Details: Lanaihale is a strenuous, full-day hike, made more so when the trail is muddy.*

GUIDES AND OUTFITTERS

A relatively new outfitter, **Lanai Eco-Adventure Centre**, P.O. Box 1394, Lanai City, HI 96763, 808/565-7373, golanai@aloha.net, www.adventurelanai.com, offers hiking, biking, and kayak/snorkel adventures. All are geared to the beginner. Cost: $69/person for two-hour trips; $89 for half-day, and $169 for full-day treks.

Ocean adventurers may want to check out **Spinning Dolphin Charters**, P.O. Box 491, Lanai City, HI 96763, 808/565-6613, or contact

TARGET: LANAI'S CLAY PIGEONS

Look, up in the sky: It's a bird, it's a rabbit, it's a clay pigeon—and the newest attraction on the island of Lanai—Lanai Pine Sporting Clays. If this sounds like just the opposite of ecotourism, it's not. The clay pigeons are biodegradable, and the targets are solar-powered.

The adventure, designed to test your hand-eye coordination, takes you deep into Lanai's interior, past dryland forest to a 15-acre trap and skeet course. There, you are fitted specifically to a gun, given instruction if you require or desire, and sent out to one of several ranges. You have the option of shooting trap, skeet, compact sporting, or sporting clays.

A typical sporting clays round consists of 100 targets attempted over a two-hour period. Shooters may attempt the course solo or in groups of six. The woodsy setting is spectacular, with views of Lanai's valleys rolling down to the surf and Maui poking up on the horizon.

A yearly fund-raising event to benefit Ducks Unlimited offers a purse of $20,000, and invites your participation. For more details contact Lanai Pine Sporting Clays at 800/321-4666 or 808/563-4545, or the hotel concierge at either the Lodge at Koele or the Manele Bay Hotel.

the hotel concierge at either the Lodge at Koele or Manele Bay Hotel. Enjoy sportfishing, sightseeing, snorkeling, and seasonal whale-watching charters aboard the 28-foot *Spinning Dolphin II*. These are six-person-maximum tours, allowing comfort and personalized service. Cost: $400/half-day; $600/full day.

Trilogy Ocean Sports Lanai, call 888/MAUI-800 (or contact the hotel concierge at either the Lodge at Koele or Manele Bay Hotel), offers snorkel sails, adventure scuba dives, cove exploration, and an eco–marine-mammal tour. Sailing excursions are on catamarans with brightly colored sails, while the cove exploration tours and scuba dives load up on smaller, faster vessels to get you to and from your destination quickly. Cost: $75/person for the eco–marine-mammal tour; $95/person for the snorkel sail; $130/person for the cove exploration tour; $140/person for the two-tank dive tour. Children 3–15 half-price.

For sport-shooters, try **Lanai Pine Sporting Clays**, 800/321-4666, or contact the hotel concierge at either the Lodge at Koele or Manele Bay Hotel. A number of shooting options are available, including skeet and wobble trap ranges. Instruction is offered, as is shooting geared for the more experienced gunner. Cost: $65/person for 50 targets; $125/person for 100 targets.

Red Rover, P.O. Box 520, Lanai City, HI 96763, 877/REDROVER (toll-free) or 808/565-7722, rents four-wheel-drive Rover Road Warriors for off-road adventure. They set you up with maps, communications equipment, a music library, and winches for getting yourself out of a jam. If you need help extricating, a rescue squad is on the way for the asking. If you'd rather let them do the driving, they offer tours in Hummers. Cost: $75/hour, two-hour minimum for the tours.

From 15-minute children's horseback rides to four-hour private trail rides into Lanai's mountain range, there's **The Stables at Koele**, P.O. Box 310, Lanai City, HI 96763, 808/565-4424, or contact the hotel concierge at either the Lodge at Koele or Manele Bay Hotel. Lessons in English and Western riding also are available. Cost: $10/person for the 15-minute children's rides; $40/person for the one-hour trail ride; $230/person for four-hour private trail rides.

CAMPING

Hulopoe Bay is the only camping facility on the island of Lanai, but it's one of the best campgrounds in Hawaii. A favorite spot for Lanai residents to spend their weekends, it's ideal for many reasons. First of all, it's right on a lovely stretch of white-sand beach, where gentle waves and great snorkeling comprise a day's work. Second, the bay is frequently visited by a school of spinner dolphins, which are as curious about you as you are about them. And finally, the facilities include picnic tables, barbecue grills, showers, and rest rooms. Six campsites available.

A permit is required for camping at Hulopoe Beach. The facility is private and run by the Lanai Company. Permits run $5, plus $5 per person per night, seven nights maximum. Reservations should be made four to six weeks in advance of travel dates. For information or reservations write P.O. Box 310, Lanai City, HI 96763, 808/565-3982.

LODGING

There are few lodging choices on Lanai, but what's here is wonderful. Both the Lodge at Koele and the Manele Bay Hotel are owned by Castle & Cooke, Inc., which also owns much of the island. The two resorts are among the most luxurious in the world. They also fall into the "high end" cost category. If you've got the budget, they're hard to beat. If you're traveling on a more modest budget, consider Hotel Lanai. In either case, you will love every minute of your stay on the Pineapple Island.

The Lodge at Koele, P.O. Box 310, Lanai City, HI 96763, 800/321-4666 or 808/565-7300, is an elegant inn in the fashion of an old English country manor, set in Lanai's upcountry near Lanai City. The 102 guest rooms and suites are tastefully decorated with four-poster beds, light and airy color schemes, and comfortable furniture. The common areas, starting with the Grand Hall and its massive stone fireplace and overstuffed couches, are at once cozy and luxurious. Afternoon tea in the Music Room is quite nice, thank you. The staff here makes you feel like the lord or lady of the manor. Rates: $325 and up.

The delightful **Manele Bay Hotel**, P.O. Box 310, Lanai City, HI 96763, 800/321-4666 or 808/565-7700, is set on a cliff overlooking Hulopoe Bay, a 20-minute shuttle ride from Lanai City. It's a more modern design with hints of a Chinese influence, but every bit as elegant as the Lodge at Koele. Manele Bay Hotel has 250 rooms and suites, many of which have sweeping ocean views. Activity here is golf-, tennis-, beach-, and pool-oriented. In the evenings, guests head off to

The Lodge at Koele

dinner at the exquisite Ihilani Restaurant or Hulopoe Court, both featuring ocean views as tasty as the food. Rates: $295 and up.

A simple, less-expensive alternative to Lanai's luxury hotels is **Hotel Lanai**, P.O. Box 520, Lanai City, HI 96763, 800/795-7211 or 808/565-7211, a charming, recently renovated country inn built in 1923. A throwback to earlier times, Hotel Lanai is located in the heart of Lanai City, in the island's cool upcountry. Natural wood floors and old-style fixtures give this 11-room hotel a charming and homey feel. Guests enjoy complimentary continental breakfast. In the evening, it feels great to sit on the lanai here and just watch the world go by. Rates: $95–$140.

FOOD

The Lodge at Koele, P.O. Box 310, Lanai City, HI 96763, 800/321-4666 or 808/565-7300, offers two public dining choices, the foremost simply called the Formal Dining Room, open for dinner nightly. The atmosphere is elegant, the food is wonderful. Try roasted summer corn and sweet-potato soup, followed by Lanai venison loin, seared *ahi* tuna, or rack of lamb. Entrées are on the pricey side for some budgets—the rack of lamb is $38, for example—but well worth the splurge if you love perfect preparations of quality fare. A good wine list, too.

As at the Lodge at Koele, there are several options for dining at **Manele Bay Hotel**, P.O. Box 310, Lanai City, HI 96763, 800/321-4666 or 808/565-7700. The Ihilani Dining Room, open for dinner nightly, is one of the best restaurants in the state. Entrées include several vegetarian selections, plus a chef's selection of items, which is paired with wines if you desire. Hulopoe Court, also open for breakfast and lunch, is a less-formal option, but still very good.

Henry Clay's Rotisserie, at the Hotel Lanai, 808/565-7211, is open for dinner nightly, offering several choices of wild game, seafood, and lobster entrées, as well as a nice selection of appetizers such as a New England clam chowder and "rajun cajun" shrimp. It is a less-expensive alternative to the luxury resorts, and like the Hotel Lanai, in which it is housed, boasts a low-key, homey ambiance.

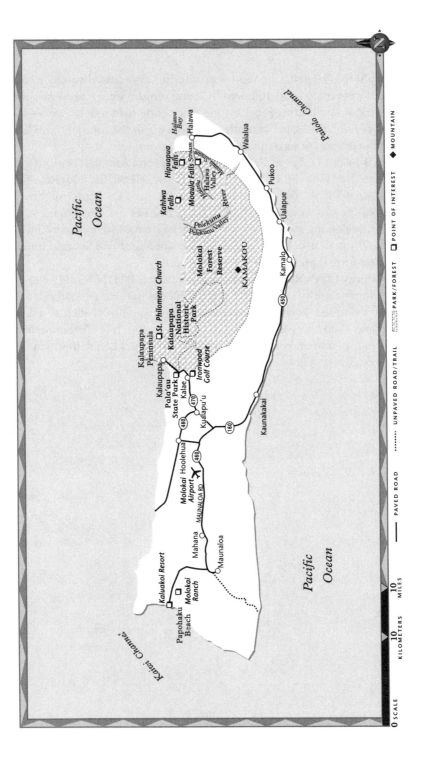

MOLOKAI—THE FRIENDLY ISLE

7

In the middle of the Hawaiian archipelago, the island of Molokai is just 26 miles off the southeast shore of Oahu. But it is far, far away in most other categories.

Molokai is undeveloped, for the most part. There are not many lodging choices on the island, even fewer restaurants, and two golf courses. And if you ask any of the island's 6,000 residents, they're likely to tell you that that's plenty of development already—maybe even too much!

Orientation/Lay of the Land

After a few years of closure, lovely Halawa Valley on the far eastern tip of the island is now open again for exploration. The rugged North Shore, with its towering ocean cliffs and awe-inspiring vistas, is as exciting to explore on foot as it is remote. And the renowned mule ride down to Kalaupapa Peninsula, where Belgian priest Father Damien de Veuster went to care for the victims of Hansen's disease—otherwise known as leprosy—is also accessible after a couple years of respite.

On the western end of the island, Molokai Ranch may have finally found an identity. The ranch has constructed three "eco-camps"

195

Molokai Ranch's Kaupoa Beach

designed to entice the adventure traveler to the island for fun in the water, on horseback and bicycle, and on foot. Ranch accommodations are in "tentalows" or yurts, beam-supported structures with canvas walls. Meals are served in open-air pavilions, and the experience is like a luxury summer camp for the whole family.

The main town on Molokai is Kaunakakai, located on the central southern shore of this index-finger–shaped island. Kaunakakai is a throwback to earlier times. You'll swear that things have not changed much in 75 years, and you would be correct. From Kaunakakai to either end of Molokai is roughly 20 miles. The island is 37 miles long and 10 miles wide at its widest point.

Molokai's western half is arid and dry, with wonderful sand dunes leading down to miles of deserted beach. Molokai Ranch is headquartered in Maunaloa Town, once a center for the island's agriculture industry. Also on the western tip of Molokai is Kaluakoi Resort and Golf Course, the island's only effort at commercial tourism as the rest of Hawaii knows it.

The eastern half of the island is greener, with tall mountains looking down into fertile valleys and deep canyons. Halawa Valley invites hiking and exploration, but other parts of eastern Molokai are inaccessible—and some parts you don't want to trespass even if they appear accessible. This is pot-growing country, and some of these protective farmers shoot first and ask questions later. It all adds to the description of Molokai as a Wild, Wild West kind of place.

Nature/Adventure Activities

Since Molokai is so undeveloped, it is a perfect destination for the adventure traveler. In addition to having the best eco-resort in Hawaii (Molokai Ranch), the island is a hiker's paradise: Choose from mountain, valley, and shoreline hikes. The fact that there has been so little development means that much of the island's natural area has been preserved.

Flora and Fauna

The eastern end of Molokai is particularly significant to environmentalists. The Nature Conservancy holds long-term lease rights to 2,774 pristine acres in the heart of the eastern Molokai's mountains, the Kamakou Preserve. The State of Hawaii owns or controls much of the balance of the land in an area called Molokai Forest Reserve. Both of these wilderness areas are bastions for many of Hawaii's most endangered plant and bird species.

Some areas in the deepest reaches of the forest are completely inaccessible, including to the introduced species that have damaged the native ecosystems in so much of Hawaii. For this reason, Molokai's deep forest harbors some of the state's best native plant species.

There are, however, some very good hikes into more accessible areas, and the Kamakou Preserve is one of the best. Here, more than 200 endemic plants thrive, and several endemic birds. The birds here include *'apapane*, Hawaii *amakihi*, and the brilliant red *i'iwi*. Two other

197

species, the *oloma'o*—a thrush—and the Molokai creeper, both of which used to be spotted here, are now either critically endangered or extinct. The more-arid western end of Molokai teems with deer, wild turkey, pheasant, and other introduced creatures.

History, Culture, and Customs

Visitors to the Friendly Isle will find a way of life that moves at a much slower pace than most of the world. Jets don't scream in and out of the airport. In fact, the airport cannot accommodate most jets.

There are no high-rises or freeways. There's not even a stoplight. And people just don't seem to get wound up about too many things over here. This is one of the island's great charms: If you're planning a visit to Molokai, you've got to slow down!

To the rest of the world, Molokai is best known for the leper colony that was established on the remote northern peninsula of Kalaupapa in the mid-1800s, and for the work of Father Damien, who spent much of his life in the Kalaupapa settlement caring for the people who were banished there.

But there is really quite a bit more to this unassuming island than you might imagine. For one thing, more than half of its population is native Hawaiian. In part, this explains why there is so much resistance to what the rest of the world calls "progress." The people of Molokai live a much more traditional Hawaiian lifestyle. One person's progress is another person's intrusion.

In ancient times, the warriors of Molokai were feared and respected by warriors from the other Hawaiian islands. And the kahuna were thought to possess great power. Even today, evidence of this spiritual history remains in the many *heiau* found on the island.

Hula is generally thought to have had its origins on Molokai. Cattle ranching and the *paniolo* lifestyle also have a long and storied past here.

Aquaculture was an important element in Molokai's early days. Almost 50 fishponds once lined the southern shore of the island, some of which have survived and are still in use.

Agriculture, too, has always played a major role in Molokai's economy and way of life. First, individual farmers grew sweet potatoes,

BIRTH OF THE HULA

Hula is thought to have originated on Molokai. At Ka'ana on the slopes of Maunaloa in West Molokai, the goddess Laka is said to have danced the first hula. She then traveled throughout the islands teaching others the graceful movements and chants that have today been passed down through many generations of kumu hula *(master dancers).*

Each May, this traditional dance is celebrated in a festival called Molokai Ka Hula Piko—A Celebration of the Birth of Hula on Molokai. The day of dance is preceded by a week of lectures on hula and tours to the historic sites that are celebrated in the dance.

To make arrangements to attend this popular cultural festival, contact the Molokai Visitors Association, 800/800-6367 or 808/553-3867. Considering the island's limited accommodations, it's best to plan far in advance to visit during this week.

bananas, and taro. Later, as larger agribusiness moved in and acquired land, pineapple became the number-one crop. With the end of pineapple production in 1982—by then the island's largest employer—Molokai began a still-ongoing period of economic difficulty.

Tourism was considered, and one resort was built. But ambitious plans for several others fizzled, leaving Kaluakoi Resort an industry in search of a critical mass.

Nowadays, watermelon, coffee beans, vegetables, and herbs are the principal crops. Molokai Ranch, which owns roughly one-third of the island, has built the tourism base somewhat with their eco-camps. And perhaps things are finally looking a little brighter for Molokai's economy.

Local residents will wait and see. Change is slow here, sometimes frustratingly so for those who would like to plant Molokai's flag on Hawaii's tourism map. But looked at in the broad perspective of time, considering what the residents of Molokai see has happened to Waikiki and Kaanapali, Kona and Lihue—a bustling development pattern they do not wish to see in their own backyards—perhaps Molokai's brooding pace and slow approach to development is a blessing in disguise.

Visitor Information

Visitors are welcomed at the **Molokai Visitors Association**, in Kaunakakai at the intersection of Kam Highway and Wharf Road. You can stop by Monday through Friday during normal business hours; or contact the association at P.O. Box 90, Kaunakakai, HI 96748, 800/800-6367 or 808/553-3867 for an appointment or to have information sent to you. The association's Web site, which provides information on Molokai companies, services, and products, is at www.molokai-hawaii.com.

Information specific to **Molokai Ranch** and their offerings can be obtained by writing Molokai Ranch, P.O. Box 259, Maunaloa, HI 96770; or phoning toll-free 877/726-4656. The ranch's Web site address is www.molokai-ranch.com.

The Nature Conservancy of Hawaii provides information about their preserves and hikes on Molokai and elsewhere. Contact them on Molokai at P.O. Box 220, Kualapu'u, HI 96757, 808/553-5236; or in Honolulu at 1116 Smith St., #201, Honolulu, HI 96817, 808/537-4508.

Getting There

Flights to Molokai are more limited than they are to Maui, the Big Island, or Kauai. But both Hawaiian Airlines and Aloha Island Air have several regularly scheduled daily flights. Be prepared for smaller aircraft—both carriers use propeller jets into the small airport.

When you land, one thing you'll want to consider is renting a four-wheel-drive vehicle to do some exploring. All over the island are miles of dirt roads leading to deserted beaches, or inland roads winding through the Molokai outback. A word of caution: Make sure that what you are renting is actually what you are getting. Some unhappy customers have reported that they booked a four-wheel-drive, but the four-wheel-drive feature had been permanently disabled; or that they were contractually forbidden to take the four-wheel-drive vehicles off the main roads.

Again, fewer rental-car choices are available here. If you have a favorite company, check with them to see if they are represented. If not, Budget and Dollar car-rental offices are at the airport, and Island Kine Rentals is in Kaunakakai.

NATURE AND ADVENTURE SIGHTS ON MOLOKAI

Halawa Valley

On the far eastern tip of the island, this was once a thriving population center with more than 1,500 families living up and down the fertile valley floor. Evidence suggests that people have been living in Halawa Valley for almost 1,300 years, with artifacts found dating back to A.D. 650, making it one of the earliest settlements in the chain.

In 1946, one of the most destructive tsunamis ever to hit the Hawaiian Islands struck. Hardest hit were the town of Hilo on the Big Island, and Molokai's Halawa Valley. The onrush of water and the ensuing backwash were devastating. Afterwards, most of the families who had lived in Halawa Valley for generations left.

Today this idyllic three-mile-long valley is one of Molokai's most scenic destinations, and is open for hiking tours with a local guide. Visitors now may join storyteller Pilipo Solotario, who was born and raised in the valley, on hikes to the twin-tiered **Moaula Falls** and pool.

The valley is filled with wild ferns, mango and guava trees, and sacred sites from traditional Hawaii. On the day-long hike, Solotario shares his memories of growing up in the tropical valley, recalling the 1946 tidal wave that wiped out a thriving taro industry and sent inhabitants fleeing for their lives.

Details: For more information call Halawa Falls Cultural Hike at 808/553-4355.

Ironwood Golf Course

An inexpensive nine-holer in mountains above Kaunakakai, this is as far from Pebble Beach as you may ever get and still have an ocean view.

Russell Woo/The Nature Conservancy

Kamakou Preserve

It's fun, local-style golf, where most everyone walks the course. Carts are available if you need or want one, but don't. Relax, have fun, and enjoy the cool setting at this 1,200-foot elevation. Plus, it's only $10 for nine holes; $14 for 18 holes. This is how golf was originally played.
Details: *Call 808/567-6000 for directions and tee times.*

Kalaupapa Peninsula

Talk about a contradiction: On the north shore of Molokai, on the exquisitely picturesque Kalaupapa Peninsula, one of Hawaii's least-proud moments took place. In the late 1800s, fearing the spread of dreaded Hansen's disease—leprosy—people from around the islands were rounded up and banished to this remote shore. Despite the fact that there was no solid evidence that leprosy was contagious, people were separated from their families and society and sent to Kalaupapa to live out their days in a beautiful, tough wilderness.

Into this emotional and difficult circumstance came a Belgian priest by the name of Father Damien de Veuster, whose life mission became caring for the people at Kalaupapa's infamous leper colony. Father Damien's church, **St. Philomena**, stands lovingly restored today as a reminder of his selfless work and dedication to the leprosy victims.

Visitors to Molokai these days can take mule rides down the vertical sea cliffs to the Kalaupapa leper colony with veteran mule skinner Buzzy Sproat. A dazzling view of Molokai's north shore unfolds as you descend the 1,700 feet of elevation in 26 switchbacks on the back of a steady mule.

The trail was originally cut into the face of the cliffs in 1886 by Manual Joao Farinha, an immigrant to Hawaii from Madeira, following the course of an ancient Hawaiian footpath. It was used to transport guests to Kalaupapa and haul supplies.

Once down the cliffs, today's mule riders hook up with **Damien Tours** for an excursion through the leper colony (some 44 long-time residents still live here, plus an additional 40 workers), and a visit to St. Philomena Church to hear the history of Kalaupapa and the tales of the people who lived here. This is followed by a picnic lunch at Judd Park overlooking the scenic north coast of the island.

Hiking in is now possible and easier due to the renovation of the three-mile **Kalaupapa Pali Trail** by the National Park Service in 1994. It's the same trail used by the mule trips. Hiking down provides the opportunity to stop at will to admire the magnificent views, as well as the option to explore a little more of the north shore than an organized tour might offer.

If you're hiking, though, be aware that you need an invitation from a resident or a reservation with Damien Tours to enter, as Kalaupapa is a restricted area.

Pala'au State Park is at the end of the road, past where the mule tours meet at the top of the cliffs. From Pala'au, the views of the coastline below are stunning. There are picnic table here and a campground. Chances are you'll have the place to yourself.

Details: The mule ride is a 7½-hour trip, not all of it (thankfully) in the saddle. Riders are advised to dress comfortably, long pants suggested. Bring your own water and snacks. Don't forget the camera. Age 16 and older only.

Kamakou Preserve

The Nature Conservancy offers monthly hikes into this 2,774-acre preserve in the heart of the eastern Molokai mountains, a stronghold for many of Hawaii's most endangered species. Since 1982, the conservancy has worked to preserve and restore this area, instituting programs to reduce the presence and impact of alien species. They have also constructed boardwalks in some areas to make exploration easier and less muddy—and they do get their share of rain up here: some 15 feet per year, to be precise.

Getting to Kamakou Preserve, named after the highest mountain peak on Molokai, is a definite four-wheel-drive excursion and can be a little hairy, particularly in wet weather. But what a rare treat to be able to witness life at this 4,000-foot elevation, in one of the most pristine environments on earth.

Once there, your most accessible hiking option is a three-mile round-trip hike that should take roughly four hours. Your hike leads through **Pepeʻopae Bog**, an area of dwarf ohia trees, mosses, and lichens that thrive in this ecosystem, which has been largely undisturbed for thousands of years. Farther on, you'll pass a scenic overlook into **Pelekunu Valley**, another Nature Conservancy preserve. On clear days, the view from this overlook is quite dramatic.

This rarified preserve is home to more than 200 endemic plant species, and several endemic birds. In this latter category are the *ʻapapane* and Hawaii *amakihi*.

Your Nature Conservancy guides are knowledgeable in identifying these bird and plant species, and will also provide current information about their status.

Details: The Nature Conservancy hikes often fill up quite a long time in advance, so plan early and make arrangements if you want to go. Because it's such a rare treat to hike into these pristine areas, these trips are very popular among Hawaii residents from all islands. Take rain gear—the area gets wet — and be prepared to get muddy.

Molokai Ranch

This is a 54,000-acre spread on the arid western end of the island.

MOLOKAI'S BEST BEACH

by Rick Carroll

Author Rick Carroll has studied Hawaii's beaches extensively.
Here is his choice for the best beach on Molokai.

*While some claim **Papohaku Beach** is Hawaii's biggest (it's not; Polihale on Kauai is), it is the biggest, longest beach on Molokai: two miles of golden sand, 100 yards wide with high dunes in the foreshore.*

Broad, often empty, Papohaku stretches two miles on the far side of 110-foot Pu'u O Kaiaka, a black lava-rock landmark. Otherwise deserted, this beach has a 26-mile channel view of Oahu and Waikiki's bright lights.

Swimming is risky due to a shore break and strong undertow, so save this beach for long walks.

Known as Molokai's center of *paniolo* (cowboy) activity for many years, today the ranch offers horseback riding and a whole lot more.

Guests are housed in one of three camps: Paniolo Camp, Kolo Cliffs Camp, and Kaupoa Beach Camp. Each camp is set up around a different theme, but guests can engage in most of the activities offered at all three. For example, if you decide to make the oceanfront **Kaupoa Beach Camp** your home during your visit, you are offered a variety of ocean- and beach-related activities. These include ocean kayaking, snorkeling, and outrigger canoe sailing with experienced local guides. But you are also encouraged to go mountain biking on the miles of cow trails leading from Maunaloa Town down to the ocean.

Similarly, at **Paniolo Camp** horseback activities are stressed, such as a roundup and a trail ride. But you can also head down to the beach, or go mountain biking.

Guests at Kaupoa and Paniolo stay in "tentalows," bungalow-like

Molokai Ranch "tentalows"

© George Fuller

tents mounted on wooden platforms. These are not your run-of-the-mill tents; each has a queen-size bed, solar-powered lights, and private bathroom where you can watch the stars while showering. Guests at the more remote **Kolo Cliffs Camp** stay in yurts, structures similar to those at Kaupoa and Paniolo Camps—but yurts are round.

All meals are served buffet-style in an open-air dining pavilion. Breakfasts include cereals, fruits, muffins, and eggs; lunch consists of sandwiches or burgers, salads, and chips; and the hearty dinners generally consist of steaks, salads, a fresh-fish dish, and dessert.

Make of your stay what you will. For parents, this is adventure summer camp for the whole family—and you know what? Parents have just as much fun as their kids! But couples can also make it a romantic getaway and spend their time in tandem kayaks, getting on mountain bikes and heading out on their own, or wandering miles of secluded beach.

One of the most pleasing aspects of the camps is after dinner sitting and "talking story" with the locals. The night sky is ablaze with stars and there's not a city light around to dim them. Off in the distance over the water... what is that glow against the sky? Oh, that's Honolulu, a million miles away.

Details: *For more information or reservations write to Molokai Ranch, P.O. Box 259, Maunaloa, HI 96770; or phone toll-free 877/726-4656.*

GUIDES AND OUTFITTERS

Richard Marks is the only licensed operator of tours to Kalaupapa Peninsula. His company, **Damien Tours**, P.O. Box 13, Kalaupapa, HI 96742, 808/567-6171, offers four-hour historical tours of Kalaupapa Peninsula and Father Damien's church. The peninsula is a restricted area, and you must have a reservation with Damien Tours to go beyond the top of the trail. (If you are part of the Molokai Mule Ride, this is taken care of for you.) Bring your own lunch; no one under 16 allowed. Tour begins at 9:45 a.m. Cost: $30/person.

Molokai Mule Ride, Box 200, Kualapu'u, HI 96757, 800/567-7550 or 808/567-6088, will take you via mule down the highest sea cliffs in the world to the leper colony at Kalaupapa. A dazzling view is spread out before you as you descend the 1,700 feet of elevation in 26 switchbacks. Cost is $135/person.

Hikers, take note: **Nature Conservancy of Hawaii**, P.O. Box 220, Kualapu'u, HI 96757, 808/553-5236, leads monthly hikes onto conservancy land at Kamakou Preserve, as well as monthly hikes in the Moomomi Sand Dunes. Also, **Halawa Falls Cultural Hike** (P.O. Box 863, Kaunakakai, HI 96748, 808/553-4355) offers guided hiking tours into beautiful Halawa Valley with Hawaiian storyteller Pilipo Solotario. Solotario, who grew up in Halawa Valley, educates hikers about the history and culture of the valley and then leads hikes to a waterfall. Costs are $25/person; $15 children under 12.

For an all-around eco-adventure, check out **Molokai Ranch**, P.O. Box 259, Maunaloa, HI 96770, 877/726-4656 (toll-free). Stay in one of three "eco-camps" and participate in a variety of activities, including horseback riding, ocean kayaking, mountain biking, and outrigger sailing. Cost: $215–$245/person/night. Includes all meals and most activities.

LODGING

There are very few lodging choices on Molokai. The one resort on the island, Kaluakoi Resort, has been of questionable quality in recent years. That's why it isn't listed here. There is no legal camping on Molokai.

Molokai Ranch

With solar-powered lights and solar-heated showers, Molokai Ranch takes a clue from the sun on how to be eco-friendly.

Molokai Ranch, P.O. Box 259, Maunaloa, HI 96770, 877/726-4656 (toll-free) is an adventure-traveler's paradise. The ranch offers accommodations packages at three separate "camps." The units, called "tentalows" or yurts, are canvas-walled structures with support beams, solar-powered lights, and individually solar-heated showers. (A full description of Molokai Ranch is found in Nature and Adventure Sights, above.) Rates: $215–$245 per person per night, including all meals, ground transportation, gratuities, and taxes.

For the B&B feel, check out **Hale o Keo Keo** (through Hawaii's Best Bed & Breakfasts), in Waialua on the east end of Molokai, 800/262-9912 or 808/885-4550. This quaint, lovely two-bedroom beach house is situated on some old fishponds and a beach on the lush eastern end of Molokai. Guests are delighted to find Hawaiian quilts on the beds, and a variety of local-style furnishings. Full kitchen, living room. This may not be the Ritz, but Molokai isn't Manhattan. Rates: $150 for up to five people.

Paniolo Hale (through Hawaii's Best Bed & Breakfasts), at Kaluakoi Resort, 800/262-9912 or 808/885-4550, offers individually owned condominium units with kitchens, washer/dryer units, and screened porches, on the grounds of Kaluakoi Resort on the west end of Molokai. Guests have privileges at the golf course and other resort facilities. The condos are within walking distance of Papohaku Beach, one of the longest stretches of white-sand beach in Hawaii. Rates: $95–$195, depending on unit.

FOOD

There are very few dining choices on Molokai. Many visitors opt to do their own cooking if they are staying in a condo or accommodations with a kitchen. Remember that if you're staying at Molokai Ranch, meals are included.

When on Molokai, do as the Molokaians: Go to **Kanemitsu Bakery**, in the heart of Kaunakakai, 808/553-5855. The baked-nightly Molokai sweet breads and stone cookies are delicious and taken as gifts throughout the state. Local-style breakfasts and plate lunches are available in a small sit-down area, but the real reason to come here is the baked goodies. If you want a real treat, you can show up at the back door of the bakery after 10:30 p.m. and get your bread hot from the oven. Run by the Kanemitsu family since 1935. Open for breakfast and lunch Wed–Mon; closed Tue.

The Village Grill at Maunaloa Town, on the main street of Maunaloa, 808/552-0012, serves up a selection of burgers, sandwiches, and local favorites such as chicken katsu and loco moco for lunch; and steaks, ribs, prime rib, and fresh fish for dinner. There is also a *keiki* (kids') menu, and a couple of pizzas if you need a pizza fix. It's hearty food, in keeping with the *paniolo* lifestyle of Molokai Ranch. Open for lunch Mon–Fri. and dinner nightly,

Outpost Natural Foods, in downtown Kaunakakai, 808/553-5857, is a combination natural-foods store and vegetarian lunch bar offering a welcome option in food on Molokai, where the choices are so few. You can purchase fresh produce, bulk foods, and juices in the store portion. Open 9 a.m.–6 p.m. Sun–Thu; 9 a.m.– 3:30 p.m. Fri; closed Sat.

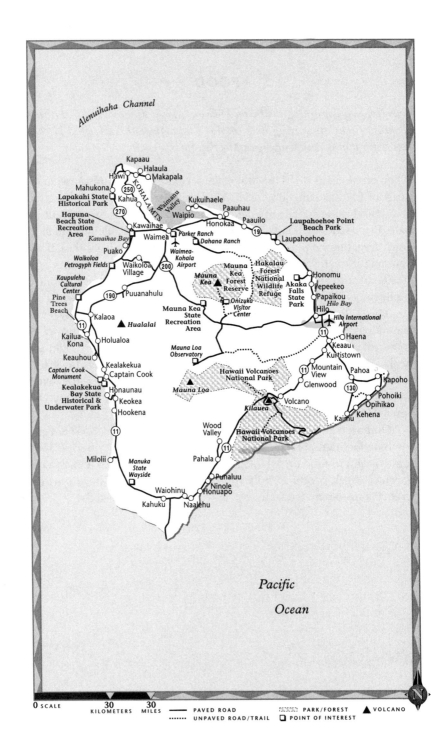

Alenuihaha Channel

Kapaau
Halaula
Hawi Makapala
Mahukona KOHALA MTS
Lapakahi State 250
Historical Park Kahua Kukuihaele
270 Paauhau
Hapuna Waipio
Beach State Kawaihae Paauilo
Recreation Honokaa 19
Area Kawaihae Bay Waimea Laupahoehoe Point
Puako Parker Ranch Beach Park
Dahana Ranch Laupahoehoe
Waikoloa Waimea-
Petroglyph Fields Waikoloa Kohala
Village Airport Mauna Hakalau
200 Kea Forest Honomu
Kaupulehu Forest National Akaka Pepeekeo
Cultural 190 Puuanahulu Mauna Reserve Wildlife Falls Papaikou
Center Kea Refuge State Hilo Bay
Pine Park
Trees Mauna Kea Onizuka Hilo
Beach Kalaoa Hualalai State Visitor Hilo International
Recreation Center Airport
Kailua- Area Haena
Kona Holualoa Keaau
Keauhou Kurtistown
Mauna Loa
Captain Cook Observatory Mountain Pahoa
Monument Kealakekua View
Captain Cook Hawaii Volcanoes Glenwood 130 Kapoho
Kealakekua National Park 11
Bay State Honaunau Mauna Loa Pohoiki
Historical & Keokea Opihikao
Underwater Park Hookena Kilauea Volcano Kaimu Kehena
Wood Hawaii Volcanoes
Valley National Park
11
Milolii Manuka Pahala
State
Wayside Punaluu
Waiohinu Ninole
Kahuku Naalehu Honuapo

Pacific

Ocean

N

0 SCALE   30   30   —— PAVED ROAD   PARK/FOREST   ▲ VOLCANO
     KILOMETERS MILES ········ UNPAVED ROAD/TRAIL   ☐ POINT OF INTEREST

HAWAII—THE BIG ISLAND

8

The principal story of the Big Island of Hawaii is one of creation and destruction. It is a story of millennia passing and raw elements of nature superimposed against a landscape so innately beautiful that everyone who sees it proclaims it paradise. It is also a story of a spiritual people whose legends and beliefs have been passed from generation to generation.

There are five volcanoes that form the face of the island, from the active (Kilauea, Mauna Loa, Hualalai) to the dormant (Mauna Kea) to the extinct (Kohala). This abundance of activity speaks to the fact that in the sea beneath the island are the most active tectonic plates in the world.

Meanwhile, at the summits of Mauna Kea and Mauna Loa, snow is common during the winter months. This raw and lovely dichotomy of fire and ice is what the Big Island is all about—and what you'll likely remember long after your trip is over.

Visitors can view all of this from close range, and relax on the beach, too. The sunny Kona and Kohala coasts are a playground for fun in the sun. These many diverse things make the Big Island of Hawaii the favorite island of locals and visitors alike, and that's saying a lot, considering the steep competition from the rest of the islands.

Orientation/Lay of the Land

The island of Hawaii—known as "the Big Island" to differentiate it from the state as a whole—is a wonderful study in the contrasts of nature, climate, and lifestyle.

On one end of the island, the raw force of nature is on display, as Kilauea Volcano has been spewing bright red lava down her slopes and into the sea for more than 15 years now. Considered a "friendly flow," this magnificent spectacle can be viewed by helicopter and—from a safe distance—on foot. Kilauea is part of Hawaii Volcanoes National Park, and is its principal attraction. The park also encompasses another active volcano, Mauna Loa, which is more difficult to visit by car but provides some great hiking.

Roughly 30 minutes down the eastern slope of Mauna Loa at the waterfront is the lovely, slow-paced town of Hilo, where residents outnumber tourists by a long shot. The major event of the year in Hilo is the Merrie Monarch Festival, which brings together Hawaii's finest hula dancers for a weekend of dance and celebration of traditional Hawaiian culture.

Formerly a key shipping port for the state's sugarcane industry, Hilo today provides a glimpse of what life on the neighbor islands used to be like. The waters outside Hilo Bay still provide a good living for fishers, and to get a real sense of this you should make your way to the daily Suisan Fish Auction, where Big Island chefs bid for the freshest catch. Although the downtown area has been redeveloped to some extent in recent years with chic restaurants, theaters, and trendy shops, Hilo is still one of Hawaii's quaint, low-key towns.

On the other side of the island are the recreation and sports capital of Hawaii, Kona, and the Kohala Coast, where visitors find a stretch of sunny, lava-strewn coastline dotted with luxurious resorts: Four Seasons Resort Hualalai, Kona Village Resort, Hilton Waikoloa Village (formerly Hyatt Regency Waikoloa), Mauna Lani Bay Hotel & Bungalows, Orchid at Mauna Lani, Hapuna Beach Prince, and Mauna Kea Beach Hotel.

Annual activities in Kona include the Hawaii International Billfish Tournament, marlin fishing's finest hour; the Ironman Triathlon; and the Kona Coffee Festival. The Kona-Kohala area is also a good base for exploration of Mauna Kea and the observatories on her summit; the Hawi and North Kohala region, an emerging ecotourism destination; and the Captain Cook–Kealakekua area, just south of Kona, where you can swim and dive in protected Kealakekua Bay; and for touring the working coffee farms (and tasting their product) also just south of Kona.

If you're making the Kona-Kohala side of the island your base, reserve time to see the Hilo side—and vice versa.

The other option is to stay in a bed-and-breakfast in Kamuela or on the Hamakua Coast. It gets a little colder and rainier in these regions, but the tradeoff is greenery—lush, tropical greenery. Waimea, on the northwestern slope of Mauna Kea, is the island's center of *paniolo* (cowboy) activity. Parker Ranch, one of the largest private working cattle ranches in the United States, encompasses much of the area, offering a visitors center for guests to see what life has been like for the cowboys here for the past 150 years.

The Hamakua Coast was once a thriving sugar-producing region, but with sugarcane in decline in Hawaii for the past decade or more, the towns along this beautiful coast are looking at ways to retool themselves for a new economy. Visit now, before too much change takes place.

Either of these areas will also make a great base for activities and exploration of Mauna Kea, the lush Waipio Valley, and environs.

Nature/Adventure Activities
Appropriately, the Big Island offers a lot of big options for adventure travel, and too many places to visit. Hikers will find more trails and treks than they have time for. Snorkelers and divers may never want to come up for air. And adventurers with a thirst for sailing and fishing won't be disappointed.

Flora and Fauna
The Big Island is unique in that visitors will find just about every climatic zone on the planet here, often very close together. Scientists

Current Events, Hawaii's Big Island

Hawaiian sailing canoe

have thus far identified close to 150 climatic zones around the world, and most occur somewhere on Hawaii. This gives the island a rare setting for flora and fauna of many species.

For example, in the misty elevations of Hawaii Volcanoes National Park, bird-watchers revel in the variety of species that commonly can be spotted at areas such as Kipuka Puaulu, also called Bird Park. Here, across Highway 11 from the main visitor sites, birders are treated to several endemic species, such as *oma'o, elepaio* (monarch flycatcher), and *'apapane* (crimson honeycreeper). The lovely red and brown *i'iwi* bird (honeycreeper) is also occasionally spotted here, although it prefers a higher elevation.

A little farther up the slope of Mauna Loa, approximately 10 miles, you will be at the 6,600-foot level. In this climatic zone you are likely to encounter the red-billed leiothrix, as well as a contingent of Kalij pheasants. At this elevation, if you're lucky, you may also encounter the *pueo* (short-eared) owl or the *i'o* (Hawaiian hawk). Both of these birds tend to fly over open areas where they can hunt rodents.

Down at the coast, where the lava flow has created new land over the years, many seabird species are common. And inside some of the hardened lava tubes at Hawaii Volcanoes National Park, less-visible species of animals thrive, such as happy face spiders, centipedes, and millipedes.

It is this type of diversity—in addition to the obvious geologic phenomena—that makes Hawaii Volcanoes National Park such a treasure.

On the slopes of Mauna Kea are climatic zones similar to those found on Mauna Loa. But since Mauna Kea's summit is higher, and its flanks do not extend to the ocean, several distinctions also occur. At the highest elevations of Mauna Kea, a particular species of silversword is found, similar to the one found on Maui's Haleakala. Also up here is the endangered *palila* (a yellow and gray honeycreeper), which eats seedpods of the *mamane* tree, found only on the subalpine slopes of Mauna Kea.

Along the Kohala Coast, rare anchialine pools occur, brackish water that is home to some tiny red shrimp and red coralline algae. These pools are generally found near the ocean, but have also been discovered up to two miles inland. On the Kohala Coast these ponds and their tiny inhabitants have been preserved by developers (although sometimes not without a fight), and several hotels now offer educational tours of these rare natural occurrences.

History, Culture, and Customs

Several human events have shaped the history of the Big Island over the centuries, but perhaps none more than the birth of Kamehameha—who would become Hawaii's unifying king—in the North Kohala area around 1758, and the death of Captain Cook at Kealakekua Bay some 21 years later, in 1779.

Cook sailed his ship, the *Resolution*, into the protected waters of Kealakekua Bay and was greeted as a returning god, for it is believed the Hawaiians thought he was their god Lono. His visit showed the Hawaiians many things for the first time, such as worked metal, fittings for sailing ships, and ultimately, firearms. This last piece of show-and-tell cost him his life, for it revealed him as a threat rather than a god to the Hawaiians, and in a skirmish over a ship's rudder, Cook, several of his men, and many Hawaiians died. Today, a monument at Kealakekua Bay marks the spot of his demise.

Despite its tragic ending, Cook's visit to the islands did make an indelible impression on the young warrior Kamehameha, who apparently was savvy enough to see the opportunity presented by European firearms and tools. Throughout his life, Kamehameha surrounded himself with European friends and advisors, and their influence cannot be minimized in his efforts to establish a thriving kingdom in the islands. By 1791, Kamehameha had united the Big Island; by 1810 he ruled all the islands except Kauai and Niihau.

One area of great European influence was the economy. For example, Captain George Vancouver landed the first cattle and sheep on the Big Island in 1793 and presented them to Kamehameha. Vancouver returned again the following year with more cattle and persuaded the king to prevent the killing of the animals until they could multiply. Multiply they did, until great herds of wild cattle roamed the island, destroying crops and native forests as they went.

In 1803 the first horses—wild mustangs of Moorish and Arabian descent—arrived on Hawaii to help in herding and controlling the cattle. To encourage his people, Kamehameha learned to ride. Within decades, an entire culture and tradition of Hawaiian cowboys was thriving, and still thrives to this day. So, too, does the cattle industry, as evidenced by the approximately 300 beef cattle farms in operation on the Big Island.

Interestingly, Hawaii's cowboys—called *paniolos*—were taught their craft by vaqueros from Spanish California who arrived on the Big Island in 1832 at the request of Kamehameha III. Among other things, the vaqueros taught the Hawaiians the craft of making saddles, lariats, and bell spurs.

In the lower foothills of Mauna Loa, near Kona, the first coffee trees were planted in 1828. Nowadays, coffee is grown on some 600 farms in the Kona district and is a mainstay of the island's economy.

Sugarcane, too, was first grown commercially around this time, in

1835. The wetter regions of the Hamakua Coast proved ideal for sugar-cane, and it, too, became one of the state's main cash crops for more than 150 years.

Macadamias, those addictively wonderful little nuts, are a relative newcomer, having been first planted commercially in 1921. With the Big Island producing roughly 96 percent of the state's total output of macadamias, these nuts are an important part of the Big Island's economy, and an even more important ingredient in many recipes. What, without macadamias, would chefs use to crust the *ahi*?

Although Pacific storms seem to miss the Big Island, tsunamis have devastated Hilo more than once, in 1946 and 1960. Still, the people of Hilo—like residents island wide—love the Big Island for its diversity of climate, uniqueness of physical characteristics, and opportunities for a healthy lifestyle. It is thought of by all residents of the Aloha State as an island with great "mana."

The Big Island is the newest and by far the largest of the Hawaiian islands, combining beauty, spirituality, and natural phenomena. Kilauea—one of five volcanoes that make up the landscape of the island—has been erupting for close to two decades now, issuing molten lava in fiery rivers toward the ocean, adding new land every day.

And although Kilauea's current and relatively constant eruptions have been the focus of volcano enthusiasts since Hawaii was first inhabited, all of the Big Island's volcanoes have blown their tops at some point. What the Hawaiians believe is that Madame Pele, the fire goddess, is speaking with each eruption, giving her people messages.

One legend of Pele attributes an eruption of Hualalai to her fury. In 1790, the story goes, an enemy of King Kamehameha was advancing with his troops. Pele was angered that such a challenge would be made against the popular and prophetic king, so she exploded a vent on Hualalai, shooting poisonous gases and lava down on the 80 rival warriors. Within a year all peoples of the Big Island were united under Kamehameha.

Perhaps more than anything else, it is the raw force of the island's volcanoes that contributes to the awestruck reaction people have when they first arrive here. Indeed, as you land at Kona's airport, lava stretches as far as the eye can see. A common reaction is, "Where are we—the moon?" And the lava does look lunarlike.

Of the island's five volcanoes, three are classified as active: Kilauea, Mauna Loa, and Hualalai. Kilauea and Mauna Loa are most active. In addition to Kilauea's current eruption (since 1983), Mauna Loa has erupted 33 times since 1843; the most recent was in 1984. Hualalai has had six vents erupt since 1700, with the Kona airport being built right on top of one of the larger flows; the most recent was in 1801.

Mauna Kea is classified as dormant, with its most recent eruption estimated to have taken place 4,000 to 6,000 years ago. And Kohala, the oldest volcano on the Big Island, is considered extinct; its most recent eruption is estimated to have occurred 120,000 years ago.

Anything in the lava's path is destroyed, given back to Madame Pele. Just ask the former residents of Kalapana, whose town was burned to the ground by the onslaught of one of Kilauea's flows in 1990.

But there is also renewal in this powerful process. Witness the spate of resort development along the Kohala Coast, all built upon ancient lava flows. And witness Loihi, the newest land on the planet, now being formed under the ocean's surface near the coast of the Big Island. Or the petroglyph fields near Waikoloa and Mauna Lani, where the old Hawaiians went to create rock carvings and offer prayers.

With all of this raw power, this creation and destruction taking place right before their eyes, is it any wonder that Hawaiians consider the Big Island such a spiritual place?

Festivals and Tournaments

The Big Island hosts a number of major festivals and competitions throughout the year. The first is **Merrie Monarch Festival**, named in honor of King David Kalakaua. This dance festival has been held annually since 1964, occurring in Hilo around Easter weekend. Hula *halau* (troupes) statewide practice the entire year to compete in this festival. It is one of the most exciting and colorful cultural events held in Hawaii. Categories of hula include traditional and modern men's and women's dance, although everybody always has a soft spot for the *keiki* (children) performers. Recent years have also seen dancers from other parts of the United States coming over for the competition as well. If Hawaiian culture and tradition interest you, this is one event you should not miss. For further information and dates, call 808/935-9168.

The prestigious fishing event **Hawaiian International Billfish Tournament** has been held since 1959. Teams from Hawaii, the U.S. Mainland, Australia, Japan, and elsewhere come to see who can land the biggest game fish over a five-day period. Normally staged in August, this tournament has been called "the Olympics of big-game fishing," and the waters off Kona are where it's held. Blue and black marlin, sailfish, and others are prized. It's not much of a spectator sport when the boats are at sea, but Honokohau Harbor is abuzz with activity each morning as the boats prepare to shove off for the day, and again in the afternoon when they return to port with their catches. For further information and dates, call 808/329-6155.

The **Aloha Festivals** take place each September, with events held on all islands. One of the best places to take in the festivities is the *paniolo* town of Waimea, on the slopes of Mauna Kea. Events here include a *pa'u* parade, where horses and riders are both decked out in colorful leis; a falsetto singing competition (a tradition in Hawaii); and lots of food, arts, and crafts. Plus, you'll be hard-pressed to find a friendlier, more scenic town than "the Rainbow City," Waimea. For further information and dates, call 808/885-8086.

A Big Island tradition since 1980, the **Ironman Triathlon** has grown in stature each year, it seems. Nowadays the best athletes in the world come to Kona each October to compete in this grueling test of fortitude and stamina. Nearly 1,500 participants have entered in recent years. Competition starts with a 2.4-mile ocean swim at Kailua Pier, continues with a 112-mile bicycle course that leads along a steaming-hot stretch of highway bordered by lava to Hawi on the far northern coast and back to Kona, and concludes with an agonizing 26.2-mile run. Some 20,000 people show up to cheer, sympathize with, and hand water to the participants. For further information and dates, call 808/329-0063.

Held the first week of November—the middle of coffee harvest season—the **Kona Coffee Festival** is billed as Hawaii's oldest food festival.

This is a fun event where farmers enter their coffee beans for judging in a variety of categories, including fragrance, taste, and body. (What? Not buzz?) You too can test the varieties, talk to the farmers, and take home some excellent joe. Other events include lei-making, art exhibits, and mill tours. For further information and dates, call 808/326-7820.

Visitor Information

There are many ways to get the best current information about the Big Island. The **Hawaii Visitors & Convention Bureau** is always a good source. They provide brochures, maps, and practical tips for travel to all the islands. Contact them before you visit, or drop by when you're on Oahu: 2270 Kalakaua Ave., Suite 801, Honolulu, HI 96815, in the heart of Waikiki; 808/923-1811 or 800/GO-HAWAII; www.gohawaii.com.

A similar service specifically geared to the Big Island is provided by the **Big Island Visitors Bureau**. They are happy to provide information; call 808/961-5797, fax 808/961-2126, or write 250 Keawe St., Hilo, HI 96720. Their Kona office is at 75-5719 W. Alii Dr., Kailua-Kona, HI 96740.

For information specifically on Hawaii Volcanoes National Park before you arrive, contact **National Park Service**, Prince Kuhio Federal Bldg., 300 Ala Moana Blvd., Rm. 6305, Honolulu, HI 96813; 808/541-2693.

Other useful Web sites include the **Hawaii Ecotourism Association**'s locations, www.planet-hawaii.com/hea/ and www.alternative-hawaii.com. A fantastic and informative site for those interested in learning more about Hawaii's volcanoes is the **United States Geological Survey**'s www.hvo.wr.usgs.gov/volcanoes.

Getting There

You can fly into either Kona or Hilo on regularly scheduled and frequent jet flights from Honolulu. You can now also fly directly into the Kona airport from the west coast of the Mainland on Hawaiian Airlines or United Airlines. All major car-rental companies are located at both airports.

Clearly, with a 300-mile coastline and such distinct sites to visit, you'll want to spend at least four or five days on the Big Island. Getting around is best done with a rental car or van, since reliable public transportation does not exist and taxis become expensive.

HAWAII VOLCANOES NATIONAL PARK

Hawaii Volcanoes National Park is considered home of Madame Pele, the goddess of fire in Hawaiian creation mythology. She is said to live in Halemaʻumaʻu Crater, within Kilauea Caldera. Today, Pele is still respected. Visitors will occasionally encounter a bottle of gin wrapped in ti leaves, left upon a lava formation near Halemaʻumaʻu. Do not touch! It's an offering to the fire goddess.

General information about Hawaii Volcanoes National Park, camping information, eruption updates, and special services can be obtained by calling park headquarters at 808/985-6000. Dining, lodging, and cabin reservations information is available at 808/967-7321.

You may also contact the National Park Service, Prince Kuhio Federal Bldg., 300 Ala Moana Blvd., Rm. 6305, Honolulu, HI 96813; 808/541-2693. A Web site that's particularly interesting to those wishing to learn more about Hawaii's volcanoes is the U. S. Geological Survey's www.hvo.wr.usgs.gov/volcanoes.

Orientation/Lay of the Land

The number-one visitor attraction in the State of Hawaii, Hawaii Volcanoes National Park encompasses two of the most active volcanoes in the world, Kilauea and Mauna Loa. The park is roughly 377 square miles, and extends from the summit of Mauna Loa—13,677 feet above sea level—down to the Pacific, where Kilauea has been pushing lava from a vent called Puʻu Oʻo into the ocean since 1983, creating the newest land on earth.

Getting here is easy. The best way to do it, if you're making Hawaii Volcanoes National Park a primary part of your visit to the Big Island, is to fly into Hilo, rent a vehicle, and drive the 30 miles up Highway 11. The other option, if you're staying on the Kona-Kohala side of the island, is to

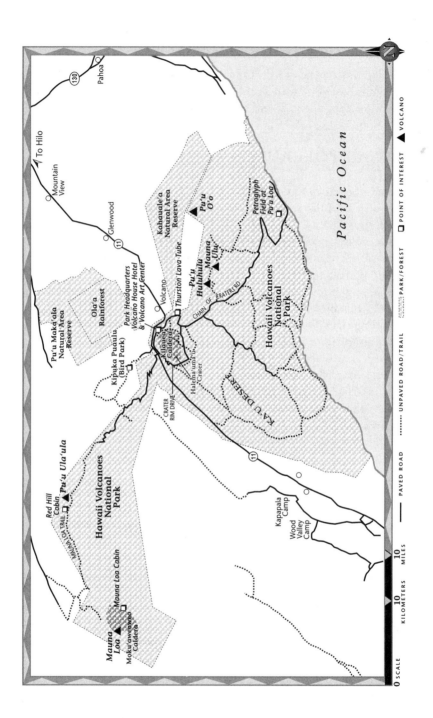

make the drive from there. It's approximately 96 miles from Kona, but the drive takes several hours because of the winding, scenic road that leads through some of the most isolated towns on the Big Island.

The third option, and one that is very popular if time is limited, is to take a helicopter tour over the park. You'll see areas that you cannot access on foot, and get a bird's-eye view of historic and current lava flows. Helicopter companies are found in Kona, in Hilo, and on the Kohala Coast. Expect to pay $75 to $100 per person for these aerial tours.

There are some 150 miles of trails leading through the park, many of which can be accessed with a short walk from a parking area. There are also two visitor centers where you can read about the park and its history, flora, and fauna. And there are two scenic drives. Additionally, more-strenuous hikes are possible on Mauna Loa. If this is your aim, be prepared with proper gear and warm clothing—it gets cold at the upper elevations, even in midsummer.

Remember, it's imperative to make reservations in advance for accommodations in Volcano Village, as there are no major hotels in the area, and the bed-and-breakfasts can fill up quickly, particularly on holidays.

Flora and Fauna

The flora and fauna of the park are quite diverse, owing to the many different climatic zones. Bird-watchers enjoy a wide variety of species commonly spotted at areas such as Kipuka Puaulu, or Bird Park. Here, across Highway 11 from the main visitor sites, birders are treated to several endemic species, such as *oma'o, elepaio* (monarch flycatcher), *amakihi,* and *'apapane* (crimson honeycreeper). The lovely *i'iwi* (honeycreeper) is also occasionally spotted here.

Ascend the slope of Mauna Loa for approximately 10 miles, and you'll be at the 6,600-foot level. In this climatic zone, keep an eye out for the red-billed leiothrix, as well as pretty Kalij pheasants. If you're lucky, you may also encounter *pueo* (short-eared) owls or *i'o* (Hawaiian hawks) as they fly over open areas, hunting their next rodent meal.

Take a look down at the coast. This is where the lava flow has

HAWAII

created new land over the years, and many seabird species—including the pelagic petrel and the shearwater—have decided to call this area home. It's a haven for three of the five remaining endangered hawksbill turtles; their nesting sites are found on this park's beaches. Inside some of the hardened lava tubes at the park, less-visible species of animals thrive, such as happy face spiders, centipedes, and millipedes. Hawaii's state bird, the nene goose, is also present here. Although its numbers have increased in recent years due to protection and propagation programs, they are still low enough for the nene to be considered endangered.

As for the park's flora, again there is great diversity. The most common tree in the park is the ohia lehua—found from sea level to Mauna Loa's higher slopes—which produces a bright red flower. The Ola'a Rainforest, on the windward side of Kilauea, garners more than 100 inches of rain per year. The ohia lehua tree forms the canopy for much of the rain forest here, and the *hapu'u*—tree fern—grows in the fertile earth below.

Hawaiian woodworkers formerly found plentiful koa-tree forests in the park. But the forests have become increasingly spare, and many woodworkers—traditional craftspeople prized in the islands—now take their raw materials only from fallen trees. Luckily, some of Hawaii's best koa forests still exist inside Hawaii Volcanoes National Park.

Other common tree species found inside the park's boundaries include the ubiquitous coconut palm and *mamane* trees; common shrubs include the *ohelo* and *pukiawe*. The *ohelo* was used in many traditional Hawaiian ways, including construction of homes and the making of weapons. Its bright red fruit was crushed and used as a dye.

History, Culture, and Customs
The island of Hawaii sits almost in the middle of the Pacific plate, a huge, jagged piece of the earth's crust that is moving some four inches per year to the northwest. Under the southwest portion of the island is what scientists call a "stationary hot spot," where molten lava builds and then issues from the planet's interior. As the Pacific plate moves over the hot spot, lava builds and islands are created. Consider for a moment

that Midway Island, some 1,300 miles to the northwest and once the size of the Big Island, was created in this manner in this particular spot. Today, maybe 35 million years later, Midway is just an atoll in a distant sea. It is this amazing geologic process that we learn about and witness in action when visiting Hawaii Volcanoes National Park.

The first non-Hawaiians to visit Kilauea were a group of New England missionaries led by the Reverend William Ellis, in 1823. Two decades later another expedition visited, led by Commander Charles Wilkes. Wilkes and his crew spent several weeks at the summit of Mauna Loa, making scientific observations, before retreating to Kilauea Caldera.

The first Volcano House was built in 1846 to serve the needs of the growing number of travelers to the area. One of these travelers was none other than Mark Twain, who toured in 1866, and proclaimed, "Here was room for the imagination to work!"

Over the years, Volcano House has been expanded and remodeled many times. Today it serves as the primary accommodations within the park, and is also popular as a place to warm the hands in front of the huge fireplace after a day of exploring in the often cold and foggy park.

Hawaii Volcanoes National Park was established in 1916, largely due to the lobbying efforts of Lorrin Thurston, then publisher of the *Honolulu Pacific Commercial Advertiser* newspaper. In 1906 he began a campaign to make the area public, and in 1912 was joined in his efforts by Thomas Jaggar, who had come to Hawaii to establish the Hawaii Volcano Observatory. On August 1, 1916, President Woodrow Wilson granted their pleas, making the area a national park.

The first areas protected under national park status were the summits of Kilauea and Mauna Loa on the Big Island, and the summit of Haleakala on Maui. In time, Kilauea Caldera, the Ka'u Desert, the Ola'a Rainforest and more of Mauna Loa's slopes were added.

In 1961 Haleakala became a separate national park. But due to the active status of Kilauea and Mauna Loa, more attention is centered upon them as volcanoes. In 1980 the United Nations Educational, Scientific, and Cultural Organization (UNESCO) named Hawaii Volcanoes National Park an International Biosphere Reserve for the stark and amazing diversity of its ecologic zones, and in 1982 UNESCO named the park a World Heritage Site.

NATURE AND ADVENTURE SIGHTS IN HAWAII VOLCANOES NATIONAL PARK

Kilauea Visitors Center, Park Headquarters, and Volcano House Complex

There are so many ways to visit Hawaii Volcanoes National Park that you probably won't have time to take advantage of them all. You can hike easily or strenuously, camp out or find a cute bed-and-breakfast, helicopter over, or remain still and bird-watch for hours on end.

Any visit should start at the **Kilauea Visitors Center and Park Headquarters**. Here you'll learn about the park, its history, and what you will be looking at when you get inside. A half-hour movie on volcanic eruptions plays every hour, and there are displays on the geologic processes and the flora and fauna of the park. A shop inside the Visitors Center sells videos, maps, and books about Kilauea and Hawaii. Park Headquarters is also where you'll need to get your permit for overnight camping if this is on your agenda.

A short walk away, but part of the same complex, is **Volcano House Hotel and Restaurant** and the **Volcano Art Center**, which is getting a new home in Volcano Village. Volcano House has been through several owners and incarnations since it was first established at its present location on the lip of Kilauea Caldera in 1846. The current hotel was built in 1941, with additions made in 1953. Extensive renovation and restoration were done in 1989.

One of the most fascinating details of the hotel is the lava stone fireplace, which employees swear has been burning continuously for more than 60 years. Here, in front of the fire, Mark Twain warmed his hands in 1866, as did Franklin D. Roosevelt in 1934. You'll want to, too; this 4,000-foot-elevation area of the park can get damp and cold, particularly during winter.

All dining facilities at Volcano House overlook the caldera, which can be an awesome sight. Often, plumes of steam vent through the crusted lava. And it's not unusual in the evening to see fog settle in. Save your best spooky stories for nighttime around here!

Details: *The Kilauea Visitors Center, Park Headquarters, and Volcano House are located just inside the park's gate off Highway 11, roughly a 30-*

VOLCANO ART CENTER

There are special places on earth where the life force, spiritual presence, and physical reality come together to create a powerful attraction for artists. For over a thousand years, Kilauea Volcano has been such a place. Since 1974, the Volcano Art Center (VAC) has been a catalyst for the creativity of artists, writers, and musicians; and has served as a place where science, nature, and art meet in a truly dynamic environment.

To further this creative force, VAC is developing a new arts-and-education campus on a 7.4-acre site named Niaulani. The location, between Volcano Village and the boundary of Hawaii Volcanoes National Park, is stunning. Dominated by a native rain forest of ohia, olapa, and koa, the new facilities will be low key, nestled into the forest.

Nature trails will thread through the forest, offering visitors and artists quiet places to meditate and gain inspiration. Downed trees discovered on-site, as well as a group of invasive non-native trees, are being milled for reuse in building construction. Buildings will incorporate energy-efficient technology, as well as vernacular design elements typical of historic homes in the area.

A fully equipped hot-glass studio, areas for woodcarving and metal work, studios for fiber arts and painting, classrooms for Hawaiian language and natural sciences study and clean arts, a small lecture/performance hall, housing for visiting artists, plus VAC offices are all on the drawing boards.

Construction of the main administration, education, and studio art buildings is expected to be complete by the year 2000. Fund-raising opportunities include direct donations, planned gifts, and naming opportunities.

To learn more about how you can be a part of this place, contact Marilyn Nicholson, Executive Director, VAC, P.O. Box 104, Hawaii Volcanoes National Park, HI 96718; phone 808/967-8222; fax 808/967-8512; e-mail: vacmln@gte.net.

minute drive from Hilo. The park is open 24 hours a day, 365 days per year. You must purchase an entrance permit, which is valid for seven days. Entrance fee is $10 per vehicle and $5 per hiker, bicyclist, or motorcycle. (Golden Eagle Passports are honored here.) For general information, call 808/985-6000.

It's a good idea to make reservations if you'd like to stay at Volcano House or the camper cabins at Namakani Paio, particularly in summer months. Call 808/967-7321 for information and reservations. There is no charge for overnight camping permits, obtained at Park Headquarters.

Crater Rim

An 11-mile loop trail, this moderately strenuous hike takes you on a journey around the rim of Kilauea Caldera. Along the way you pass through desert and rain forest, and see steam vents, sulfur banks, and lots of lava from various flows. Several other trails intersect the Crater Rim loop, including the Halema'uma'u Trail, Kilauea Iki, and Byron Ledge Trail. But each of these should be undertaken separately. The Crater Rim is actually a fairly easy trail to walk, with much of it paved. What becomes moderately strenuous about it is the length.

Details: The trail starts at Park Headquarters. Allow an entire day to complete this hike.

Crater Rim and Chain of Craters Drives

There are two main driving trips you can take inside the park. One is an 11-mile jaunt around **Crater Rim Drive** that begins and ends at Kilauea Visitors Center and Park Headquarters. From Crater Rim Drive you will have access to many of the park's most popular destinations, such as the **Thomas A. Jaggar Museum**, where visitors can see ongoing video presentations of volcanic eruptions, seismic equipment relating to the adjacent Hawaiian Volcano Observatory (not open to the public), and wonderful overlooks into Kilauea Caldera.

Other easy stops along Crater Rim Drive include **Halema'uma'u Crater Overlook**, a 10-minute walk into a historic lava flow from a paved parking area; and Thurston Lava Tube, a 20-minute walk through a fern forest and lava tube from a paved parking area.

The second driving excursion is the 46-mile round trip down **Chain of Craters Road**, from the 4,000-foot level to sea level in a quick 20 miles. The road dead-ends where a recent lava flow overran the pavement. This trip can take most of a day if you adopt a leisurely pace and take in the sights.

Several side trips and short hikes are found along Chain of Craters Road. One of the most fascinating stops is the **petroglyph field at Pu'u Loa**. This collection of some 15,000 traditional Hawaiian rock carvings—roughly a one-mile walk from the highway—has been occasionally threatened by lava flows, so it may or may not still be there when you arrive.

Hiking from the end of Chain of Craters Road will give you the closest vantage point on land to the current lava flow from Pu'u O'o vent. The best time to view the lava is at night, when the red glow against the dark sky is brightest. But use your head and be careful. Even though rangers try to keep you at a safe distance, they are not always there. The lava fields can be very dangerous, and several overly enthusiastic visitors have lost their lives down here.

Chain of Craters Road formerly continued along the coast and on into Hilo, but lava from the ongoing eruption of Pu'u O'o—which destroyed the village of Kalapana, a park visitor center, and the famous Black Sand Beach—also destroyed the highway. Seeing it provides a reminder of exactly how powerful the forces of nature can be.

Details: Thomas A. Jaggar Museum is open 8:30 a.m.–5 p.m. daily. Call 808/985-6049 for information. Get eruption updates by asking at Park Headquarters, or by calling 808/985-6000.

Kilauea Iki

This challenging four-mile loop takes roughly two to four hours. The trail descends 400 feet through rain forest, across the Kilauea crater rim floor, past a cinder cone. Hikers return via the rim of the crater. Take drinking water and expect some steep and rocky terrain.

Details: The trailhead is off Crater Rim Drive, on the eastern side of the park. It's across from Thurston Lava Tube, and is well marked. Contact Park Headquarters for trail conditions.

Kipuka Puaulu

Also called Bird Park, this easy one-mile loop hike takes you on a trail through a lushly forested area of the park where bird-watching is at its best. Since this area is not inside the gates of the main area of Hawaii Volcanoes National Park, it is less visited, which is just fine with bird-lovers—and with the birds! Also lots of rare plants and shrubs here. Although you can complete the hike in an hour, you'll probably want to linger—allow more time.

Details: *Kipuka Puaulu is off Mauna Loa Road. Coming from Volcano Village or the main entrance to the park, Mauna Loa Road is a right-hand turn off Highway 11. The trailhead is a short drive from there, and clearly marked.*

Mauna Loa

Getting to the summit of Mauna Loa and back is a strenuous, four-day hike, and should be undertaken only with great care and precaution. Even so, there is no guarantee that you will not encounter difficulty. If you are fully informed and prepared, it can be a magnificent journey.

Unlike Mauna Kea, Mauna Loa has no road leading to the summit, so hiking up is the only choice. The trailhead begins at the end of Mauna Loa Road, at an elevation of 6,662 feet. The trail follows Mauna Loa's Northeast Rift Zone and rises through native forests, where you'll see koa trees as well as an abundance of ohia and *mamane* trees, until you get above the tree line at roughly 8,500 feet. In addition to the wonderful trees, part of the thrill of this leg of the journey is the chance to see some of Hawaii's endangered birds such as the *amakihi*, a native honeycreeper that feeds on the yellow flowers of the *mamane.*

Most backpackers will split the journey into two parts, staying overnight in a cabin at the 10,035-foot level, an area called **Puʻu Ulaʻula**, or Red Hill. From the trailhead, this part of the hike should take roughly four to five hours and will realize a 3,400-foot gain in elevation. At Red Hill you'll find **Red Hill Cabin**, which is outfitted with eight bunks (available on a first-come, first-served basis), pit toilets, and a water-catchment tank.

The second part of the trek is steeper and takes considerably

VIEWING THE LAVA FLOW

Helicopter tours may be the best way to see the lava flow, and there are plenty of companies from which to choose. You can climb onboard at the airports in Hilo or Kona, or at a heliport near Waikoloa on the Kohala Coast. The whirlybirds then make their way to Kilauea and hover above some of the most fascinating sights in the park, including several passes over red-hot lava if it's flowing. It can be a little disconcerting when you feel the chopper's floorboards getting hot, but it is as safe as any helicopter tour. The aerial bird's-eye view is also best for photography.

The other magnificent view of the lava flow is by sea. American Hawaii Cruises, as part of its week-long island tour, shoves off from Hilo in the late afternoon. As the good ship Independence *rounds the easternmost tip of the Big Island and starts its overnight chug to Kona, passengers are treated to a marvelous sight. If the volcano is active, there, running down the side of the mountain and into the Pacific, is a long, bright red ribbon of lava. From your vantage point several miles out to sea, this otherworldly sight glows against the night sky. Awestruck passengers stand on deck and watch for close to an hour until the volcano has passed from view; only then can many of them speak.*

longer to go a shorter distance. Be prepared to ascend an additional 3,200 feet to reach the south rim of **Moku'aweoweo Caldera**, which is at the 13,250-foot level. The hike from Red Hill to the crater rim should take eight to 12 hours. There is also a sleeping shelter here, the **Mauna Loa Cabin**, with 12 bunks, a water-catchment tank, and pit toilets.

Mauna Loa Cabin is the starting point for a half-day hike around the caldera to the true summit of **Mauna Loa** at 13,677 feet. Once there, you are rewarded with stunning vistas, rare flora and fauna, and almost total solitude. It may not be what you see on posters depicting

Hawaii, but the panorama across the Big Island from Mauna Loa's summit is one of the most magnificent vistas you'll ever see.

The best time of year to undertake this hike is summer, but even then be aware that temperatures drop below freezing at night. It does snow toward the summit during winter months, and it can get foggy any time of year. The trail is well marked with stone cairns, called *ahu*. Rangers advise that you remain aware of the *ahu*, particularly in foggy conditions, as it is easy to become lost on the mountain.

Rangers also remind you that Mauna Loa is an active volcano, and that eruptions are always possible. Stay upslope from flows and upwind from volcanic gasses. Altitude sickness and dizziness are common at this elevation.

Preparations for this unusual Hawaiian adventure include warm clothing, sunscreen, sunglasses, head covering, enough water and food, and an emergency plan. Many people take cellular phones with them for emergencies these days, but always let someone know that you're going.

Details: The trailhead is off Mauna Loa Road. A backcountry permit is required, and can be obtained from Park Headquarters at no cost. You are required to hike out everything you hiked in—do not bury your trash. Stays are limited to three nights per site. Treat all catchment water before drinking.

Pu'u Huluhulu

A moderate three-mile hike over 1973 and 1974 lava flows, this trail takes you to the top of a cinder cone. There is not a lot of elevation change on this round-trip hike until you get to the base of the cinder cone, and from there it's only 150 feet up. From the top of the *pu'u* (cinder cone) some good views of Kilauea's Pu'u O'o—the vent that has been erupting since 1983—await you.

Details: The trailhead is off Chain of Craters Road.

Thurston Lava Tube

This is a quick and easy hike of less than .5 mile, taking only 20 minutes to complete. It leads into a lush fern forest and through a massive lava tube. Named after one of the park's greatest advocates, Lorrin

Thurston, the lava tube requires a stair-climb to enter and exit. It is one of the most popular—and busiest—trails in the park, but one that's thoroughly enjoyable for all family members.
Details: *The trailhead is off Crater Rim Drive, clearly marked.*

GUIDES AND OUTFITTERS

Aerial views of the Big Island are sometimes the best ways to see what's happening in the volcanoes. One of the best and safest helicopter tour companies around is **Blue Hawaiian Helicopters**, Hilo International Airport, Hilo; from the U.S. Mainland call 800/745-BLUE; from Hawaii call 808/961-5600. Blue Hawaiian flies out of both Hilo International Airport and the Waikoloa heliport. From Waikoloa the tour lasts two hours and includes Mauna Loa's lower slopes, the active lava flow from Kilauea, and a brief landing in Hilo. It then proceeds down the Hamakua Coast and into the Waipio Valley, where passengers are treated to close-up views of lush greenery and towering waterfalls. The tour from Hilo lasts 50 minutes and flies over Kilauea only, including the active lava flow. Cost for the two-hour tour from Waikoloa is $305/person; for the 50-minute tour from Hilo, $140/person.

American Hawaii Cruises, 2100 N. Nimitz Hwy., Honolulu, 800/765-7000 or 808/847-3172, offers a classic 1950s cruise ship that makes its way around the Hawaiian islands weekly, so you can see Hawaii by sea. Sea cruises reveal a Hawaii seldom seen even by residents—the sea cliffs of Molokai, Kauai's Na Pali Coast, the Big Island's erupting volcano, and whales, seabirds, and spinner dolphins. American Hawaii Cruises' SS *Independence*, a vintage 682-foot steamship, sails every Saturday on weekly interisland cruises from Honolulu's Aloha Tower. Call for costs.

On land, there's **Hawaii Forest & Trail**, Box 2975, Kailua-Kona, HI 96745, 800/464-1933 or 808/322-8881. This company, well respected for its leadership in the ecotours area, is operated by Rob and Cindy Pacheco, who conduct many of the tours personally. The volcano tours take you to the active flow, on some hiking trails, and to other points of interest. The drive over and back from the Kona side is via the Saddle

Road and along the scenic Hamakua Coast. Cost for the all-day tour is
$130/person, lunch included.

CAMPING

*Camping may be on your list of things to do in Hawaii, but you may not want
to do it at Hawaii Volcanoes National Park. The facilities are limited—and it
gets cold up here! Be prepared. For information call 808/985-6000.*

Namakani Paio is the only camping facility within the park boundaries,
aside from the designated backcountry sites. A drive-in campground,
it's located three miles from the park entrance on Highway 11. There
are eating shelters with picnic tables, wheelchair-accessible rest rooms,
and fireplaces without wood. Collecting firewood is prohibited inside
the park, so bring your own. Same thing with water; it may be unavail-
able, so bring your own. Use of these facilities is free, and on a first-
come, first-served basis. Stays are limited to seven days per year.

There are also some camper cabins at Namakani Paio, operated by
Volcano House. The cabins are unheated, and contain one double bed
and two single bunks. For these you do need a reservation.

LODGING

One of the pleasures of staying in the Volcano area is that the colder
climate has caused many lodges and bed-and-breakfasts to build fireplaces in their rooms and common areas. There may not be any hotels
in the area—with the exception of rustic Volcano House, which I do
not recommend—but you can choose from several great, romantic
bed-and-breakfasts in nearby Volcano Village. Volcano Village is adjacent to the park, and is so small that there are no street addresses. Call
Hawaii's Best Bed & Breakfasts for reservations and information about
the B&Bs they represent.

At **Carson's Volcano Cottage**, P.O. Box 503, Volcano Village, HI
96785, 800/845-LAVA or 808/967-7683, you're bound to find fire-

places, hot tubs, and nicely manicured gardens. A rustic building outfitted with collectibles and antiques, this is a charming selection set amid the rain forest of Volcano Village. Rates start at $85 and range to $165, depending on room.

Another Volcano Village find is **Chalet Kilauea—The Inn at Volcano**, Box 998 Wright Rd., Volcano Village, HI 96785, 800/937-7786 or 808/967-7786. Owners Lisha and Brian Crawford have created six romantic theme suites in this lovingly restored inn. Set amid a fern forest in Volcano Village, guests have their choice of themes: Out of Africa, Owners, Treehouse, Oriental Jade, Continental Lace, or Hapu'u Forest. Each suite has been decorated with treasures from the Crawfords' travels. Marble bathrooms, whirlpool tubs, and gourmet breakfasts add to the charm and luxury. Rates run from $135 to $395 for the larger suite.

In the heart of Volcano Village, **Hi'iaka House** (through Hawaii's Best Bed & Breakfasts), in Volcano Village, 800/262-9912 or 808/885-4550, is a cute, two-bedroom, 1½-bath house artfully appointed with many tasteful touches. The structure was built in 1939 and has been preserved nicely over the years. The owner, who lives nearby, will greet you when you arrive, then you're on your own in this private home. Breakfast provisions provided. Rates are $95 for two persons; $15/each additional person. Two-night minimum stay.

Hydrangea Cottage & Mountain House (through Hawaii's Best Bed & Breakfasts), in Volcano Village, 800/262-9912 or 808/885-4550, is a beautifully landscaped three-acre romantic getaway. It's particularly lovely in summer when the hydrangeas bloom blue and brilliant pink. The elegant cottage has a full kitchen, fireplace, and floor-to-ceiling windows in the bedroom and living room, and opens onto a tropical rain forest. The adjacent three-bedroom house features two master suites, each with living room and fireplace. Rates are $135 for the cottage; $150 for Mountain House suites; $50 for the small additional room (sleeps two). Minimum stay is two nights in all accommodations.

Lorna and Albert Jeyte run **Kilauea Lodge**, P.O. Box 116, Volcano, HI 96785, 808/967-7366, one of the best places to stay and dine in Volcano Village. This elegantly restored wood and lava-stone lodge, built in 1938, is a great home base while exploring Hawaii Volcanoes National Park. Set amid tall ferns and the ubiquitous mist that makes Volcano Village such a unique environment, the chalet-like lodge features a roaring fireplace, cozy sofas, and excellent European cooking, often done by Albert. The lodge martini will warm your weary soul. Wonderful for a romantic adventure. There are 14 units available, all with private baths, eight with fireplaces (some wood-burning, some gas). Rates start at $110 and go to $145, double occupancy, and include breakfast.

Volcano Rainforest Retreat (through Hawaii's Best Bed & Breakfasts), in Volcano Village, 800/262-9912 or 808/885-4550, is one of the best accommodations choices you can make up here. Built in a Japanese monastery style, this private, comfortable cottage is perfect for artists and lovers. A Japanese *furo* bath in a gazebo surrounded by ferns is part of the rental. A full kitchen, living area with wood-burning stove, spacious sleeping loft, and downstairs bath with an oversize tub opening directly to the forest outdoors round out the offering. A new, smaller "Forest Hale" has been added, with queen bed, wood-burning stove, small bath, and tea corner. Rates are $115 for two people for Forest Hale (two-person maximum); $135 for the original cottage; $15/each additional person. Minimum two-night stay.

A two-bedroom fairy-tale cottage, **Volcano Teapot** (through Hawaii's Best Bed & Breakfasts), in Volcano Village, 800/262-9912 or 808/885-4550, is a cute little red structure and a wonderful place to hang your hat for a couple of days in Volcano Village. Built around 1900, it has a cozy wood-burning stove and a full kitchen. One bedroom has a double bed, the other has two singles. Rates are $105 for two people; $15/each additional person. Minimum two-night stay.

FOOD

For all the wonderful bed-and-breakfasts that are in Volcano Village, there are surprisingly few restaurants. **Kilauea Lodge**, P.O. Box 116, Volcano, HI 96785, 808/967-7366, is open for breakfast and dinner daily. With excellent European-style cuisine, often prepared by owner Albert Jeyte, the award-winning dining room here is a culinary adventure. A house specialty is *hasenpfeffer* (braised rabbit in a hearty hunter's wine sauce), but there is something for every taste. Although the menu changes daily, several favorites seem to crop up frequently, including chicken Albert, a boneless breast of chicken folded around mushrooms, cheddar cheese, and shrimp. There is always a vegetarian dish on the menu, as well as the fresh fish of the day in a choice of preparations. If you're in the mood for a steak, they serve delicious beef from Parker Ranch, on the other side of the island. Reservations recommended.

If you're going crazy for espresso, **Steam Vent Cafe**, Huanani Road, Volcano Village, 808/985-8744, is the place. Espressos, cappuccinos, lattes, bagels, and muffins... you'll feel right at home. You'll also find healthy sandwiches and salads on the lunch menu, and all-day treats such as brownies, cookies, and macadamia-nut pies in the deli case. Open daily for breakfast, lunch, and dinner.

Named after executive chef Surt Thammountha, **Surt's at Volcano Village**, Old Volcano Rd., Volcano Village, 808/967-8511, serves what they call "Asian-European Fusion Cuisine." If you think that's a mouthful, wait 'til you get a fork into their food. Entrées include eggplant chicken, sautéed chili squid with basil, fresh fish of the day in a variety of preparations, and a vegetarian curry. Sensitive to the needs of vegetarian diners, the chef will prepare any dish without meat. Surt's is popular with locals and visitors alike; reservations are recommended for dinner. Open for lunch and dinner daily.

The food may rely more on quantity than quality here, but the setting at **Volcano House**, Hawaii Volcanoes National Park, 808/967-7321, is unbeatable. This historic lodge is built right at the edge of Kilauea Caldera, and the views are often stunning, often eerie, and always something special. The Ka Ohelo dining room offers a buffet-style breakfast and lunch, then becomes the fine-dining option for dinner. Uncle George's Lounge is the other option, serving sandwiches and snacks all day. Best reason to dine here is the view, so make reservations to get here early. Open for breakfast, lunch, and dinner daily.

KAMUELA TO HILO

The area of the Big Island from Kamuela to Hilo encompasses one of the prettiest small towns in America, some of the most beautiful coastline in Hawaii, the world's tallest mountain (if measured from the ocean floor), some wonderful waterfalls, and the Big Island's seat of government.

Good visitor information can be obtained on by contacting the Big Island Visitors Bureau at 808/329-7787 or 808/961-5797. They also have a Web site at www.bigisland.org. Specific information on Hakalau Forest National Wildlife Refuge is available by calling 808/933-6915.

A Web site for those interested in Hawaii's *paniolos* can be found at www.rodeohawaii.com. Two Web sites specific to those interested in hiking and bird-watching adventures on this side of the island are offered, one by Hawaii Forest & Trail, www.hawaii-forest.com; and another by Hawaiian Walkways, www.hawaiianwalkways.com.

Orientation/Lay of the Land

The main route traversing this 54-mile stretch of land is Highway 19. Using Kamuela as your starting point, you travel east through Parker Ranch country, home of Hawaii's cowboys; past Waipio Valley and the small town of Honokaa; along a verdant headland above the Hamakua Coast, which once was planted with sugarcane as far as the eye could see; past Rainbow and Akaka Falls; and on into Hilo.

This section of the Big Island is similar in some ways to Maui's Hana Highway, in that it is remote, beautiful, and as lush as one expects Hawaii to be. In this sense it is a stark contrast to the Kona-Kohala Coast, which is a wonderland of brown and black lava. This area also tends to get more rain, which is why it is so green. If you decide to explore the Hamakua Coast—and you should—take a sweater and a rain jacket.

Kamuela—also known as Waimea—is in the foothills of Mauna Kea's western flank, roughly an hour's travel from the Kona airport. You'll be tempted to call Kamuela "Rainbow City" due to the many and varied rainbows you'll see here practically every day. In Hawaiian there are more

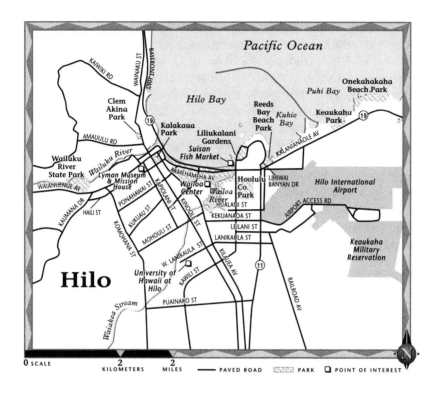

Pacific Ocean

Hilo Bay

Hilo

than 10 words for different rainbows, and you'll see all of them in Kamuela.

This attractive town was and still is the supply center for the 225,000-acre Parker Ranch. But over the past 15 years it has grown considerably, as its relaxing lifestyle and endearing charm have made it one of Hawaii's favorite second-home and get-away-from-it-all communities. Nowadays, visitors will find all the amenities of a modern small town—great restaurants, trendy shopping, coffee bars—combined with an old Hawaii *paniolo* ambiance that makes Kamuela irresistible.

Towering over Kamuela is Mauna Kea, considered the world's tallest mountain if measured from the ocean floor, at 33,476 feet. Even so, at 13,796 feet above sea level it is the tallest peak in Hawaii, 119 feet taller than its neighbor, Mauna Loa. At Mauna Kea's summit are 10 telescopes belonging to several nations, including the largest telescope in the world. Kamuela is the best access point to Mauna Kea.

As you follow Highway 19 east out of Kamuela, you'll drive past the northern boundary of Parker Ranch and emerge at the coastline near the small town of Honokaa. You can either keep going down the Hamakua Coast or take Highway 240 for a side trip to Waipio Valley. If you have any spare time at all, take the side trip, even if it's only for a picnic at the Waipio Valley Lookout. Several informative plaques at the overlook give you a brief description of the dramatic and wide valley you're viewing. If you have more time, hiking and other adventures can be had in Waipio Valley and neighboring Waimanu Valley.

The road from Honokaa to Hilo is about as scenic as any you'll find in Hawaii. It is along this stretch that you'll find Akaka Falls, Rainbow Falls, and several other waterfalls. A side trip on Highway 61 will take you closer to the coast, and is well worth the time.

All this will lead you into Hilo, the Big Island's seat of government. Once a bustling seaport city for the sugarcane industry along the Hamakua Coast, today Hilo is a laid-back community looking for new ways to drive its economy. Hunting for antiques downtown is always fun, and you'll find fine food and a glimpse of what Hawaii looked like back in 1920.

You can start your exploration of this section of Hawaii from either Hilo or Kona. Daily and frequent flights into both airports are offered by Hawaiian Airlines and Aloha Airlines. When you get to the Big Island, rent a car. All major car-rental companies are found at either airport, and driving is the best way to get around.

Flora and Fauna
One of the most significant areas of flora and fauna within this particular section of the Big Island is Mauna Kea. Reaching 13,796 in elevation, Mauna Kea is Hawaii's tallest peak. At lower elevations the mountain slopes are covered with native *mamane* trees, which flower a beautiful yellow in summer. A particular type of honeycreeper, the *palila*, is found only on Mauna Kea's lower slopes, attracted by the pods from the *mamane*. A species of the silversword plant is also found on Mauna Kea.

Another interesting area of Mauna Kea that very few visitors see, due to the difficulty of access, is Hakalau Forest National Wildlife Refuge. Located on the northeastern flank of the mountain, some 16 miles down a rugged four-wheel-drive road, not only is this area geographically tough to visit, but also the refuge is open to the public only one weekend a month. Those who do visit will find healthy forests of koa and ohia trees, and communities of birds enjoying their isolation from humans. Bird life includes *'akepa*, Hawaii creeper, *i'iwi*, *'apapane*, *elepaio*, *oma'o*, and Hawaii *amakihi*.

Waipio and Waimanu Valleys, near Honokaa, were once population centers, with inhabitants growing taro and farming the fertile soil. The 1946 tsunami wiped out many homes and farms, and the area never recovered its human population.

But one species' tragedy is another's good fortune, and today these areas are grown over with wild vegetation and provide important habitat for many plant and bird species, as well as for Hawaii's only native land mammal, the hoary bat. This small creature, with a wingspan of roughly 12 inches at full growth, emerges only at night to hunt insects.

Waimanu Valley, the more isolated of the two, is protected because of its unusual estuary, which is fed by waterfalls from the valley walls. The freshwater streams here are home to two native mollusks, shrimp, and mullets. Birders here will find black-crowned night heron and the endangered *koloa* duck.

Akaka Falls State Park is more the groomed, lush Hawaii one has come to expect from Hawaii Visitors & Convention Bureau marketing campaigns. Here, visitors find tall stands of coconut trees, bamboo, ferns of various types, torch ginger, plumeria, flowers of all colors and shapes, and waterfalls plummeting over tall cliffs. Several species of introduced birds are common here, including the northern cardinal and yellow finch.

History, Culture, and Customs

The *paniolo* town of Kamuela is fascinating as the heart of Hawaii's cowboy country. Its roots are as a supply town to the cattle industry, chiefly to Parker Ranch, the 225,000-acre working cattle ranch that

© George Fuller

Pa'u Parade rider

occupies most of the land in the area.

Parker Ranch dates back to 1847, when Kamehameha III granted John Parker a small plot of land, which he eventually expanded. But the history of cattle here goes back even farther. Captain George Vancouver brought the first cattle to the Big Island in 1793 and presented them as a gift to Kamehameha I, son of an *ali'i* (royal) family, who two years earlier had united the Big Island under his rule. Vancouver brought more cattle the following year, and soon large herds of wild cattle roamed the island, destroying crops and native forests as they went.

In 1803 the first horses arrived on the Big Island from Spanish California to be used in herding and controlling the cattle. Other horses came from Great Britain and the United States. Kamehameha was fascinated with the animals, and took up riding as a means of encouraging the *paniolo* lifestyle in Hawaii. Within decades an entire culture and tradition of Hawaiian cowboys was thriving, and still thrives to this day. By some counts, the Big Island's cattle and livestock industry nowadays accounts for approximately $25 million in annual sales.

Hawaii's *paniolo* are well known in the islands for wearing festive leis and hats decorated with brightly colored flowers or beautiful feather bands. The cowboy credited for this tradition is Jack Purdy, one of Kamuela's original settlers. Purdy married a Hawaiian of royal blood and their offspring have been instrumental in continuing the *paniolo* lifestyle in Kamuela.

Ikua Purdy, one of Jack Purdy's grandsons, became the first Hawaiian nominated to the National Cowboy Hall of Fame in 1996. One story of Ikua Purdy often told on the Big Island is of his 1908 trip to Cheyenne, Wyoming, to compete in Frontier Days with two fellow *paniolos*, Archie Ka'au'a and Jack Low. Mainland cowboys didn't know what to make of these Hawaiians, so foreign were they to anything normally seen in Wyoming. When all was said and done, however, Ikua Purdy was crowned world rodeo steer-roping champion. Ka'au'a placed third and Low sixth.

Hawaiian cowboys were suddenly well respected. The annual Pa'u Parade, held as part of the Aloha Festivals, celebrates the *paniolo* tradition in the islands, and the sight of horses and riders decorated in flower leis is quite something to behold.

There is also a *paniolo* tradition along the Hamakua Coast, but really it is the sugarcane industry that shaped the lifestyles along this beautiful coast. Starting at Honokaa and stretching to Hilo, the towns are small and spread perhaps 10 to 15 miles from one another. They were basically company towns for many years, that workers from the sugarcane fields came home to in the evenings. Today, with much of the sugarcane production halted due to fallen prices, these small towns are looking for new ways to support their economies.

Hilo, the island's seat of government, has been inhabited since around A.D. 1100 The first Polynesian settlers found Hilo Bay an ideal location to farm and fish. There is more than enough rain on this side of the island to provide fertile soil for almost any crop, and the waters have always been friendly fishing grounds.

By the late 1800s and early 1900s, the protected bay had become an important port. A number of wharves were built, a breakwater was constructed, and a railroad brought the tons of sugarcane down from the Hamakua Coast. Unfortunately, protected as Hilo is from storm seas, nothing could protect it from the two devastating tsunamis that hit the town, one in 1946, the other in 1960. In both instances, much of the downtown portion of the city, as well as the railroad, was destroyed. As you drive through Hilo today, you'll notice a wide, unbuilt area that extends from the bay to downtown. Even though it is prime real estate, Hilo has learned from the past. Anything built here is simply tempting fate.

The Merrie Monarch Festival, Hawaii's premier celebration of hula and traditional culture, is held each year in Hilo near Easter week.

HAWAII'S HORSE COMMUNICATOR

I leaned on the corral rail and watched Nakoa touch the horse. He started at the head, running his hand behind the young animal's ears, down its nose. He stroked its muscular neck, its belly, ran his hand along its flank, patted it gently on the rump. He repeated the process on the other side.

Then he got on—first from the left, then from the right. I had never seen anyone mount a horse from the right side. I looked at Bud, who was standing beside me. Bud was a cowboy from Texas. He had come to Dahana Ranch, on the slopes of Mauna Kea, to learn from Daniel H. Nakoa, Hawaii's horse communicator.

"Nakoa makes the horse relaxed and feel good before getting on," Bud said. "What horses learn first they'll stick with the rest of their lives. That's why it's important to train them like this early."

Nakoa was working on getting the horse comfortable on both sides, getting on, getting off, walking around it, touching. Soon, the horse lowered its head. Nakoa smiled.

"The trick is to make him get his head down," said Bud. "Nakoa calls that 'submitting.' Where I came from we call it 'breaking a horse down.' Some guys want the horse naked in the pen, no halter. They want to walk up and look the horse in the eye—confrontational. But Nakoa makes the horse relaxed and feel good before he gets on."

After taking care of the horses, we went inside Dahana Ranch's tack room to talk.

"People come to me and they want to learn about horses," Nakoa said. "But they end up learning about themselves, and that helps them with the horses.

"I had three kapuna," Nakoa said, referring to the Hawaiian

tradition of learning from elders. "First was Henry Keamalu. Then Joe Kahananui. Then Joe Pea. None of them ever had anything to do with horses, but I use what they taught me.

"For example, you have to be able to ride your horse before you ever see him," Nakoa said. "Once I walk into that circle out there, I already know what's going to happen."

That ability to visualize is key in traditional Polynesian culture. Nainoa Thompson, Hawaii's premier celestial navigator, tells a story about how he learned to navigate from an elder. "He asked me, 'Can you see Tahiti?'" Thompson says. "I said, 'Yes. In my mind.' Even though we were thousands of miles away, my teacher said, 'Good, because if you ever lose that vision, you will become lost at sea.'"

"I teach that you must treat the horse like an athlete. Do you love a horse like a cat, take it on your lap and fondle it? No. Do you play with one like a dog? No. Respect it like an athlete," said Nakoa.

The Hawaiian paniolo (cowboy) tradition is strong on the Big Island, particularly up around Dahana Ranch. Nakoa is part of that culture and deeply respects that tradition. He uses a copy of his father's first-generation paniolo saddle as a reminder of his heritage.

If you go see him, and ride with him on the green slopes of Mauna Kea, he will tell you all about the different generations of saddles used by the paniolos on the Big Island, and about the cowboys themselves.

He's not a horse whisperer, he wants you to know. That's Hollywood.

"I never say a word, because the horse doesn't understand you anyway," Nakoa said. "I want people to learn about life through horses—and about horses through life."

NATURE AND ADVENTURE SIGHTS
FROM KAMUELA TO HILO

Akaka Falls State Park

Akaka Falls State Park is a manicured, gardenlike park set in the eastern foothills of Mauna Kea. Tall stands of coconut trees, bamboo, ferns, and a spellbinding array of flowers, such as torch ginger, orchids, hibiscus, perfumed plumeria, and many other species, await you on this half-mile paved loop trail, as do views of two waterfalls plunging over tall cliffs. The waterfalls, Kihuna and Akaka, both drop more than 400 feet. Kihuna Falls spills into a pool above Akaka Falls, and Akaka Falls plummets into Kolekole Stream.

Several species of introduced birds are common here, including the northern cardinal and yellow finch. Even though the trail is short (.5 mile), there are several steep areas and several stairs to walk. This side trip is well worth the time.

Details: *Driving east on Highway 19 from Honokaa to Hilo, turn right onto Highway 220, just past the town of Honomu. Continue on this road for several miles until you come to a parking area at highway's end. You'll find the trailhead there.*

Laupahoehoe Point Beach Park

At this scenic beach park and camping area on a point overlooking a particularly lovely stretch of coastline, the waters are too rough for swimming and sometimes too rough for fishing. It's a great spot for exploration and a picnic, though, and for re-reading the story of how Mark Twain, who ventured to the Big Island in 1866, did firsthand interviews with Captain Josiah Mitchell and several members of his crew who washed up at Laupahoehoe in a longboat after their ship, the *Hornet*, caught fire near the equator south of Hawaii. Twain's account of the *Hornet* and the crew's 43 days in the open sea was first published in the *Sacramento Union* newspaper and later, in different form, in several magazines.

Laupahoehoe (the name of a type of lava) Point is aptly named, as black lava from ancient flows creates much of the landscape here.

Good bird-watching is to be had here, too, mostly of seabirds.

You'll spot black noddies, tropic birds, and split-tailed shearwaters. It's a beautiful area of the Hamakua Coast often missed by tourists. If you're looking for an isolated area to camp, this is it.

Details: Roughly 17 miles north of Hilo on Highway 19 you'll see a sign for Laupahoehoe Point Beach Park. Go down this road roughly 1.5 miles to the park. The road is paved, but narrow.

To read about Mark Twain's visit, and about the other novelists who made their way through Hawaii in earlier times, get Mad About Islands *by A. Grove Day (Mutual Publishing, 1997).*

Mauna Kea

This is one journey you should take, just to say you've been there. Mauna Kea's summit is 13,796 feet above sea level. Its elevation makes for crystal-clear skies an average of 360 days per year, and that's why 10 telescopes belonging to various nations are set up on Mauna Kea. They include the largest telescopes in the world—Kecks I and II, with 30-foot mirrors—NASA's and the United Kingdom's infrared telescopes, telescopes that work on millimeter/submillimeter wavelengths, and several other types of highly sophisticated instruments. Nations represented in this optimum location for observing the stars include Canada, France, Great Britain, the Netherlands, Japan, Chile, and Argentina, in addition to the United States. Unfortunately, because time on the telescopes is so valuable, most of the observatories are not open to the public.

Just below the telescopes is **Lake Waiau**, one of the highest lakes in the United States, at 13,020 feet above sea level. Around the lake are several quarry sites where ancient Hawaiians dug for the basalt they used to carve adzes. This area is called **Mauna Kea Ice Age Natural Area Reserve**, and is protected by the state.

It is recommended that you take your time getting to Mauna Kea's summit—altitude sickness is common. Pregnant women, small children, and the obese or unfit should stay below at the 9,300-foot **Onizuka Visitor Center**, named for Ellison Onizuka, Hawaii's first astronaut. You can peer at the night sky through a nine-inch telescope at 7 p.m. every Friday and Saturday at the center.

On the catwalk, University of Hawaii telescope, Mauna Kea

J. Penisten

The Onizuka center has several displays that discuss the observatories' work, as well as information on Mauna Kea's fascinating geology. If you are so inclined, take a stroll outside the visitor center to see the endangered silversword plants that grow here.

Driving the rest of the way to the summit is allowed in four-wheel-drive vehicles only, as the road is gravel and conditions can sometimes be tricky. But it's a beautiful drive, particularly that first moment when you realize that you are *above* the clouds!

Mauna Kea's summit is capped in snow several months of the year—in Hawaiian the name translates to "white mountain"—and it is possible to ski her slopes in winter. Dick Tillson, a Honolulu engineer who surveyed Mauna Kea on skis in 1965 and named the popular and easily accessible Poi Bowl (it's a .75-mile run with 500 feet of vertical drop), discovered that old Hawaiian trails converge at the ski bowls.

The skiing is rough and occasionally rocky, but the temptation to ski in the morning and swim at the beach by noon is irresistible to hardcore skiers.

Details: *Highway 200 is also called the Saddle Road because it traverses the saddle between Mauna Kea and Mauna Loa. It can be accessed off Highway 190, the "upper road" from Kona to Kamuela, or from Hilo, where it's a little more difficult to find. It intersects with Highway 19, but don't blink—you're likely to miss the not-well-marked turn. The Saddle Road is the only access to Mauna Kea.*

Unfortunately, most car-rental companies do not allow you to take their vehicles all the way to the summit. Some don't even want you on the Saddle Road. So ask before you rent. One company that rents four-wheel-drives is Harper's of Hilo, 808/969-1478. Luckily, a tour is available, and this may be the best and most relaxing way to go. The outfitter is listed below in the Guides and Outfitters section. As for skiing, there are occasionally outfitters based in Kamuela who will rent you gear. At the time of this writing, however, no such outfitter could be found.

Find out about hours, times, etc., at Onizuka Visitor Center, at the 9,300-foot level, calling 808/961-2180.

Be prepared for cold weather! Bring a heavy sweater for daytime trips, and a parka for after dark. Evening temperatures average 40–55 degrees in summer, 26–50 degrees in winter.

Mauna Kea Lower Slopes

A couple of outfitters offer horseback rides on the lower slopes of Mauna Kea. Since this is the heart of Hawaii's *paniolo* country, not only are these rides scenic—on a clear day it's some of the greenest country and bluest sky you'll ever see—but also most of the guides are eager to share their *paniolo* knowledge with you. You'll learn about traditional Spanish/Mexican saddle making, lariat and bell-spur crafting, Hawaii's most famous cowboys, and how the Big Island came to be such a *paniolo* hot spot.

Most of the rides start near Kamuela and proceed through the green cattle country of Mauna Kea's foothills. Although you may think of trail rides as being a nose-to-tail experience for the inexperienced, up here you'll find range rides on working cattle horses. You don't have to be an expert rider, but your horse won't bore you, either.

Details: *Take warm, waterproof clothing with you. The area is green because it rains frequently. Dahana Ranch, the most respected horseback riding outfitter is listed in Guides and Outfitters, below.*

Waipio Valley

Long ago this lush, tropical place was the valley of kings; it is said to have been a popular retreat for the Big Island's *ali'i*. From the black-sand bay at its mouth, Waipio sweeps back six miles between vertical walls laced by 2,000-foot-high twin falls.

Waipio and neighboring Waimanu Valleys, near Honokaa, were at one point in the not-too-distant past population centers for the Hawaiian people. Here, 40,000 Hawaiians lived in a garden of Eden surrounded by taro, red bananas, wild guavas, and waterfalls. Farming was the people's mainstay, as just about everything grew in the fertile soil of these lush valleys. Where the valleys reached the beach, fishing was popular. Misfortune struck, though, when the 1946 tsunami wiped out many homes and farms, and the area has never again been such a vital force for the Hawaiian people.

Today both Waipio and Waimanu Valleys are perfect for hiking and bird-watching. Both are grown over with vegetation, providing important habitat for many plant and bird species, as well as for Hawaii's only native land mammal, the hoary bat. This small creature—the full-grown adult wingspan is roughly 12 inches—comes out only at night to hunt insects. And there is a human population as well, perhaps 50 people still tending fields of taro, fishing, hunting, and soaking up the ambiance of this special place.

The isolated **Waimanu Valley** is protected by an estuary, unusual in that it's fed by waterfalls from the valley walls. You may find some native mollusks, shrimp, and mullets in these freshwater streams, and in the sky, black-crowned night heron and the endangered *koloa* duck.

Hiking from the Waipio Valley Lookout to Waimanu Valley and back is a strenuous, three-day trek, covering some 17 miles. But you are rewarded with spectacular views, some blessed isolation in healthy forests and wetlands, and five waterfalls in the valley.

The first leg of the journey takes you down the steep road to the floor of Waipio Valley. This is the same road used by all traffic, and it's narrow, so give way to vehicles trying to make their way. Once down, you will ford Waipio Stream. This is often most easily done where the stream hits the beach, as it can be hazardous farther up.

Saddle Road Pu'u (cinder cone)

You can get from there to the far wall of the valley either on the beach, which is more strenuous going with a backpack, or via a trail just inside the trees. You'll soon come to a fork. Take the fork that leads up the switchbacks. This is called **Muliwai Trail**, and it is the only way into Waimanu Valley. Here you'll see some of the more breathtaking views of the entire hike.

Soon you'll be in a forest of ironwood, eucalyptus, monkey pod, and Norfolk pines. You'll cross several gulches and another stream, and hike past a waterfall where a tranquil pool beckons you for a swim. When you emerge at the top of Waimanu Valley, another wonderful view awaits. Roughly a 90-minute hike remains to the campsite on the valley floor.

If hiking is on your list in Hawaii, this one should not be missed. In many ways, it's a better trail in better shape than Kauai's famed Na Pali Coast.

Less-strenuous hikes can be made in Waipio Valley; hikes here can vary in length from two hours to all day. The shorter hikes reveal good views of tall waterfalls, and you can get your feet wet crossing several streams. Because Waipio Valley does have a small human population, please pay attention to property signs and show respect for the local residents.

Two companies offer horseback rides along the Waipio Valley floor. Both are led by knowledgeable guides who provide stories about the valley's history and people. Because the valley terrain is rough the horses will be walking, as anything faster is a danger to animal and rider. This is one of the best ways to see the valley—the horses do most of the worrying about where to step, and you can relax and enjoy the scenic views.

A wagon tour is another good way to see the valley. These creaking, mule-drawn wagons are fun for families and for those who may not wish or be able to walk the rough terrain.

Details: Follow Highway 19 east out of Kamuela. Near the town of Honokaa, take Highway 240 to Waipio Valley. The road dead-ends into a parking area at Waipio Valley Lookout.

Because the road leading down to the valley floor is so steep, both the wagon tour and the horseback rides meet you in the small town of Kukuihaele, near the Waipio Lookout, and take you in a four-wheel-drive down to the valley floor where you meet your horse or buggy.

A permit is required for camping in Waimanu Valley, and can be obtained from the Division of Forestry and Wildlife, 1643 Kilauea Ave., Hilo, HI 96720, 808/933-4221.

GUIDES AND OUTFITTERS

Mauna Kea Summit Adventures/Paradise Safaris, P.O. Box 9027, Kailua-Kona, HI 96745, 888/322-2366 or 808/322-2366, will pick you up at your hotel (if you're staying on the Kona-Kohala Coast), and take you to the very heights of the Big Island—the summit of Mauna Kea. They stop to acclimate at the 9,300-foot Onizuka Visitor Center (named for Hawaii's astronaut, Ellison Onizuka, who died in the space-shuttle *Challenger* disaster), before ascending to the top. Once at the summit, you'll stay for 45 minutes to an hour and take in the sunset from this incredible vantage point. Photo opportunities abound. The tour then descends to a more comfortable level for stargazing and hot-chocolate sipping (it's cold up here!). You should count on a 7½-hour day. Cost is $135/person, and includes soup, sandwiches, gloves, and a parka, for which you'll be more than thankful.

To explore some of the Big Island's less-discovered natural gems, check out **Hawaiian Walkways**, P.O. Box 2193, Kamuela, HI 96743, 800/457-7759 or 808/775-0372. Owner Hugh Montgomery will guide your way. One popular hike leads you through eucalyptus forests, past a 50-foot waterfall, and along a stream to a high rim above Waipio Valley. Along the way you'll get an education about Hawaii's ancient and historic trails; the geology, botany, and cultural stories of Hawaii; and what we must do to protect and preserve these beautiful islands. This is a rare treat with knowledgeable guides. Cost is $75/person/half-day; $110/full day; $125–$150 for custom trips.

A leader in the ecotours area, **Hawaii Forest & Trail**, Box 2975, Kailua-Kona, HI 96745, 800/464-1933 or 808/322-8881, conducts two tours of interest in the area of the Big Island. One is a bird-watching trip into Hakalau Forest National Wildlife Refuge on Mauna Kea's northeastern slopes. This tour is highly recommended if you are interested in birding here, as access is very difficult (and cannot be done in a rental car) otherwise. The other tour is bird-watching/rain forest–discovery, and also takes you into the Pu'u O'o area on Mauna Kea's lower slopes. Cost is $130/person for either tour.

Horseback riding options abound in this region. **Dahana Ranch**, P.O. Box 1293, Kamuela, HI 96743, 808/885-0057, is a working horse ranch offering horseback rides of varying lengths on the lower slopes of Mauna Kea. The owner is a "horse communicator" and on the rides he talks about Hawaiian *paniolo* traditions. You can take a 2½-hour cattle-drive ride, or a shorter, 1½-hour, four-mile ranch ride. The terrain is lovely and the views go on forever. Bring a warm coat—it can get chilly up here. Cost is $55/person for the 1½-hour ride; $100/person for the 2½-hour cattle drive. The longer ride includes lunch.

Another choice is **Mauna Kea Stables**, c/o Mauna Kea Beach Hotel, One Mauna Kea Beach Dr., Kamuela, 808/885-4288 or 808/882-7222. Operated by the Mauna Kea Beach Hotel, the stables are located up-country in Kamuela. They offer rides onto Parker Ranch pastureland,

THE BIG ISLAND'S BEST BEACHES

by Rick Carroll

Author Rick Carroll has studied Hawaii's beaches extensively.
Here are his choices for the best beaches on the Big Island.

Best Beach—Mahai'ula

*On the left side of the aircraft as you fly into Kailua-Kona it flashes
like a half-remembered dream: a gold-sand beach with an oasis of
palms on the black lava coast. Now you see it, now you don't.*

*It's easy to find, now that a new sign on Queen Kaahumanu
Highway points the way to Kaha Kai State Park and Mahai'ula
Beach, one of the Big Island's best. Turn left at the sign 2.6 miles
past Keahole Airport.*

*An unpaved, mile-long trail winds through the 1801 lava flow
(itself a natural spectacle) and suddenly you've found this remote,
secluded beach on the site of an ancient fishing village on
Mahai'ula Bay. A two-mile trail leads to Pu'u Kili, a 342-foot-high
cinder cone with a peerless Kona Coast view.*

Best Sunset—Kaunaoa

*I am standing on my lanai at Mauna Kea Beach Hotel on the Big
Island watching a blood-red sun sink into a cobalt sea through
green coco palms. Snowcapped Mauna Kea, at nearly 14,000 feet
the highest peak in the tropical Pacific, looms in the distance while
the last sun rays light a line of fire across the water. Sunset beaches
are everywhere, but none like this.*

*Kaunaoa was "discovered" more than 30 years ago by
Laurance Rockefeller, who sailed by, dropped anchor, and built
Hawaii's first grand beach hotel, which soon became America's favorite corporate retreat. Wide and flat, the half-moon beach lies
between two lava headlands. The gentle water is perfect for swimming laps or plotting your next merger-acquisition.*

where you'll get some wonderful views. Choose either a one-or two-hour ride. Mauna Kea Stables' rides are geared for those with less horse experience (not less horse sense) than the rides offered by Dahana Ranch. Cost is $40/person for the one-hour ride; $70/person for the two-hour ride.

To explore Waipio Valley by horseback, there's **Waipio Na Alapa Stables**, P.O. Box 992, Honokaa, HI 96727, 808/775-0419. Guides meet riders in the small village of Kukuihaele near the Waipio Valley Lookout, and take them in a four-wheel-drive vehicle down the steep road to the valley floor. From there, you enjoy a gentle, two-hour horseback ride through rain forest and past old Hawaiian settlements. Guides tell you about life in this valley from ancient times to present. Cost is $75/person.

CAMPING

There are several County of Hawaii–operated beach parks along the Hamakua Coast that allow camping, but the only one recommended is Laupahoehoe Point Beach Park. All require permits that cost $3 per day for adults; $1 per day for children 13–17; 50 cents per day for children under 12. Further information and permits can be obtained up to a year in advance (starting in November) by visiting or contacting the Department of Parks and Recreation, 25 Aupuni St., Hilo, HI 96720; 808/961-8311.

Laupahoehoe Point Beach Park off Highway 19 is situated along a rugged stretch of coastline. The views are wonderful, as is the solitude. Not many tourists use this park, and it's fair to describe it as "roughing it," although restroom facilities, showers, and fresh water are available. The area can get wet, particularly in winter months, so be prepared. Swimming is definitely not recommended here due to dangerous surf, and even fishing can be perilous when the waters are rough.

The State of Hawaii oversees cabins for rent at Mauna Kea State Recreation Area. Daily rates vary depending on the number of people and size of the cabin, but do not exceed $10 per person. Reservations are taken a year in advance at the Division of State Parks, 75 Aupuni St., Hilo, HI 96720; 808/974-6200.

Waimanu Valley is also under state jurisdiction, but a separate division handles the permits. Information can be obtained from the Division of Forestry and Wildlife, 1643 Kilauea Ave., Hilo, HI 96720, 808/974-4221. There is no charge for the campsites, but it's required that you make a reservation no earlier than 30 days before your planned campout.

Mauna Kea State Recreation Area, just off the Saddle Road, is an isolated area several miles from the actual road that leads to Mauna Kea's summit. Housekeeping cabins are available here, with kitchens, showers, linens, and bedding. You are at the 6,300-foot level, and it's a good place to acclimate before ascending the mountain. Several good trails lead from the state recreation area, and some unusual flora and fauna live in the area. No tent camping allowed.

The camping area on the floor of isolated **Waimanu Valley** is reached only by a difficult, three-day hike (in and out). You start the hike at Waipio Valley Lookout, and can reach the campsite in a good day's hike. The many rewards along the way include panoramic views of the Pacific and Waipio and Waimanu Valleys, healthy forests of ironwood and eucalyptus, and the chance to spot some of Hawaii's colorful flora and fauna.

A camping permit is required for the valley, and there are nine designated campsites. The area is beautiful, with great hiking trails, waterfalls, and swimming ponds. You must pack in or treat your own water, and pack your own food and other gear in and out. Outhouses are available. Waimanu Valley may be remote, but it is one of the Big Island's hidden gems.

LODGING

Makai Hale (through Hawaii's Best Bed & Breakfasts), near Kamuela, 800/262-9912 or 808/885-4550, is a private home close to the beaches of Mauna Kea and Hapuna, yet also a short drive to Kamuela. It's in a sunny area of the Kohala Range, so the pool and Jacuzzi are welcome additions. Expansive ocean views include good whale-watching in winter. Highly recommended. Rates: $105; plus $65 for second room (if needed) that sleeps two.

Another B&B in Kamuela is **Tina's Country Cottage** (through Hawaii's Best Bed & Breakfasts), 800/262-9912 or 808/885-4550. A two-bedroom, two-bath cottage overlooking well-groomed gardens, expansive lawns, and the green hills of the Kohala Range, this is a gem. The cottage is complete with full kitchen, woodstove, and a lanai on which you can relax after a day exploring nearby Kamuela. Rates: $105; $15/additional person. Sleeps four; minimum two-night stay.

A lovely river ambles by the two historic, restored cottages that make up **Waimea Gardens Cottage** (through Hawaii's Best Bed & Breakfasts), in Kamuela, 800/262-9912 or 808/885-4550. Both cottages are equipped with full kitchens and baths, have hardwood floors, and are wonderfully decorated with antique furnishings. One has a wood-burning fireplace. Ranked "Excellent" by the American Bed & Breakfast Association. Rates: $135.

Set on a bluff overlooking Hilo Bay, **Bay House** (through Hawaii's Best Bed & Breakfasts), in Hilo, 800/262-9912 or 808/885-4550, is a newer home convenient to downtown Hilo and environs. A physician and his family own the property and live in private quarters in the house. Guests have their own foyer, which leads to the two rooms. Both rooms have ocean views and private decks. A continental breakfast is served each morning. Rates: $95.

Shipman House Bed & Breakfast Inn, 131 Kaiulani St., Hilo, 800/627-8447 or 808/934-8002, is Hilo's finest accommodation. Built in 1899, this historic Victorian mansion is situated on 5.5 lush acres planted with palms, ferns, and many other tropical species. A stream and waterfall grace the estate, which has hosted Hawaii's last queen, Liliuokalani, as well as Jack London, who was so charmed he stayed here for an entire month. Rates: $130–$150; additional $10 for single-night stays.

Waipio Wayside Bed and Breakfast Inn, P.O. Box 840, Honokaa, 808/775-0275 or 800/833-8849, is a treat. This 1936 sugar-plantation house was rescued by Jacqueline Horne and restored to full glory. Today, the five-room inn is full of antique wicker, hand-painted silk curtains, and Chinese rugs. It sits on 1.5 acres, on a bluff above the Pacific near

Waipio Valley, with wide ocean views from the lanai, gazebo, and library. At this traditional B&B, a full, hot, sit-down breakfast is served at 8 a.m., "as organic as possible." Rates: $95 for the one room with detached bath; $115 for others, which have attached baths.

FOOD

Zagat Survey rated **Aioli's**, Hwy. 19 and Opelo Rd., Opelo Plaza, Kamuela, 808/885-6325, "Excellent" in 1998. The food here is good and quite reasonable, and the restaurant is a great place to stop for lunch, with healthy sandwiches, soups, and salads on the menu. Most of their breads, cookies, and desserts are homemade. Dinner menu changes every two weeks, but is likely to include taste treats such as herb-crusted prime rib, rack of lamb, or roasted turkey. Vegetarian dishes are always offered, such as pasta with crunchy sprouts, shiitake mushrooms, and cheese. No liquor license, but no corkage fee, either. Open Tue–Sun for lunch and dinner. Closed Mon.

Chef Hans-Peter Hager runs a tight ship at **Edelweiss**, on Hwy. 19, Kamuela, 808/885-6800. Always mentioned as one of the Big Island's best restaurants, its specialty appetizers include escargot with spinach and cheese; the Continental dinner menu highlights several German dishes. One of the most popular items is the rack of lamb for one or two, basted in garlic with mustard and herbs. Fresh fish is most often *opakapaka* (pink snapper) in butter-wine sauce. Wines include Opus One by the glass. Open Tue–Sat for lunch and dinner.

At **Merriman's**, Hwy. 19 and Opelo Rd., Opelo Plaza, Kamuela, 808/885-6822, Peter Merriman is a whiz kid in the kitchen. He's considered one of the top chefs in the state, and when you dine here you'll understand why. Favorite dishes dominate the menu, such as the Kalua pig and goat cheese quesadilla with papaya-plum dipping sauce for an appetizer. His fresh fish is either sauteed with pineapple vinaigrette, sesame-crusted and sauteed with spicy *lilikoi* sauce, or herb-grilled on mango chutney with coconut lime sauce. Several vegetable dishes are always available. Open for lunch Mon–Fri, dinner nightly.

Starting with 33 different toppings for pizza, **Cafe Pesto**, Historic S.

Hata Bldg., Hilo, 808/969-6640, has a wide variety of menu selections from which to choose. These include pastas, risottos, salads, calzones, and lots of vegetarian dishes. The dinner menu includes a few appetizers worth noting, such as the crab cakes with honey-miso vinaigrette, and the sesame-crusted Hamakua goat cheese with eggplant. Entrée specialties include fresh local fish in several preparations. Open for lunch and dinner daily

Tex Drive Inn, on Hwy. 19, Honokaa, 808/775-0598, is where the locals go for local food. The Portuguese bean soup, plate lunches, and hot *malasadas* (sugar-coated, deep-fried bread) are the most popular items. Eat indoors or out. It may not be health food, Martha, but if you want to sample local food and color, Tex is the place to go. Open daily for breakfast, lunch, and dinner.

KONA-KOHALA COAST

The Kona-Kohala Coast has long been a playground for fun in the sun, from the time of Hawaiian *aliʻi* (royalty) to today, when visitors from around the globe come to enjoy the dry climate, many beaches, and adventures by the bushel.

Very little rain falls on this side of the Big Island each year—less than nine inches along the Kohala Coast—making the landscape significantly different from what you'll see in Hilo or along the Hamakua Coast. When they land for the first time at the Kona airport, built on top of an ancient lava flow, most people's reaction is, "Where are we, the moon?"

Information about the Kona-Kohala Coast can be obtained from the Big Island Visitors Bureau, 808/329-7787 or 808/961-5797. They also have a Web site at www.bigisland.org. Kona has its own Web site: www.konaweb.com.

Orientation/Lay of the Land

Parts of the Kohala Coast do indeed look like a lunar landscape, with long miles of *pahoehoe* (black, swirling, smooth) and *aʻa* (sharp, brown, clustered) lava leading from the mountains to the sea. But there are

HAWAII'S LUNAR LANDSCAPE

The natural inclination of first-time visitors to the Kona-Kohala Coast is to remark, "This isn't what Hawaii is supposed to look like."

No, the colors are shades of brown, instead of green. The terrain looks more like what you'd expect from a distant planet than the tropics. It is a volcanic island supposedly inhabited by the punitive goddess Pele, and its demeanor doesn't let you forget that fact for a moment.

Indeed, the island is still growing. Kilauea has been erupting for close to 20 years, adding some 100 square miles of land mass to the island. And though the lava flow, which can be viewed at Hawaii Volcanoes National Park, poses no threat to those who view it—it's classified as a "friendly flow"—the people who live on the Big Island do not discount Pele's power. And neither do many tourists, but only after it's too late.

Hawaiian folk knowledge warns that you should never take lava stones away from the beds where they were found. But many visitors ignore the advice—for a little while.

"We get literally thousands of pounds of lava rocks mailed back to us from the Mainland each year," said my guide Ski. "People contract strange illnesses, fall victim to financial disaster, begin having unnerving dreams and experiences. It's because they have taken lava rocks from Pele's bed."

pockets of paradise here, too, many of them hidden. For example, dozens of unmarked roads lead from the main highway, Highway 19, through the lava fields to oases by the Pacific. Locals know that some of the best beaches on the Kohala Coast are found along this stretch just north of the airport, but few visitor guides give up the secret.

Golfing along the Kohala Coast

This is the most popular side of the island for visitors, and the better resorts are here, too, including Mauna Kea Resort, Mauna Lani Resort, Waikoloa Resort, Kona Village Resort, and Hualalai. From your base in Kona, or at one of the resorts on the Kohala Coast, you can explore to your heart's content. Take the time to go to North Kohala, less commercial than Kona, and see some delightful small towns: Hawi, Kapaau, Kawaihae. Go into the stores and "talk story" with the owners. You'll discover with them a side of Hawaii not often found by visitors.

Several major golf events have taken place at the Kohala resorts' golf courses, including the Senior Skins Game at Mauna Lani and the Senior PGA MasterCard Championship at Hualalai. These luxury properties also host several culinary events throughout the year, including Cuisines of the Sun at Mauna Lani and the Winter Wine Escape at the Hapuna Beach Prince Hotel.

The southern end of this segment does receive more rain than the Kohala Coast, set as it is in the lee of Mauna Loa. This climate encompasses much of the best of Kona's coffee country. Many of these estate farmers will welcome you to their farms and show you how the only commercially grown coffee in the United States is farmed and roasted.

Here too is Kealakekua Bay, where you can snorkel in the protected waters and view the monument marking where Captain James Cook was killed in a skirmish with the Hawaiians in 1779. A short drive farther down the road will take you to Puuhonua O Honaunau, a traditional place of refuge that still is sacred to modern Hawaiians.

Kona itself is a fun-filled village of restaurants, shops, and trinket stands. This active town is headquarters for the Ironman Triathlon, Hawaiian International Billfish Tournament, Queen Liliuokalani Outrigger Canoe Races, and Kona Coffee Cultural Festival.

As with other areas of the Big Island, the best way to get out and explore is with a rental vehicle. Getting to Kona is simple, with Hawaiian Airlines and Aloha Airlines both offering frequent flights from Honolulu. United Airlines offers direct flights into Kona from the Mainland's west coast. All major car-rental companies are located at the Kona airport.

Flora and Fauna

One of the few underwater parks in the United States is found at Kealakekua Bay State Underwater Park. Fishing or otherwise disturbing the sea life here is prohibited, making it a superb spot for snorkeling and diving. The protected waters of Kealakekua Bay are home to many fish species. Consequently, the cliffs surrounding the bay are also home to several seabird species that find good fishing here, notably the elegant white tropic bird.

If you sign up for one of the many snorkel tours to Kealakekua Bay, your guides will also know where to view eels that will often come out of the rock walls to greet you. If you're lucky, you can sometimes spot spinner dolphins in the area.

The deeper waters off Kona have long been known as a prime spot for blue and black marlin. But they are equally good for spotting turtles, humpback whales (in winter), and dolphins.

The Kohala Coast is home to rare anchialine pools (brackish water that holds some minuscule red shrimp and red coralline algae). Resort developers realize the natural significance of these ponds and their tiny inhabitants and take care to preserve them. And several hotels now

Philip Rosenberg

*Family enjoying the ocean
at Honaunau*

offer educational tours of these uncommon natural occurrences. The best examples of these anchialine pools are found in the rock shelves between the Hilton Waikoloa Village and the Royal Waikoloan.

Also along this lava-strewn coast are feral goats and donkeys, shrubbing on what grasses and scrub they can find, and seeking shade from the sun under *kiawe* trees that grow in the lava fields. At dusk you can often see a trip of goats on the Waikoloa Kings' golf course, helping the mowers with their task.

At Lapakahi State Historical Park is a marine life conservation district, but it is nowhere near as hospitable for snorkeling or fish-viewing as Kealakekua Bay. The mountain slopes of Hualalai and Kohala are good for bird-watching. Several endemic species can be commonly spotted, including the Hawaii *amakihi*, the *'apapane*, and occasionally the *i'iwi*. A wider variety of introduced birds can also be seen.

History, Culture, and Customs

Surrounded by volcanoes, the Kona-Kohala Coast is one of the state's most geologically interesting areas. Of the island's five volcanoes, four look out over this particular stretch of coast: Hualalai, Mauna Loa, Mauna Kea, and Kohala. If four volcanoes aren't enough, a fifth, Haleakala, looms across the channel on Maui.

Two of these volcanoes are classified as active: Mauna Loa and Hualalai. Although volcanologists will tell you that the two issue "friendly flows," meaning that resort guests don't have to worry about

KAUPULEHU CULTURAL CENTER

A must-see experience is the Kaupulehu Cultural Center at Four Seasons Resort Hualalai. This 1,100-square-foot center uses a variety of methods to tell the story of Hawaii and its people. Of special note is a huge saltwater aquarium that contains many of the fish found on the reefs around the island, an inlaid-wood floor map of the Pacific, and interpretive guides who will sit and "talk story" with you all day. If you are interested in the cultural history of Hawaii, this award-winning center is one of the best places to learn more. For more information on the Kaupulehu Cultural Center at Four Seasons Resort Hualalai, call 808/325-8000.

being engulfed in a lava storm, Mauna Loa has experienced 33 eruptions since 1843; the most recent was in 1984. Hualalai has had six separate vents erupt since 1700, with the current Kona airport being built on top of one of the larger flows; the most recent was in 1801.

Mauna Kea is classified as dormant, its most recent eruption estimated to have taken place 4,000 to 6,000 years ago. And Kohala, the Big Island's oldest volcano, is considered extinct; its most recent eruption is estimated to have occurred 120,000 years ago. To the untrained eye, Kohala barely looks like a volcano anymore. Its slopes are green and pastured, and there is no hint of a crater to be seen.

All of the different eruptions and ensuing flows create distinct types of lava. As you drive north from Kona, you'll see sharp brown *a'a* lava butted against swirling black *pahoehoe*, and sometimes both in the same lava field. People take white stones from the beaches and spell out "Donny Will You Marry Me" and other messages on top of the dark lava rock. It all makes for a primitive kind of modern rock art. To someone who is looking at it purely from a geologic point of view, this area of the Big Island is among the newest land on earth.

The North Kohala district is said to have been the birthplace of Hawaii's greatest king, Kamehameha, around 1758. And although no one knows for certain, Kamehameha's remains are thought to be secreted in a burial cave either here or in Waipio Valley.

The first coffee tree was brought to the Big Island in 1813 by Kamehameha's Spanish interpreter and physician, Don Francisco de Paula y Marin. The Big Island's Kona district proved to be a perfect climate for growing coffee commercially, and in 1828 coffee trees were planted widely. Kona coffee, grown on some 600 farms in the Kona district, is now respected throughout the world, and distinguishes Hawaii as the only state in the union where coffee is grown commercially.

Perhaps the most significant event in Hawaii's history occurred just south of Kona at Kealakekua Bay, when British Captain James Cook and his ship, *Resolution*, dropped anchor in 1778. Cook had arrived in the middle of a significant Hawaiian ceremony and the people of the Big Island took his arrival as the return of their god Lono.

Cook's visit revealed many things to the Hawaiians, including the use of firearms. Unfortunately for Cook, his use of firearms against the Hawaiians showed them that he was not, after all, a god, and in a disagreement over a ship's rudder, Cook went ashore to do battle and was killed. Today, a monument at Kealakekua Bay marks the spot of his demise.

That one may as well be accompanied by another monument marking the demise of the Hawaiian culture, for after Cook, many other Westerners followed. The worst among them may well have been missionaries from the United States, who ultimately wrested control of the islands from the Hawaiians. It is a battle the Hawaiians are still fighting today.

NATURE AND ADVENTURE SIGHTS ALONG THE KONA-KOHALA COAST

Big Island by Air

Helicoptering over the Big Island is such a popular activity that people often joke about helicopters being the state bird. But whirlybirds really are fantastic ways to see a whole lot of the Big Island from a perspective usually reserved for birds. From either the Kona airport or the Waikoloa heliport, choose your tour and climb onboard. These experienced chopper pilots will show you the waterfalls in back of Waipio and Waimanu Valleys, the summit of Mauna Kea—which is beautiful in winter, with a white blanket of snow—down the coast to where Kilauea Volcano is erupting into the sea, and along the brilliant green Hamakua Coast.

There is no other way to see as much of the Big Island in so little time.

Details: Many companies offer helicopter tours of the Big Island, flying out of both the Kona airport and Waikoloa heliport. The best are listed below in the Guides and Outfitters section.

Kawaihae Harbor

The good sloop *Maile* is yours for the chartering. Take her for two hours or 10 days, snorkeling, listening to whales, or swimming with spinner dolphins. This well-appointed, four-cabin, 50-foot Gulfstar sloop, is piloted by charter Captain Ralph Blancato out of Kawaihae Harbor.

"Every place is unique and special," Captain Blancato says. "But the Big Island has every possible tropical element—big blue water, smoking volcanoes, secret coves, great diving, plenty of fish."

Your days aboard the *Maile* are spent snorkeling coves, and watching whales and dolphins leap out of the water. Spectacular sunsets are everyday spectacles. At sundown you search for the elusive green flash and drink French wine from crystal goblets. Former clients all rave about Captain Blancato's knowledge of the water—but they rave equally about first-mate Kalia's cooking!

The *Maile* stays primarily in Kona-Kohala waters for fishing, swimming, and dolphin play. On longer sails, if the winds are conducive, they'll also try a Maui run. If you've got the budget, this is an experience worth spending it on.

Details: Maile Charters can be reached at P.O. Box 44335, Kamuela, HI 96743, 800/726-SAIL or 808/326-5174. Trips last two hours to 10 days.

Kealakekua Bay State Underwater Park

Whether you do this snorkel-dive trip solo, or take one of the many tours offered, a visit to Kealakekua Bay State Underwater Park is one experience everyone who loves the water should have. It is a protected bay, so don't disturb the sea life here. On the other hand, because it's protected, the fish are quite friendly and prevalent.

If you opt for a tour, you meet your boat at Keauhou Pier or at a site near Kona and push off toward the south. Most of the boats are wide-body catamarans, so even though there are 50 to 100 people on board—depending on which cruise you take—you don't feel over-crowded. Juice, coffee, fruit, and muffins are often served on the sail down, and you'll get plenty of good information about the Big Island waters from the captain or crew members.

Roughly 30 to 45 minutes later, they drop anchor in Kealakekua Bay and give you some brief instruction, and off you go into the water. The bay has a friendly shelf where you're anchored, and swimming, snorkeling, and fish-watching here are easy for anyone who is at all comfortable in the water.

Colorful fish and coral abound, visibility is 100 feet, and if you follow one of the crew he or she will likely show you rock walls where eels live—and sometimes come out to gurgle hello—and other underwater treats. People have even reported seeing white-tip reef sharks resting in caves on the shelf. Don't be alarmed if you do see one—if you keep your distance and don't disturb it, these guys are not aggressive like their bigger cousins.

On the north rim of the bay you'll see a white monument marking the spot where Captain James Cook was killed in a skirmish with the Hawaiians.

After you explore the bay, you head back to the boat, where sandwiches and drinks are served for lunch. Before shoving off for home, everyone has a chance to slide or cannonball from the second deck into the water to see who can make the biggest splash. These trips are popular with families, and everyone has a grand time.

Details: *Plenty of outfitters offer the snorkel tour. A couple of the better ones are listed below under the Guides and Outfitters section. This is also a pretty easy trip to take solo. The easiest way to get to the bay by car is by heading south* *from Kona on Highway 11. In roughly 18 miles you'll come to a sign pointing you to the right and down to the bay. Another scenic drive to the bay leads north from Puuhonua O Honaunau along the coast; a third leads along winding, scenic Napo'opo'o Road near the town of Captain Cook. Snorkel gear is available for rent at many locations in Kona. Kayaks are generally available for rent at the boat ramp leading into the bay.*

Kohala Sugar Plantation Irrigation Ditch

Back in 1905, an irrigation ditch was dug to service the sugar plantations of the North Kohala District. When completed, it was hailed as an engineering marvel. Today it is one of the Big Island's newest adventures, as you can get in an inflatable kayak and paddle down the Kohala Sugar Plantation Irrigation Ditch and inspect the marvel yourself. Block out 2½ hours for this adventure, which takes you through rain forest and tunnels, and past waterfalls.

This trip is safe and fun for kids and the whole family. Your guide will give you a slice of Big Island history while you're paddling.

Details: You can make an entire day out of exploring the North Kohala District, with the kayak cruise as the centerpiece. The round-trip kayaking portion itself, including travel time to the ditch, takes roughly 2½ hours. Paddlers meet at the Sakamoto Building, diagonally across from the King Kamehameha statue in Kapaau. A van will take you to and from the ditch.

Kona Coast

The fish exploded out of the sea like a rocket. It flashed and thrashed and fought the line. *Ono,* also known as wahoo, are one of Hawaii's great sport fish to catch and eat. But they come bigger than that out in the waters off Kona, too. As the shelf drops off and the water gets deeper, the fish get bigger. Blue and black marlin, some weighing as much as 1,000 pounds, are not uncommon. Neither are sailfish, *ahi,* or mahimahi.

The best time of year for the big fish is August, around the time of the **Hawaiian International Billfish Tournament.** This event, which has been held in Kona's waters since 1959, draws teams from all over the globe to see who can land the biggest game fish over a five-day period.

Dozens of fishing charters are available. Some specialize in night fishing—which is a different type of thrill—some in light-tackle fishing, and some in tag-and-release fishing. In tag-and-release, the fish is not killed; this is becoming popular as a way to help preserve the billfish population.

Details: Call the Kona Charter Skippers Association for information 808/329-3600; or drive down to Honokohau Harbor and have a look at the boats for yourself. If you're interested in taking your catch home with you, say so up front. Some boats do not allow this, some wish to split the catch with you, and some are tag-and-release

Biking along Kohala, Route 20

Kirk Lee Aeder—Imoco Media

only. It's up to you to find the boat that meets your needs before you go.

For more information and this year's dates of the Hawaiian International Billfish Tournament, call 808/ 329-6155.

Pine Trees Beach

Just south of the Kona airport, a good spot to go biking is at the beach called Pine Trees, at the Natural Energy Lab. The riding trail begins 50 yards north of the parking lot. The trailhead is lava, but soon enough you'll be pedaling in sand. You follow the coast for roughly 1.2 miles, finding some great views, nice shade trees, and good beaching opportunities. The trail ends at Hoona Historical Preserve. Follow the same trail back to the parking lot and then you can head south for a two-mile beach ride.

Details: Combined, there is roughly 6.5 miles of trail to ride at Pine Trees, a beginner-level ride at sea level. Plan 1½ to two hours round trip. For more information on the Pine Trees ride, or other rides on the Big Island, call Big Island Mountain Bike Association at 808/961-4452; or Hawaiian Pedals at 808/329-2294.

THE PETROGLYPH FIELDS

The goddess Pele must have been upset.

"This is the biggest wind in recent memory," remarked Ski, his hair flattened against one side of his head as the trees behind him blustered in the offshore flurry.

An hour earlier, total calm. But, quick as a snap of the fingers, Pele had sent a howling wind, just as Ski was about to show me into the petroglyph fields at Waikoloa.

A sign? Maybe, but we proceeded. The petroglyphs, or rock carvings, had captured my imagination as soon as I had heard about them, and Ski was the expert.

"This area," he said with a sweep of the arm, "is like a House of Records. People would come to this field to carve a petroglyph as a sort of prayer for, and record of, their children."

Why? "The island has very strong mana," said Ski. "The ancient Yaqui Indians believed that the earth was criss-crossed with lines of power. And where those lines intersected, those were the places of greatest power. Well, the Hawaiians believed in places of power, too. And this was one of those places."

Pele is the fire goddess who lives on Kilauea. "When Pele is upset," warned Ski, "watch out."

The lava field in which we stood is evidence of her fury. In 1790, an enemy of King Kamehameha I was advancing with his troops. Angered, Pele exploded a vent on Hualalai, shooting lava down on the rival warriors.

Thus, when the wind whipped up we wondered what Pele had in mind.

"Circles and dots are the predominant theme of this field— semicircles, two circles, a dot in the center with a circle around

it," said Ski. "These are the places where the piko ceremony took place recording the birth of children.

"What they'd do is first make the circle, then they'd wrap the umbilical cord of the child in tapa, put it in the middle of the circle, and wait overnight. When they came back, if the cord was still there the child would have a long and prosperous life. If, it was gone they would give the child to the community's care because they believed the child would become a thief."

As Ski told his story, Pele played a trick. My camera ran out of film, so I opened the back to insert a new roll. I had ripped the sprockets on the film in the rewinding process and there the whole thing lay, exposed, across the open back of the camera.

Then I broke my microphone clip. Later I discovered that most of the interview I had taped with Ski was destroyed anyway; the wind noise was so great against the microphone that little else was intelligible. Anything else, Pele?

Ski offered some guidance. "This carving on top of my staff is an owl," he said. "It's what the Hawaiians call 'aumakua'—like totems, they're guardians. If you notice, one aumakua is facing backward, one faces my right, and the other looks up at the sky. I've got a little protection with me whenever I carry this stick."

Today there are virtually no "petro" makers left. Hawaiian culture as it once was will take some time to recover, a process that has already begun. With people like Ski studying it, the process is in good hands. Another encouraging trend also currently exists: The hotels that have been built along the Kohala Coast have hired people knowledgeable in areas such as petroglyphs, and they are happy to share their knowledge with travelers.

Making peace with Pele, that's up to you.

© George Fuller

Petroglyph at Waikoloa

Waikoloa Petroglyph Fields

The Hawaiians believed that the earth was criss-crossed with lines of power, and where these lines intersected the power was greatest. The petroglyph fields at Waikoloa, along the King's Trail, is one of those power spots.

The nearby hotels, the Royal Waikoloan and the Hilton Waikoloa Village, offer walking tours to view the rock carvings. You'll see male and female figures, circles with *pukas* in the center, and other petroglyphs. Various theories have been forwarded over the years as to the meaning of these carvings (see sidebar), but current thinking is that they are a sort of House of Records, where elders went to record the birth of children and make offerings for their well-being.

Details: Park in the King's Shops parking lot and take a short walk to the lava fields. Plenty of signs show you the way. Plan an hour or so for the full tour. There is no charge, but be respectful: Pele is watching.

GUIDES AND OUTFITTERS

Blue Hawaiian Helicopters, Waikoloa heliport, 800/745-BLUE or 808/961-5600, flies out of both the Waikoloa heliport and Hilo International Airport. The two-hour tour includes Mauna Loa's lower slopes, the active lava flow from Kilauea, a brief landing in Hilo, and a trip down the Hamakua Coast and into the Waipio Valley, where passengers enjoy close-up views of lush greenery and towering waterfalls. Cost: $305/person.

If sailing, snorkeling, and hiking sound like a great way to spend a few vacation days, **Eye of the Whale Marine/Wilderness Adventures**, P.O. Box 1269, Kapaau, HI 96755, 800/659-3544 or 808/889-0227, will appeal to you. An eco-friendly series of marine excursions includes winter whale-watching, and dolphin-watching and snorkeling the rest of the year. Naturalists lead the hiking trips, and will introduce you to Hawaii's natural history, identification of tropical flora, and the development of the coral reef ecosystems. These trips are for all ages and experience levels, and all are personally guided by owner Mark Grandoni. Cost varies depending on type of trip.

Another catch of a tour is offered by **Whale Watch Learning Adventures**, P.O. Box 139, Holualoa, HI 96725, 808/322-0028. Captain Dan McSweeney takes groups on year-round whale-watching cruises off the Kona Coast. In addition to the migratory humpback whales—seen December through April in these waters—these voyages will locate other species that are in residence year-round. They include pilot, sperm, and false killer whales, as well as beaked, pygmy killer, and melon-headed whales. Plan on three hours for the trip. Cost: $49.50/person.

A snorkeler's delight is **Fair Wind Snorkel, Scuba & Snuba Cruises**, 78-7130 Kaleiopapa St., Kailua-Kona, 800/677-9461 or 808/322-2788, www.fair-wind.com. The *Fair Wind II* is a 60-foot catamaran specifically designed for snorkel cruises. Owned by a *kamaaina* family, it provides everything you'll need for underwater exploration of Kealakekua Bay, including snorkels and fins. They also have prescription masks if you need one. This ship features a 15-foot water slide, a high-dive platform, breakfast, and lunch. Expect a 4½-hour trip. Cost: $72/adults; $40/children 6–17; children 5 and under free.

Kohala Mountain Kayak Cruise, P.O. Box 660, Kapaau, HI 96755, 808/889-6922, offers kayak cruises down the Kohala Sugar Plantation Irrigation Ditch, through rain forest, and past waterfalls. Good for family adventures. Cost: $75/person; $55/children 5–18 years old.

Maile Charters, P.O. Box 44335, Kamuela, HI 96743, 800/726-SAIL or 808/326-5174, will customize sailing charters for you from two hours to 10 days for snorkeling, swimming, and whale-watching, leaving from Kawaihae Harbor. Cost: $3,300/three-day sail for four passengers; $4,400/five-day sail for four passengers. All meals included.

Back on land, **Hawaii Forest & Trail**, P.O. Box 2975, Kailua-Kona, HI 96745, 800/464-1933 or 808/322-8881, offers guided nature adventures to private-access areas in Kona and Kohala, in groups of no more than 10. This well-respected company, run by naturalists Rob and Cindy Pacheco, will show you a Hawaii few tourists ever see. You'll walk under waterfalls, through tropical rain forests, and past stands of towering ferns, flowering lehua, and stately koa trees. Along the way you may spot some of Hawaii's rarest birds, as the areas to which you'll be going are pristine habitat. Hawaii Forest & Trail provides all the gear you'll need, including water, day packs, hiking sticks, and binoculars. They even serve lunch. Cost: $130/person.

CAMPING

The County of Hawaii operates several Kona-Kohala–area beach parks that allow camping. All require permits that cost $3 per day for adults; $1 per day for children 13–17; and 50 cents per day for children under 12. Further information and permits can be obtained up to a year in advance (starting in November) by visiting or contacting the Department of Parks and Recreation, 25 Aupuni St., Hilo, HI 96720; 808/961-8311. Two of the better campsites are listed below.

In the North Kohala District, **Mahukona Beach Park** was a small port facility run by Kohala Sugar Company. Diving is good here, with lots of artifacts to be seen, such as a sunken ship, an anchor and chain, and other objects. The camping facilities include rest rooms, showers, and picnic tables.

On a point of land at the entrance to Kawaihae Harbor, **Samuel M. Spencer Beach Park** offers good camping, rest rooms, showers, drinking water, and picnic facilities. There's also good swimming and snorkeling. Follow Highway 19 north from Kona; turn left onto Highway 270 toward Kawaihae and left following the signs to Spencer Beach Park.

The State of Hawaii oversees camping at Hapuna Beach State Recreation Area. Reservations are taken a year in advance at the Division of State Parks, 75 Aupuni St., Hilo, HI 96720; 808/974-6200.

Hapuna Beach State Recreation Area is the premier state-operated camping area along the Kona-Kohala Coast. Six A-frame structures are available for campers, along with all the amenities: restroom facilities, showers, fresh water, picnic tables, and ample parking. But the best thing about camping here is the beach. Wake in the morning to one of the most beautiful stretches of white-sand beach in the state. Swimming, snorkeling, and body-surfing are excellent here. A 25-minute trail leads to Kaunaoa Beach, adjacent to Mauna Kea Beach Hotel. Kaunaoa is a lovely crescent-shaped beach, also considered one of the state's best.

LODGING

Along the Kona-Kohala Coast are several of the finest oceanfront luxury resorts in the world. Their amenities include spa facilities, golf courses, tennis courts, pools, beaches, and five-star dining. If you have the budget to stay in this type of property, use it here. This collection of world-class resorts is without equal. The Kona Kohala Resort Association will be happy to help you arrange lodging reservations. Contact them at 69-275 Waikoloa Beach Dr., Kohala Coast, HI 96743; 800/318-3637 or 808/885-4915.

There are also a couple of properties in a different key from which to choose. They may not have all the amenities of the luxury resorts, but they are charming in their own right.

Why anyone ever leaves **Kona Village Resort**, P.O. Box 1299, Kailua-Kona, HI 96745, 800/367-5290 or 808/325-5555, is a wonder. Along the Kona-Kohala Coast, where an ancient Hawaiian village once stood, on 82 coastal acres of palms and tropical flowers, is a peaceful, thatched-roofed village by the blue Pacific. Quite a bit of work has been done here in the last couple of years to create new amenities, including a tennis center, a spa and workout facility, and a massage/therapy area. This wonderful getaway, with no phones, televisions, or clocks, is a great spot to jump into the Pacific and experience Hawaii's colorful undersea life, or to use as home base as you stay on land and explore the Big Island's myriad natural treasures. It is pricey for some budgets, but if you're

▼△▼△▼△▼△▼△▼△▼

Kalahiki Cottage

This 15,000-acre working ranch is reputedly home to several of Hawaii's endangered native crows. On the premises is a rain forest and a sanctuary of endangered native birds. One of the highlights of staying here is the guided tour of these precious areas.

▼△▼△▼△▼△▼△▼△▼

looking for a splurge hotel, this is one of the best in Hawaii. Rates: $425, all meals included.

The newest resort along the Kohala Coast, **Four Seasons Resort Hualalai**, P.O. Box 1119, Kailua-Kona, HI 96745, 808/325-8000, has combined all the best elements of resort development in Hawaii from the last 35 years into one great property. The 243 spacious guest rooms and suites are tastefully decorated with comfortable furniture, dark woods, and Hawaiian art; the low-rise structure fits harmoniously into the landscape; the pools and common areas are inviting, yet private; the restaurants are wonderful and relaxing; and you're right at the surf's edge. In addition to several traditional pools, the property features a saltwater swimming pool loaded with colorful tropical fish. Rates: $50–$625, double occupancy.

Holualoa Inn, P.O. Box 222, Holualoa, HI 96725, 800/392-1812 or 808/324-1121, is a small, elegant inn set in the midst of Kona coffee country in an area called Holualoa, known as a haven for artists and craftspeople. The inn has six spacious and tastefully appointed rooms, and guests have access to a pool and Jacuzzi. It sits on a mountainside overlooking the Kona Coast. They grow their own coffee here and serve it with breakfast each morning in the dining room. The rooftop gazebo is a great spot for watching the sunset. Rates: $135–$175, double occupancy; $30/night for third person.

The one-bedroom ranch cottage **Kalahiki Cottage** (through Hawaii's Best Bed & Breakfasts), near Kona, 800/262-9912 or 808/885-4550, is a nature-lover's delight. Located on a 15,000-acre working cattle ranch, it's filled with antiques and heirlooms, and guests have access to a swimming pool and Jacuzzi. Kona is near by car, but many people opt to stay in and cook in the full kitchen. One of the highlights of Kalahiki is that a guided tour of the rain forest and endangered native bird sanctuary on the property is offered for an additional fee. Rates: $150 for the cottage; $115 for separate room in main house.

Another spot near Kona is **Puanani** (through Hawaii's Best Bed & Breakfasts), 800/262-9912 or 808/885-4550. Two suites are on the lower level of this private home, and a separate, one-bedroom cottage is also available. The owners, who live upstairs, have a landscaping business and have made Puanani a showcase of their talents. Both suites open onto a beautiful garden lanai with swimming pool, Jacuzzi, barbecue area, and wide views of the West Hawaii coastline. One suite and the cottage have full kitchens. An exercise room is also at your disposal. Rates are $95–$115.

FOOD

Canoe House at Mauna Lani, Mauna Lani Bay Hotel and Bungalows, 808/885-6622, is an oceanfront restaurant memorable not only for great food—although it shines in that arena—but for the serene, open-air ambiance. The cuisine is Pacific Rim, a blending of flavors from East and West. The signature appetizer is nori-wrapped tempura *ahi* with soy mustard sauce. Although you won't go wrong with any entrée on this menu, they always seem to do especially well with fresh fish. An impressive wine list adds to the evening's pleasure. Expect to spend around $100 for two. Open for dinner nightly.

On the oceanfront in Kona is **Huggos**, 35-5828 Kahakai Rd., Kailua-Kona, 808/329-1493. The delightful waterside setting distinguishes this restaurant. The lunch menu features wraps, sandwiches, burgers, and salads. The dinner menu has a wide selection of items, including fresh fish in several preparations—the grilled *ono* filets in a spicy coconut kiwi sauce are great—steaks, pastas, and the house specialty: barbecued beef ribs. Tasty desserts, such as a massive Hualalai ice-cream pie, await if you clean your plate. Get here early, as the daily sunset extravaganza is worth watching from your vantage point on the water. In the evenings, the bar has live music if you feel like moving your feet. Open for lunch Mon–Fri and dinner daily.

Sam Choy's, 73-5576 Kouhola St., Kailua-Kona 808/326-1545, is

KONA COFFEE

While you're on the Big Island, take a Kona coffee country tour if you have the time. Many of the small farms are clustered in the hills just south of Kona, down to Kealakekua Bay. Most of the farmers will welcome your visit and show you the fine art of coffee-growing. Several commercial shops and stores along Highways 11 and 180 sell Kona coffee and can help guide you in your search. Coffee trees bloom in spring, issuing a white flower. During summer the green coffee beans appear on the branches, gradually turning red. Harvest is between September and January. For information on Kona coffee country tours, call 808/326-7820.

very popular with residents for breakfast and lunch. It's the brainchild of Sam Choy, a Big Island chef who made good and now has restaurants on several islands. What you get at this location is loads of local food at very reasonable prices. If you would like to do as the locals do in Kona, go to Sam Choy's for breakfast and order the "loco moco," eggs over rice with brown gravy. Open for breakfast and lunch daily, and for dinner Tue–Sat.

Hualalai Club Grille, at Hualalai Golf Course, 808/325-8000, has a relaxed, country-club atmosphere combined with wonderful food, making this a good choice for lunch or dinner. If you enjoy golf, ask for a table overlooking the 18th green of the Jack Nicklaus–designed golf course and watch the players come in as you enjoy your meal. An excellent selection of gourmet pizzas is offered, such as Kona lobster with pesto. Hearty sandwiches and pastas are on the lunch menu, along with salads. Dinner entrées include steaks, fresh fish, pizzas, and pastas. An extensive wine list rounds out the offerings. Open for lunch and dinner daily.

It's tough to order from the menu at **Roy's Waikoloa**, 250 Waikoloa Beach Dr. (King's Shops), 808/886-4321, because everything is so good. Some favorites from the appetizer menu include Szechuan spiced baby back ribs, and the honey orange–glazed roast duck nachos. Favorite dinner entrées include the cracked pepper *ahi* with herb-smashed potatoes, and the braised beef short ribs. There is also a decent wine list. But whatever you do, save room for the dark chocolate soufflé, which you must order 20 minutes in advance. In fact, get two: It's so good you won't want to share. Open for lunch and dinner daily.

If you're in the Kawaihae area, stop for good Mexican food at **Tres Hombres**, Kawaihae Shopping Center at Kawaihae Harbor, 808/882-1031. Fish tacos are the most popular item on the menu, but the garlic quesadillas and sizzling fajitas are not far behind. Fajitas come in a variety of combinations, including steak and chicken, and mahi and shrimp. If you're *really* hungry, try *el grande* burrito, a monster tortilla filled with black beans, guacamole, lettuce, tomatoes, and your choice of chicken, fish, or beef. Hombres also serves a killer margarita. (A new Kona location has opened on Alii Drive, just past the Hard Rock Café.) Open for lunch and dinner daily.

APPENDIX A
TRAVEL BASICS

While the Hawaiian islands may seem like an exotic travel destination—they certainly are far from the Mainland—the state enjoys much of the same infrastructure as the rest of the United States. However, you will encounter some differences in language, culture, and climate, so here are a few tips to help you prepare.

WHAT TO BRING
The weather in Hawaii is always good. Gentle trade winds blow year-round, and temperatures average 85 degrees from May through October; and 78 degrees November through April. Average water temperature is 74 degrees.

So what to bring depends on the activities in which you wish to engage. Bring swimwear, sunscreen, a hat for protection from the sun, shorts, and open footwear. Reefwalkers are useful for exploring rocky beaches and shorelines.

If you're interested in hiking, shorts are normally fine, unless you are going into colder zones such as Mauna Loa summit or Haleakala. Hiking boots are fine, but not necessary, as most hikes can be done in tennis shoes. For horseback riding, bring jeans or long pants. Boots are not vital.

Remember, we have no snakes, poison oak, or poison ivy in Hawaii.

Evenings are normally temperate, but if you're visiting in winter months, take a light sweater. Dinners out at nicer restaurants require slacks and aloha shirts for men, dresses or skirts for women. We call it "aloha wear" and many shops offer a wide variety of appropriate clothing. A sport coat and tie are not necessary for men.

ENTRY AND EXIT REQUIREMENTS
No special visas, passports, or tourist permits are required for U.S. citizens. Canadian citizens contact the Canadian Consulate, 550 S. Hope St., 9th floor, Los Angeles, CA 90071, 213/346-2700, for details on traveling to the United States.

HEALTH AND SAFETY
Generally speaking, Hawaii is a safe and healthy place to visit. Outdoor activities are a daily occurrence, and most are extremely safe.

There are major hospitals on all islands, however, should you run into serious health problems. The state and federal parks are monitored closely by rangers, and overnight campers are required to obtain permits so rangers are aware of the fact that people are in the area. When hiking in remote areas, check in with the ranger stations and let them know your plans. There may come a time when you're happy you did so.

Where most people get into trouble—if they are going to get into trouble—is in the water. The water is warm and inviting, and the great majority of the time it is safe. But the ocean can also have unexpected currents, rocks, and other unforeseen dangers. Again, let someone know your plans. Never dive or snorkel alone. And if the surf is high or rough, don't bite off more than you can chew. Our lifeguards are good, but don't press your luck in the ocean.

Hitchhiking is illegal on all islands as, of course, are illegal drugs. There are some areas, particularly on Oahu and the Big Island, that are well known as higher crime zones, and not as friendly to tourists. Mostly, there is no reason for you to go to these areas anyway, but since you're an adventurer, take care to avoid danger. Ask locals, such as your innkeeper or hotel concierge, which areas to avoid on the island you're visiting.

Immunization Requirements and Health Precautions
No special immunizations are required to visit Hawaii.

Food and Drinking Water
Hawaii enjoys the same high standards for food and drinking water as the rest of the United States. In some hiking and camping areas, though, fresh water may not be readily available. Be sure to plan ahead and hike in drinking water to your campsites.

TRANSPORTATION
As expected, most airlines offer flights to Hawaii. Once in Hawaii, don't expect to take public transportation, except on Oahu.

To Hawaii
The Honolulu International Airport is the hub of the Pacific. On any given day, the runways and tarmac are loaded with flights from all reaches of the globe.

From the Mainland United States, flights are frequent and available on almost all major carriers. Many charter flights are also available—albeit with far less choice of scheduling—offering travelers a less expensive alternative to commercial airlines.

United Airlines flies most people to Hawaii from the United States, with roughly 50 percent of the market share. Their routes comes from many major cities in the United States, and therefore United is likely to be convenient from a variety of gateways.

But there are less-expensive alternatives. Hawaiian Airlines is a good phone call, with fares normally from $300 to $500, depending on season. Hawaiian is limited in where they fly from, however, with flights primarily from the West Coast: San Francisco, Los Angeles, Portland, and Seattle.

Both Hawaiian and United now fly directly from many Mainland West Coast cities to Maui, the Big Island, and Kauai.

Just about every major airline flies to Hawaii, but the most common commercial carriers from the Mainland United States include Delta, Continental, and American. From Canada, Air Canada is the major carrier with daily flights to and from Canada. Canadian Airlines offers similar service.

From the West Coast, flight times are roughly five hours. There are no non-stops from East Coast cities, and it is often a welcome break to overnight in San Francisco or Los Angeles.

Not much is available in the way of sea passage, unless you're considering a cruise. If this is the case, quite a few luxury liners make Hawaii part of their offerings.

Within Hawaii

Once in Hawaii, flights are frequent between islands on Hawaiian Airlines and Aloha Airlines. Flights leave from the Inter-island Terminal at Honolulu International Airport, which is located in the main airport complex.

On Kauai, the main airport is at Lihue; on Maui, you have two choices, Kahului and Kapalua/West Maui. On the Big Island you can fly into either Kailua-Kona or Hilo; on Molokai the airport is at Kaunakakai; on Lanai it is at Lanai City.

Rental cars and vans—with all major rental companies found at the airports—are the preferred method of transportation and available on all islands. Oahu has a good bus system, called The Bus, and it's one of the best deals in the state. For one dollar, you can ride around the island all day. Unfortunately, the other islands don't have such good public transportation, and taxi fares can add up quickly.

COMMUNICATIONS

Much the same communications infrastructure found in the United States is also found in Hawaii.

Language

Although the Hawaiian language is now being taught in some schools, and studied at the University of Hawaii, English is spoken here. Still, there are some Hawaiian (and pidgin, a local slang) words that are commonly used, and we have provided a short glossary below.

a'a—sharp lava rock
ali'i—royalty

halau—troupe
hale—house
haole—Caucasian
heiau—sacred ground
i'o—hawk
kamaaina—one who is "of the land," a local
kane—man
kapu—forbidden
keiki—children
koloa—duck
kukui—a kind of nut tree
kumu hula—master dancers of the hula
mahalo—thank you
makai—toward the ocean
Maui no ka oi—Maui is the best!
mauka—mountains
menehune—the legendary "small people" of the islands
pahoehoe—smooth lava rock
paniolo—Hawaiian cowboy
pueo—short-eared owl
puka—hole
stink-eye—a harsh look
wahine—woman

Telephone Service

Hawaiian Tel provides primary phone service. All major phone cards will work for long distance—AT&T, MCI WorldCom, U.S. Sprint, etc. Long-distance phone cards can be purchased at many shops, and often you can get a good deal on them. Cellular phones will work on roam on many parts of most islands, but as yet there is no blanket coverage. Iridium phones will work anywhere in Hawaii.

Mail Service

Mail takes a little longer to get to the Mainland United States and Canada from Hawaii, particularly from more remote locales. There are post offices, UPS, FedEx, and other carriers located everywhere. Overnight service is not guaranteed, however. Most services take two days. (There is, of course, no Ground UPS.) Shipping by sea is cheap, but takes up to two weeks.

Internet Access

Hawaii has excellent Internet access. Many of the major hotels have fitted their rooms with lines dedicated for this purpose.

MONEY MATTERS

Hawaii may be a paradise, but it can be a bit pricey. However, the islands offer the services you need to make your visit as easy as possible.

Currency

U.S. dollars. Many banks and other currency exchange locations can be found for exchange of foreign currency.

Banks

Bank of Hawaii and First Hawaiian Bank dominate the market. Hours vary from branch to branch, but those branch offices found in supermarkets such as Safeway tend to be open longer hours.

ATM machines are found everywhere, and all major debit cards will work. Travelers checks can be cashed just about everywhere.

Credit Cards

All major credit cards accepted, including VISA, MasterCard, American Express, and Discover.

Taxes and Tipping

Expect hotel room tax to be applied to your hotel bills, and a general excise tax of 4.66 percent to be applied to all transactions. Tipping is optional, with 15–20 percent a common tipping amount.

CUISINE

You'll find every imaginable type of cuisine in Hawaii. These include an abundance of Chinese, Japanese, and Thai restaurants. American fare is readily available, including fast food chains.

What's more interesting, however, is Hawaii Regional Cuisine, an invention of Hawaii chefs who wished to create a distinctive approach to cooking that would combine classical and Asian influences with local ingredients. This style of cooking can be found on all the major islands.

TIME ZONE

Hawaii Standard Time. Hawaii does not abide by Daylight Savings Time. Thus, when the balance of the country is in Daylight Savings Time, Hawaii is two hours behind the West Coast and five hours behind New York; when the balance of the country reverts to standard time, Hawaii is three hours behind the West Coast, six behind New York.

APPENDIX B
ADDITIONAL RESOURCES

VISITOR INFORMATION

Hawaii Visitors & Convention
Bureau
2270 Kalakaua Avenue, Suite 801
Honolulu, HI 96815
808/923-1811 or 800/GO-HAWAII
www.gohawaii.com

Oahu Visitors Bureau
733 Bishop Street, Suite 1872
Honolulu, HI 96813
808/524-0722 or 877/525-OAHU
www.visit-oahu.com

Kauai Visitors Bureau
3016 Umi Street, Suite 207
Lihue Plaza Building
Lihue, HI 96766
808/245-3971

Maui Visitors Bureau
1727 Wili Pa Loop
Wailuku, HI 96793
808/244-3530

Molokai Visitors Association
in Kaunakakai at the intersection of
Kam Highway and Wharf Road
P.O. Box 90
Kaunakakai, HI 96748
800/800-6367 or 808/553-3867
www.molokai-hawaii.com

The Lanai Company
P.O. Box 310
Lanai City, HI 96763
800/321-4666
www.lanai-resorts.com

Big Island Visitors Bureau
250 Keawe Street
Hilo, HI 96720
or 75-5719 W. Alii Drive
Kailua-Kona, HI 96740
808/961-5797

National Park Service
Prince Kuhio Federal Building
Room 6305
300 Ala Moana Boulevard
Honolulu, HI 96813
808/541-2693 (for information
    specifically on Hawaii
    Volcanoes National Park)

State Parks Office
54 South High Street
Wailuku, HI 96793
808/984-8109
(camping on Maui)

Department of Land and
    Natural Resources
    Division of State Parks
P.O. Box 1671
Lihue, HI 96766 (hiking on Kauai)

RECOMMENDED TOUR COMPANIES

Annette's Adventures
45-403 Koa Kahiko Street
Kaneohe, HI 96744
808/235-5431

Eye of the Whale Marine/ Wilderness Adventures
P.O. Box 1269
Kapaau, HI 96755
800/659-3544

Hawaii Forest & Trail
800/464-1993, 808/322-8881
www.hawaii-forest.com

Molokai Ranch
P.O. Box 259
Maunaloa, HI 96770
877/726-4656 (toll-free)
www.molokai-ranch.com

Destination Lanai
P.O. Box 700
Lanai City, HI 96763
800/947-4774 or 808/565-7600

CONSERVATION GROUPS

Hawaii Ecotourism Association
P.O. Box 61435
Honolulu, HI 96839
877/300-7058
www.planet-hawaii.com/hea

Sierra Club
P.O. Box 2577
Honolulu, HI 96803
808/538-6616

The Nature Conservancy of Hawaii
1116 Smith Street, #201
Honolulu, HI 96817
808/537-4508

Hawaii Wildlife Fund
P.O. Box 12082
Lahaina, HI 96761
808/667-0437

RECOMMENDED READING

Discover Hawaii's Best Golf by George Fuller (Island Heritage Publishing, 1999)

Great Outdoor Adventures of Hawaii by Rick Carroll (Foghorn Press, 1991)

Hawaii by James Michener (Fawcett, 1959)

Kauai Trails by Kathy Morey (Wilderness Press, 1997)

Mad About Islands: Novelists of a Vanished Pacific by A. Grove Day (Mutual Publishing, 1987)

My Time in Hawaii by Victoria Nelson (St. Martin Press, out of print but worth looking for)

Shoal of Time: A History of the Hawaiian Islands by Gavin Daws (University of Hawaii Press, 1989)

INDEX

windsurfing, 106, 115, 145, 153
Windward Oahu, 80–91, lay of the
    land, 80–81; flora and fauna,
    81–82; nature and adventure
    sights, 82–86; guides and outfit
    ters, 86–87; camping, 87; lodg-
    ing, 87, 90; food, 90–91

Map Index
Hawaii, vi
Oahu, 44
Waikiki/Honolulu, 53
Kauai, 92
Maui, 124
Lanai, 178
Molokai, 194
The Big Island, 210
Hawaii Volcanoes National Park, 222
Hilo, 239

Guidebooks that really guide

City•Smart™ Guidebooks

Pick one for your favorite city: *Albuquerque, Anchorage, Austin, Calgary, Charlotte, Chicago, Cincinnati, Cleveland, Denver, Indianapolis, Kansas City, Memphis, Milwaukee, Minneapolis/St. Paul, Nashville, Pittsburgh, Portland, Richmond, Salt Lake City, San Antonio, San Francisco, St. Louis, Tampa/St. Petersburg, Tucson.* US $12.95 to 15.95

Retirement & Relocation Guidebooks

The World's Top Retirement Havens, Live Well in Honduras, Live Well in Ireland, Live Well in Mexico. US $15.95 to $16.95

Travel•Smart® Guidebooks

Trip planners with select recommendations to *Alaska, American Southwest, Arizona, Carolinas, Colorado, Deep South, Eastern Canada, Florida, Florida Gulf Coast, Hawaii, Illinois/Indiana, Kentucky/Tennessee, Maryland/Delaware, Michigan, Minnesota/Wisconsin, Montana/Wyoming/Idaho, New England, New Mexico, New York State, Northern California, Ohio, Pacific Northwest, Pennsylvania/New Jersey, South Florida and the Keys, Southern California, Texas, Utah, Virginias, Western Canada.* US $14.95 to $17.95

Rick Steves' Guides

See *Europe Through the Back Door* and take along guides to *France, Belgium & the Netherlands; Germany, Austria & Switzerland; Great Britain & Ireland; Italy; Scandinavia; Spain & Portugal; London; Paris;* or *Best of Europe.* US $12.95 to $21.95

Adventures in Nature

Plan your next adventure in *Alaska, Belize, Caribbean, Costa Rica, Guatemala, Hawaii, Honduras, Mexico.* US $17.95 to $18.95

Into the Heart of Jerusalem

A traveler's guide to visits, celebrations, and sojourns. US $17.95

The People's Guide to Mexico

This is so much more than a guidebook—it's a trip to Mexico in and of itself, complete with the flavor of the country and its sights, sounds, and people. US $22.95

 JOHN MUIR PUBLICATIONS
P.O. Box 613 ✦ Santa Fe, NM 87504

Available at your favorite bookstore.
For a catalog or to place an order call 800-888-7504.

John Muir Publications' guides are available at your favorite bookstore

The 100 Best Small Art Towns in America 3rd edition
Discover Creative Communities, Fresh Air, and Affordable Living
U.S. $16.95

Healing Centers & Retreats
Healthy Getaways for Every Body and Budget
U.S. $16.95

Cross-Country Ski Vacations, 2nd edition
A Guide to the Best Resorts, Lodges, and Groomed Trails in North America
U.S. $15.95

Gene Kilgore's Ranch Vacations, 5th edition
The Complete Guide to Guest and Resort, Fly-Fishing, and Cross-Country Skiing Ranches
U.S. $22.95

Yoga Vacations
A Guide to International Yoga Retreats
U.S. $16.95

Watch It Made in the U.S.A., 2nd edition
A Visitor's Guide to the Companies That Make Your Favorite Products
U.S. $17.95

The Way of the Traveler
Making Every Trip a Journey of Self-Discovery
U.S. $12.95

Kidding Around®
Guides for kids 6 to 10 years old about what to do, where to go, and how to have fun in *Atlanta, Austin, Boston, Chicago, Cleveland, Denver, Indianapolis, Kansas City, Miami, Milwaukee, Minneapolis/St. Paul, Nashville, Portland, San Francisco, Seattle, Washington D.C.*
U.S. $7.95

ABOUT THE AUTHOR

Editor and writer George Fuller has been writing about adventure and travel in the Pacific Rim for more than 15 years.

His journalism career began in Monterey, California, as a sports beat writer for the daily *Santa Cruz Morning Star*, and then features writer for the daily *Monterey Herald*. He later served as editor of *Monterey Life* magazine. In 1986 he moved to Hawaii as an editor for Davick Publications (*Aloha/RSVP* magazines), before becoming editor and associate publisher of Hemmeter Publishing. He held this position from 1988 until 1992 when the company closed its Hawaii operations and moved to New Orleans.

From 1992 to 1996 he was editor of *LINKS—The Best of Golf*. In 1996 Fuller created *Asia–Pacific Golf*, a Japanese and English–language magazine focusing on golf travel in the Pacific Rim, and also began publishing the magazine *Great Outdoor Adventures of Hawaii*.

He has six books to his credit, the most recent being *Discover Hawaii's Best Golf*, published in February 1999 (Island Heritage Publishing). He has contributed to many guidebooks, notably the *Berlitz Travelers Guide, Birnbaum Guide, CitiBank's Great Resorts of the World,* and *Guest Informant*.

Fuller has written about travel and adventure for many newspapers and magazines, including the *New York Times Magazine, Time, San Francisco Chronicle, Palm Springs Life, San Francisco Focus, GOLF Magazine, Golf Digest, LINKS, Successful Meetings, Honolulu,* and many others. He is an on-line correspondent for the PGA of America (pga.com) and Golf.com.